S0-BWB-620

What Readers Say

"A lively manuscript written by a lawyer is both an oxymoron and an unexpected pleasure. ... I was reminded of Scott Turow's first book, One-L, but only for a moment. Woodcock has all three L's and a glorious wit that makes the bumps and grind of becoming a lawyer fun for laymen as well as its target audience ...."

— Sol Stein, prizewinning novelist and playwright, author of A Feast for Lawyers, and formerly a 19-year publisher of Nobel Prize winners and best-sellers

"There's nothing like a career in law, and there's nobody else quite like Woodcock to talk about it. This should be required reading for all law students — and lawyers."

— Myrna Wigod, former Stanley H. Kaplan LSAT review course instructor; now a partner at the 200-attorney law firm of McCarter & English, Newark, New Jersey

"As an engineer and MBA (M.I.T., 1983) who has worked with accountants, lawyers and engineers for years, I can say without reservation that any student considering a career choice among those professions will understand and learn from the hardheaded perspective that Woodcock brings to the topic of becoming a lawyer."

— James F. Reda, Vice President, The Bachelder Group; Lieutenant, Coast Guard Reserve

"Highly recommended. This is a fresh new look at a subject that could use a good airing. Woodcock is brash and thought-provoking and frequently dead-on in describing the warts and joys of the legal profession. If you're contemplating — or sentenced to — a career in law, you really should read Take the Bar and Beat Me."

— David A. Horowitz, Assistant General Counsel, Advest Inc.

"For those trying to choose between law school and medical school, this humorous and sardonic insider's view of the life of a law student and lawyer, along with Samuel Shem's House of God [about medical training], will provide a fairly accurate view of what is coming."

— Dr. Margaret Brandwein, Assistant Professor of Pathology, Mount Sinai Hospital, New York, NY

"This book presents one view of lawyers and the law. I disagree with much of that view. Nevertheless, it is an amusing book, and I encourage fellow and future lawyers to read it. Law school sometimes seems like the ancient past; this brought much of it back vividly. The book has a wealth of research and humor — at times, I laughed out loud — and it conveys many realities that people should (but often don't) grasp before entering law school."

— Edward Powers, a partner at the 75-attorney law firm of Richards & O'Neil, New York City

"I hadn't planned to read it all the way through. But [Woodcock has] written a page-turner, and I have read nearly every word of it."

— Top Law School Professor (name withheld by request)

"It helps ... that Mr. Woodcock has resorted to the device — unusual, for this kind of book — of using footnotes and offering numerous supporting quotes from legal experts. [It is] clear that, whatever the author's experience may have been, he is hardly alone in the points he makes. ... This book is must reading for anyone thinking about going to law school, as well as for those who are attending or have attended ...."

— Lawrence A. Dubin, Professor of Law, University of Detroit Law School

"An accurate, dismaying picture ... that should be read by law professors, lawyers, and judges."

— Judge Lois G. Forer, author of Money and Justice: Who Owns the Courts?

TAKE THE

BAR

AND BEAT ME

An irreverent look at law school
and career choices for prelaws, law
students, advanced paralegals – and
the people who once loved them

By Raymond L. Woodcock, J.D., M.B.A.

THE CAREER PRESS
180 Fifth Ave.
Hawthorne, N.J. 07507
1-800-CAREER-1
201-427-0229 (outside U.S.)
FAX: 1-201-427-2037

© Copyright 1991 Raymond L. Woodcock, J.D., M.B.A.

All rights reserved under the Pan-American and International Copyright Conventions. This book may not be reproduced, in whole or in part, in any form or by any means, electronic or mechanical, including photocopying, recording, or by any information storage and retrieval system now known or hereafter invented, without written permission from the publisher, The Career Press.

Take the Bar and Beat Me

An Irreverent Look at Law School
and Career Choices
for Prelaws, Paralegals, Law Students
— and the People Who Once Loved Them

ISBN 1-56414-000-8, $8.95

Cover design by Dean Johnson Design, Inc.,
with relentless input from the author

Copies of this volume may be ordered by mail or phone directly from the publisher. To order by mail, please include the price of $8.95, plus $2.50 for postage and handling. For multiple copies, please include an additional $1.00 postage and handling per copy.

Send orders to: The Career Press, Inc., 180 Fifth Ave., P.O. Box 34, Hawthorne, NJ 07507. To order with your VISA or MasterCard, or to obtain information on the complete line of Career Press books, call toll-free 1-800-CAREER-1 (outside the U.S., call 201-427-0229) during East Coast business hours.

The paraphrasing on pp. 94-95 is adapted from LIABILITY: The Legal Revolution and Its Consequences, by Peter Huber. Copyright (c) 1988 by Peter Huber. Reprinted by permission of Basic Books, a division of HarperCollins Publishers Inc.

Many thanks to the WordPerfect Corporation for the judge's gavel — standard equipment with WordPerfect 5.1 — that I've used at the start of each new chapter.

Introduction

Alice in Wonderland is the best book, I believe, to introduce the lay person to the process of becoming a lawyer — if only because, as they say, it is the best book to introduce the lay person to anything. Here is a glimpse through the looking glass:

Your Application to Law School:

"I can't explain *myself*, I'm afraid, sir," said Alice, "because I'm not myself, you see."
"I don't see," said the Caterpillar.

Legal Ethics:

"Tut, tut, child," said the Duchess. "Everything's got a moral if only you can find it."

Studying for the Bar Exam:

Begin at the beginning ... and go on till you come to the end: then stop.

The ABC's of Billing Your Client:

"Take some more tea," the March Hare said to Alice, very earnestly.
"I've had nothing yet," Alice replied in an offended tone: "so I can't take more."
"You mean you can't take *less*," said the Hatter: "it's very easy to take *more* than nothing."

Don't Burn Your Bridges When You Leave the Firm:

"All right," said the Cheshire Cat; and this time it vanished quite slowly, beginning with the end of the tail, and ending with the grin, which remained some time after the rest of it had gone.

The Public's View of Attorneys:

"If it had grown up," she said to herself, "it would have made a dreadfully ugly child; but it makes a rather handsome pig, I think."

to my Mom and the Red Kid

Contents

PART I: LAW SCHOOL

PART II: ENTERING THE LAWYER'S WORLD

Analytic Table of Contents
for Relatives, Friends & Lovers

Practicing Law: Should You Get In? Should You Get Out? Should You Beg Your Friends to Avoid It?

I once dated an attorney whose previous boyfriend believed in reincarnation. More specifically, she told me that he believed he had been alive at the time of Christ, and that Jesus had put a curse on him. So when things would go wrong in his life — the one in the 20th century, I mean — he would say to her, "See? It's The Curse."

I told her this was nonsense. Her reaction? "Ray, you can't be sure of that. It could possibly have happened." And technically, she was right. I wasn't there with Jesus, so I couldn't prove that the ex-boyfriend's story was false.

But for Christ's sake, let's get real. I had to believe that the former boyfriend was a jackass — and so was she, for putting up with him.

I must say, however, that she had learned well one lesson of law school: You need to know how to make something out of nothing. A client comes to you with a bizarre story, and it's your job to explain to the jury why his/her view of events might be — indeed, *must* be — true.

It's OK to work so hard to convert the possible into the likely when you're in the courtroom. But we're not in the courtroom right now. We're in your living room, or wherever, and we're not trying to fool anyone. It's just you and me, talking about your career, your future, your life.

I want to be direct about it. You may find it entirely too easy to waste a large chunk of your life by following a series of decisions, each of which makes great sense by itself, but which, taken together, will carry you directly away from what you really wanted for yourself.

You might start, for example, by planning your career on the basis of what you read in books by famous lawyers and Harvard Law School professors. Few of us have anything in common with those kinds of people, but I suppose hope springs eternal. If those books help you form a burning belief in your own Destiny, maybe you should rely on them.

Meanwhile, those of us who are still standing down here on Earth may find it more useful to look at some of the things that can go right and wrong in the life of an ordinary, mainstream attorney, who goes to a good law school, gets a good law job, and keeps on asking questions about the whole thing.

Anything as big as the law inspires endless differences of opinion. I have but one view. For that reason, you should not limit your reading to this book. After you've finished with me — or after I've finished with you — you should stroll into your local library and sample something very different.

That, however, is not the same as saying that you can safely ignore me. You can run, but you can't hide. The law is a very hard-nosed profession, and it has a nasty habit of chewing people up and spitting them out. So if I can knock you on your tail now, before you've invested your life in a career that makes no sense for you, I figure I'm doing you a service.

I hope this book reaches its intended audience, including those who plan to go to law school, those in law school already, and those who are sending loved ones off to law school. But I hope that some of those people are *not* persuaded by what I've written. We need lawyers, especially those who can't be dissuaded by my attack. What we don't need is a bunch of lawyers who find that, for them, law is the wrong career.

The law of a nation can be a great thing. In the United States, many fine people work hard to produce our system of justice. I am pleased to know a few of those fine people personally, and I do not mean to attack either those people or the Law, in the abstract. My slings and arrows are reserved for the misfits: the people who don't belong and the ideas that make no sense.

I guess the bottom line is that I want to give you enough knowledge to make you dangerous. If you're alive and questioning; if you're refusing to just step in line and do what everyone else seems to think you should do; if you tackle, now, the questions that others won't confront until midway in their careers — if any of those things happen, then this book will have served its purpose.

In any case, I wish you all the best.

PART I
LAW SCHOOL

§1. The Decision to Do It

When you decide to go to law school, you're not just offhandedly agreeing to waste a couple of years in an entertaining way. You're consciously, nervously putting yourself on a path that makes you a different kind of person, just as surely as if you were joining the Marines.

A. Applying

Parents, teachers, and peers don't usually hold a gun to your head and make you go to law school. It's your choice.

For some future law students, it happens without question. They always wanted to be attorneys. But for most of us, it's not so cut-and-dried. We look ahead and try to decide what will pay the most and lead to the best career.

That's the way it was for me. During my last two years in college, I attended meetings and gathered information on different possible futures for myself. I thought about going off to work for some company, and I also thought about continuing on in school for another few years.[1]

I eventually decided to get an advanced degree. At that point, the choice for me was between law school and a Ph.D.

---

1. There doesn't have to be a smooth transition from college to law school. One study shows that 24% of lawyers made their decision to go to law school only after they had graduated from college and had gone to work for a while. See the Georgetown study, fn. 357, pg. 176. (Note on my style: This citation means, "Look at page 176 of the article that I've cited in my footnote no. 357.")

in political science. I quickly learned, however, that hundreds of those Ph.D.s might compete for the same position. I got the picture. It didn't make much sense to go to graduate school if I wanted to have self-respect and an income.

Still, I had reservations about law school. I wanted neither to work that hard nor to be identified with the bad things you hear about lawyers.

1. The Psychology of Applying

It finally dawned on me that I could apply to law schools, "just to see what happens." I figured I could make a better decision when I knew whether I could get into a good school. If I didn't succeed in that, I planned to try the Ph.D.

That was naive of me. I had underestimated what happens to your mind when you fill out your law school applications. They're a lot of work, and they require some thought about yourself and your future.

In particular, you have to write at least one essay for each school, responding to specific questions on the application form. Among other things, they want to know what you're hoping to get from law school, and how you think you'll fit in, and why their school appeals to you.

This may be the first time in your life that you'll have to explain to someone, carefully, that you are an adult now and that you know what you're doing with your life. Moreover, you're applying to *law* school, so you have to be especially persuasive. By the time you're done, it's not surprising if you believe your own propaganda, and are now convinced that law school is exactly the place for you.

Once you've filed the applications, you wait. You wait for weeks, watching your mail nervously, praying for a positive response from, say, Yale Law School, your favorite. And then the magical envelope appears in your mailbox. You cross yourself, maybe even pour a drink, and open it. And there, in black and white, are the words, "You've got to be kidding!"

Not really. The words of rejection are usually much kinder. But it's still a rejection. You may think you're smart. But as the letters saying "No" pour in from Harvard, Stanford, Chicago, and all the rest, all across the country, you get the message. They've rejected you because they got literally thousands of applications that were better than yours. They don't want you. You're not nearly good enough.

It makes you crave a chance to go to law school, just to show them all how good you are. And here's the point: If you had any doubt before, you're quite certain now that, in law school, you'll be among the truly *elite* young people of America. Everything else seems lackluster by comparison.

So now that you've gone for the hook, they can reel you in. Sure enough, a week or two later, you start getting letters of acceptance from some very good schools. You can hold your head up again among your friends who are also applying to law school. You're somebody after all.

I'm sure the schools don't plan it this way. And you'll still agonize over the thought that you're really gonna bite the bullet and go to law school. But you'll know the meaning of fright now. When you feared that nobody wanted you, you panicked. You looked into the abyss and had to imagine your future, not as a dynamic young attorney, but instead as a middle-aged, moth-eaten fop earning minimum wage, shelving books or washing cars, with no hopes and no challenges. Are we surprised that law school suddenly looks so good?

2. Choosing a School

In the next weeks, your excitement grows. You get obsessed with the thought that you're going to be a lawyer. If you hadn't realized it before, you begin to notice, now, that lawyers appear a lot in the newspapers and history books. You walk through the law school at your university, or one nearby, and notice how lively the law students are. They seem to talk about such significant issues. You can hardly wait to become part of it all.

You go through all this during the middle of your senior year in college. You start classes at law school six months later. But in those few months, even the college seniors who had doubts about law school grow to be quite sure that it's exactly what they want to do. They think they understand their legal future well.

Of course, a few rejections and acceptances on law school applications, and the sight of some attorneys' names in the newspapers and the history books, are not necessarily enough to persuade you to commit yourself to three years of hard study in law school. There's something else, and it's worth understanding.

It starts with the Law School Admissions Test (LSAT), which you take as part of your application process. To prepare for it, you buy a study guidebook. If you're rich, you also sign up for a $700 preparation course. Either way, you spend weeks practicing the odd kinds of questions they throw at you.

The exam itself is a case study in anxiety. When you arrive, you see people with candy bars, coffee, and potato chips; you notice that some are fondling their favorite pencil, while others have a whole pre-sharpened boxful. (Just in case they break six or eight of them during the exam, I guess.) You even see a few fanatics jump up and run out of the room and back in again, in the last few moments before the exam begins, just to stimulate themselves.

When your test scores come back, you move on to a new level of anxiety. You go back to the bookstore and buy one of the standard guides to law schools. These books have charts that tell you how likely you are, with your college grade-point average (GPA) and LSAT scores, to get into each law school. At some colleges, you can even go to your dean's office and find out how many people from your college, with your LSAT and GPA combination, applied to (and were accepted at) each law school in the U.S. last year, and the year before, and the year before that.

Armed with these materials, you can decide which schools are "sure bets," which of the better ones are "maybes," and which of the very best are worth a shot. Each application requires all that paperwork, plus a fee of $30 or more, so you try to choose well. Your goal is to cover the spectrum: If you apply to a minimum of one humble school and one elite school, you're less likely to kick yourself for shooting too low or too high, and you won't spend a year sitting around to try again.

With fees, transcripts, and other expenses, my own applications to law schools cost me about $600. I applied to a lot of schools, and I think it was the right thing to do. In a typical year, 20 percent of all law school applicants may find themselves rejected by all of the schools to which they apply, even though three out of four of those rejects probably would have been admitted if they had applied to different schools.[2]

a. The Way You'd Expect to Choose a School

Ideally, you'd like to know a lot of things before you choose among the 175 or so law schools in the U.S. that are now approved by the ABA.[3] You might have only the vaguest idea of where and what you'd like to do as a lawyer. You could use a good source of information at this point.

Let's suppose, for instance, that you'd like to practice law in California. It would be helpful to know how much you might make as a lawyer in San Francisco or Los Angeles. And then you'd like to compare this California information against comparable data for, say, New York. It's one thing to decide between Manhattan and Malibu. But for all you know at this point, the wrong law school might have you choosing, instead, between Buffalo and Bakersfield. You'd like to know this kind of thing *before* committing to a particular school.

It could also make a difference in your planning if you could learn more about being a lawyer in your target place. Is there active discrimination, in that city or state, against lawyers of your ethnic group, race, religion, or sex, by the bar association, by law firms, or by judges? On the other hand, do any of your favorite law schools have strong local alumni networks that might help you get a job?

There are other kinds of information that would be helpful to you at this point. For instance, it would be nice to have a chart that lets you go down a column entitled "Annual salary," until you reach the number that appeals to you, and then look across to the column for the city and the size of firm that interest you, and see how many hours you'll work to make that much money in that city. It could also be helpful to know how many years the typical graduate of each law school stays in his/her first law job, or how much s/he makes there, and how

---

2. Thomas O. White, ed., *The Official Guide to U.S. Law Schools, 1987-88*, the Law School Admission Council (LSAC) and the Law School Admission Services (LSAS), with the American Bar Association (ABA) and the Association of American Law Schools (AALS), 1987, pg. 6.

3. Note: if you forget the definitions of terms in this book, see the Index for the locations of those definitions.

many graduates of each school have become partners[4] in top firms or judges in important courts.

Not to mention the bar exam. You might wonder how many people from each law school fail it the first time, and of those who fail, how many *never* pass it, so that they've effectively wasted their three years in law school.[5] And you might want to know how much law school will cost, how much you'll have to borrow, and how long it will take to repay.

In short, if you were choosing among law schools according to whether they met your personal needs, you'd expect to be able to go down to the bookstore and pick up a book that contains a lot of data on questions like these.

But surprise, surprise! This is *not* how most law students go about deciding which law school to attend. It can't be, because there's no such book. In fact, even the raw data that you'd need to answer those questions isn't always published, and in some cases it's never even been collected.[6]

So now we have two unanswered questions: What makes people suddenly become so sure that they want to go to law school, and how do they know which law school they want to go to? And, come to think of it, there's a third question: Why doesn't the bookstore stock a book that answers these practical questions about your legal future?

It's not that bookstores are afraid of the subject. After all, the shelves are full of resources like your LSAT preparation book[7] and your book on how to approach the law school application process[8] and how to choose your law courses,[9] as well as war-story books about the first year of law school[10] or

---

4. Law firms are generally required to be run by lawyers, which means there is good reason to set them up as partnerships rather than as corporations. Typically, you go to a law firm as an "associate," or non-partner, and you stay there for a number of years, and if things work out well, they will make you a partner after five to eight years, depending on the firm and the city.

5. This is not an idle concern. See fn. 360.

6. This book will point out many instances of little or no data.

7. E.g., Thomas H. Martinson, *LSAT: Law School Admissions Test* (New York: Arco, 1989).

8. E.g., Jeff Deaver, *The Complete Law School Companion* (New York: John Wiley & Sons, 1984).

9. E.g., Stephen Gillers, ed., *Looking at Law School: A Student Guide from the Society of American Law Teachers*, revised ed. (New York: New American Library, 1984).

10. E.g., Scott Turow, *One-L* (New York: Warner Books, 1977).

about being a big-shot attorney,[11] and guides to the various law schools,[12] and collections of articles by lawyers in which they say why their own specialties are so good[13] or so bad.[14]

Nor are lawyers reluctant to ask questions. On the contrary, they're bright. They're driven. Even at this pre-law stage, you'd think that these students, of all people, would insist on knowing exactly what's going to happen to them in this hard, expensive process of legal education.

So how can it be that many people who enter law school know less about what they're getting than when they go out to buy a new car? You have to assume that they believe they have enough information to make their career decisions. How can they be so smart, know so little, and feel that they have the knowledge they need, all at the same time?

There is an answer. The answer is that all this information *doesn't matter.*

b. The Way You Really Choose a School

If you were going after a Ph.D. in philosophy, you'd know that one graduate school is very different from another. Unless you loved the kind of specialized work that they were doing at a particular school, you wouldn't fit in, and they probably wouldn't like you very much.

That's not how it is in law school. The ABA-approved schools all meet the same requirements, and the graduates all have to work in the same legal system, so you're a lot more likely to be studying exactly what you would have studied at some other school.

Since the schools are so similar, the choice of school might seem irrelevant. I mean, if you're destined to be at the bottom of your law school class, then no doubt you belong at a place like Harvard, whose fame will make it much easier for you to

---

11. E.g., Roy Grutman and Bill Thomas, *Lawyers and Thieves* (New York: Simon & Schuster, 1990).

12. E.g., Elliott M. Epstein et al., *Barron's Guide to Law Schools*, 8th ed. (New York: Barron's Educational Series, 1988).

13. E.g., *Full Disclosure: Do You Really Want to Be a Lawyer?* Susan J. Bell, ed., for Young Lawyers Division of ABA (Princeton: Peterson's Guides, 1989).

14. E.g., Deborah L. Arron, *Running From the Law: Why Good Lawyers Are Getting Out of the Legal System* (Seattle: Niche Press, 1989); Richard W. Moll, *The Lure of the Law: Why People Become Lawyers, and What the Profession Does to Them* (New York: Viking, 1990).

rest on your laurels. Otherwise, though, you have lots of highly comparable schools to choose among, and you'll work hard and learn a lot at any of them:

> *[A]t least 40 law schools in this country are of "superior quality." They ... produce graduates who can solve the most intellectually demanding [legal problems]. Alleged distinctions between or among these schools are distinctions in <u>image</u> ....*[15]

And that's why you care which school you get into. We agree: The schools really are similar. But that's not important. What's important is that your peers, your employers, and you yourself are going to believe that you're a cut above the crowd if you graduate from a big-image school.[16] Everyone goes to the "best" — i.e., the most prestigious — school they can, and therefore they assume that you're doing likewise. So if you go to a "loser" school, they think that's where you belong.

So no one cares about all those factual questions I was asking a moment ago. For most entering law students, the real question about a school is not whether it will give you a better education, but where it stands on the pecking order. And since a lot of people take that order so seriously, here are the top 20, according to one widely published survey:[17]

---

15. Scott Van Alstyne, "Ranking the Law Schools: The Reality of Illusion?" *American Bar Foundation ("ABF") Research Journal*, vol. 1982 [sic], 1982, pg. 684 (his emphasis). Grammar and punctuation note: (1) I have not used legal citations in footnotes. If you ever want to figure out a legal citation, consider the example "20 B.C.L. Rev. 601, 613," which means "look at page 613 of the article that begins at page 601 of volume 20 of the Boston College Law Review," as you would know from your copy of *A Uniform System of Citation*, prepared by the Law Reviews of Columbia, Harvard, Penn, and Yale and beloved of law students everywhere. (2) Sometimes, I have cut quotes down to show the author's most important words. As the *System* indicates, lawyers do not simply "paraphrase." Instead, they use brackets to indicate the addition or substitution of a word or letter (e.g., "Peter, Paul [or] Mary") and ellipses ("...") to indicate deletion of one or more words. But brackets and ellipses are ugly and distracting. So, in some places in this book, I have decided not to use them, and instead have simply indicated, in the footnote, that the quote has been paraphrased. You can check the original sources to resolve any doubt about the quality of my paraphrasings.

16. After comparing starting salaries and schools' prestige rankings, "it is clear ... law school students had an incentive ... to get to the highest rated school they could." (Ronald G. Ehrenberg, "An Economic Analysis of the Market for Law School Students," *Journal of Legal Education*, vol. 39, 1989, pg. 639.)

17. Robert J. Morse and Elizabeth A. Wagner, "Top 25 Law Schools," *U.S. News & World Report*, vol. 110, Apr. 29, 1991, pp. 74-75.

1. Yale $	*11. Georgetown $*
2. Harvard $	*12. Berkeley **
3. U. Chicago $	*13. Cornell $*
4. Stanford $	*14. Northwestern $*
5. Columbia $	*15. U. Texas **
6. U. Michigan	*16. U. So. Calif. $*
7. NYU $	*17. Vanderbilt*
8. U. Virginia *	*18. UCLA **
9. Duke	*19. U. Iowa **
10. U. Penn. $	*20. Hastings **

* out-of-state tuition well below $15,000/year
$ avg. starting salaries of grads = $65,000+

And now that you've feasted your greedy eyes, let's get back to the enterprise of figuring out what goes on here.

c. This Logic Can Lead to Funny Results

There's room to question the pecking order — not only because it pretends to detect important differences in the quality of the schools, but also because it sometimes ignores schools that seem to be quietly doing a good job of getting their graduates into high places. For instance, I was surprised, when I once paged through the *Martindale-Hubbell Law Directory*,[18] to see how many of the lawyers in good law firms had gone to obscure schools. In the same spirit, a random look at more than 600 attorneys who made it into the *Who's Who in American Law*[19] gave me this unexpected list, in descending order, of the 10 schools from which most of those attorneys had come: Harvard, Michigan, Columbia, George Washington, Virginia, Yale, Chicago, Fordham, Georgetown, and NYU.[20]

Students often don't, but should, think about more than

---

18. Produced annually in Summit, NJ. Most public libraries have a copy.
19. *Who's Who in American Law*, Marquis Who's Who, Chicago. I can't remember which edition I used.
20. My surprise went both ways. George Washington? Fordham? And where were Stanford, Berkeley, Duke, etc.? No doubt the list would have changed if I had looked at more entries. And I have grown more suspicious, in the intervening years, of the significance of a listing in *Who's Who* — probably because they listed me. But this tabulation was enough to suggest that going to a less-famous school might not be so terrible.

mere prestige. For example, one writer urges you to find out whether (a) you can take courses outside the law school in relevant subjects (business, for instance), (b) the clinical[21] courses are good, (c) the social life seems limited to beer blasts, (d) student government makes a difference, (e) you have a choice of interesting legal journals to join, and (f) the place has good physical facilities.[22]

Of course, I ignored all that and went to Columbia, mostly because it was the most prestigious school that accepted me. Columbia offered an excellent selection of legal journals and an abysmal physical and spiritual environment.

For instance, you could barely stand the student lounge. The law library's photocopiers were broken-down and primitive, despite the hundreds of students who relied on them. When a graffiti nut lost his mind with a Magic Marker on the stalls in the men's restroom, the maintenance people (who seemed to hate us anyway) responded by simply scraping off the graffiti *and* the paint, leaving bare metal that eventually rusted. The halls were perpetually half-lit, although at least that helped to hide the filthy walls, army-like metal lockers, and beat-up furniture. The security guards did nothing, unless you forgot your student I.D. card, in which case they'd promptly turn you away — never mind that you'd been coming through there every day, all year, trying to catch their eye to say hello. The students were very driven, which means that many of them did not hesitate to take books off the library shelves and leave them wherever they chose, forcing you to spend 10 minutes at a time, hunting through the entire library to find each missing volume.[23]

By way of comparison, I've recently done some work in the law library at the University of Colorado at Boulder. I

---

21. For instance, from Harvard Law School: "Clinical programs put students into dozens of organizational settings. Placements are available in a variety of fields. Student roles range from direct client representation to research and writing, policy analysis, and litigation assistance. Some courses require half or more of a student's time for a semester; others involve only ten hours a week of field work. Some courses focus on lawyering skills, while others emphasize doctrine, policy, theory, or ethics." (Paraphrased from the 1989-90 catalog.)

22. Sally F. Goldfarb, *Inside the Law Schools: A Guide by Students, for Students*, 4th ed. (New York: E.P. Dutton, 1986), pp. 14-15.

23. Columbia has improved its physical plant since then. That did me no good, of course. As for its spiritual environment, I have not seen indications that it leads the struggle to make legal education more sensible or decent.

think we snobs at Columbia would have looked on this school with disdain. It's not ancient, or famous, or expensive.

But they're friendly, at least by New York standards, and they seem to trust each other out there. The students have their own assigned desks in the library, where they leave pens, notebooks, sweaters, even their briefcases — not just for a few minutes, but over the entire Christmas break. Nobody seems to steal anything.

All of the photocopiers at Boulder are modern, and they've all been working whenever I've visited. I wanted to use them, so I bought a copy card[24] at the front desk for $20. With $17 worth of copies still on the card, I forgot about it and walked away, leaving it in the machine. An hour later, I remembered it and went racing back, to find that some honest soul had turned it in at the front desk. I did it again a couple of days later, and, again, it was waiting for me up front. A woman there said the same thing had happened to her.

It blew me away. Columbia was not like this. If I'd dropped my copy card at Columbia, people would have followed me to see if I was going to drop anything else. I wished I had known, when applying to law school, how different one school's students can be from another in terms of warmth and respect.

Most prelaw students don't deeply investigate the question of which law school would be best for them personally. Certainly not if it's a choice between Columbia and Boulder. The pecking order is hard to buck. You'd need an awfully good reason to reject a top school.

That's what the statistics say, anyway. The big-name schools get literally thousands of applications for a few hundred spaces, and those applications come from the college students with the best GPAs and LSAT scores. There's no denying the importance of prestige in this process.

So you wind up with a funny result. The students who are brightest and most questioning get in line behind one another, applying to the same schools in the same ways for the same reasons. They come a long way, in a very short time, from

---

24. "Copy cards" are like credit cards. They are magnetically programmed to allow a certain number of copies, so that you don't have to carry a lot of change or interrupt yourself each time to put in another dime.

their initial doubts about going to law school.

But why? What is so compelling about law school and/or the practice of law? What grabs you and makes you shout, "Yes! Yes! That's for me!"

The answer is, you do this because you've got a dream. You buy into a projection, partially true and partially false, that's displayed for you by older people — mostly lawyers — who have their own ideas of what the law is all about.

B. Wanting It Badly

When you graduate from college, you may be young, but you're not an idiot. If you're hardheaded enough to imagine yourself as a lawyer, then you're probably hardheaded enough to demand specific statements on why you should become one. In response to your demand, you will hear a number of reasons that you may find very persuasive. A few were especially important to me and to many of my peers.

1. Diversity

First off, you may be seduced by the thought that, with a law degree, you can do almost anything you'd like. As one lawyer put it,

> *For someone not sure of his interests or how long he wants to commit himself to one profession, law is an attractive starting point. ... There is also security in knowing that if a second profession fails, one has the option of returning to the challenging and secure practice of law.*[25]

The people who want you to consider law school are very careful to remind you that it's OK if you're indecisive about your future. For example, within the last few years, the law school authorities said this in their highly popular book, *The Official Guide to U.S. Law Schools*, formerly known as the *Prelaw Handbook*:

---

25. Charles Z. Cohen, *Your Future as a Lawyer* (New York: Richards Rosen Press, 1977), pg. 89.

> *The law touches virtually every aspect of not only American society as a whole but of our lives as individuals .... American law practice is so diverse that it is difficult to describe what the "typical" lawyer does. Each lawyer works with different clients and different legal problems. ... A legal career is diverse enough to satisfy nearly any preference ....*[26]

It's true that the law is everywhere we turn, and that lawyers are the ones who work with that law. Also, lawyers do many things besides practicing law. They become corporation executives, politicians, and Hollywood script-writers. You name it, and you can find lawyers doing it.

There are many roles within the law. There are advocates, who argue on behalf of the client; counselors, who advise the client on his/her options; and negotiators, who do a little of each. We might add that there are drones, who churn out reams of paper; grubs, whose thankless library labors allow the glamorous advocate to pour forth brilliant insights; and hatchet-people, who "facilitate" matters that are too petty to warrant much attention from the big-time lawyers.

We probably shouldn't go too far with this notion that the law is infinitely diverse, however. There are limits. Otherwise, we wouldn't call it "law." We'd just call it "working for a living." Law doesn't train you to ride broncos or design highways. Your years of law study and practice will lead you to jobs and attitudes that are very different from those of non-lawyers.

Law schools do offer a diverse selection of courses. But they're all law courses. If you want to get into another field, you have to go outside the law school.

Similarly, you'll find variety after graduating, when you go into law practice and get introduced to a number of subjects. But I emphasize *introduce.* It's one thing to be a lawyer who gets to learn a little bit about, say, farming, while defending a farmer who's been sued. It's quite another thing to go back to that farmer after the lawsuit is over and see if he has the least interest in hiring you to work with him there on the farm.

---

26. *Official Guide,* fn. 2, pg. 3.

You can take your law degree and your pride out into the nonlegal job market, but unless you've got marketable nonlegal skills, you're apt to come back a humbler person.

The point is, you're getting diverse training, but it's diverse only for purposes of practicing law. You'll have, at most, one or two nonlegal areas in which, after a number of years, you may know enough to be able to consider a second career. In this sense, law really isn't all that different from any number of other pursuits.

Lawyers can indeed *become* almost anything else, once they've gotten their basic training in law school. But why in the world would we give law the credit for that? These are some of the brightest people in the country. They could have gone into those other fields right at the start. The question isn't whether law school helped them to reach these nonlegal positions. It's whether they wasted a lot of time with law instead of proceeding directly to where they ended up.

In lieu of diversity in the job market, you might be intrigued by diversity in the classroom. You can tell yourself that law school will surround you with unique, special people. But you might want to think about what got these people into law school. The fact is, a lot of them are extreme nerds. Flamboyant they're not. They've proved that they can study endlessly. You should plan on doing some searching if you want to find stimulating friends.

You'll definitely find talented people in law school. But talents require feeding. If someone is willing to devote the time that law school demands, they've probably decided that their other talents weren't really that great or important. They're voting against, not in favor of, self-expansion.

You can benefit from asking yourself what kind of diversity you're seeking from your legal education. If you just want an excuse to pass three years without making any serious decisions, this will do, although you could probably find alternatives that would be more fun, productive, and affordable.

I've criticized the notion that the law is diverse. But I did admit that lawyers do wind up doing a wide variety of things. Isn't that good enough?

Look again, if you will, at that last quote from *The Official Guide*, and particularly the last sentence of it. It expresses a slightly different idea. It says, not that lawyers as a group are diverse, but that any individual lawyer's career can be "diverse enough to satisfy nearly any preference." That makes law school much more tempting. It sounds as though, once you become a lawyer, you'll get to decide whether to spend your days working with one, or three, or a dozen different kinds of law and people and activities.

Unfortunately, that's so wrong that I can't believe they wrote it. It may be that lawyers do many different things. But each individual lawyer is apt to be stuck doing the same thing over and over again.[27]   Just because one ant goes in one direction and another ant goes in another direction doesn't mean that every ant is free to go in any direction.[28]

A lawyer is a professional.   That requires him/her to become highly skilled in a few specific ways.   People don't hire lawyers who'll have fun and make it up as they go along. Clients want a lawyer who has proved him/herself under fire in the same kind of situation many times before.   If you practice law in an area that excites you, that's great, because you'll be doing a lot of it.   But if you want to spend your career on a free ride around the intellectual world, I wish you luck. It's possible to get that kind of legal experience, but it's not likely. That's just not how most legal careers work.[29]

People who spend too much time studying in college sometimes lose track of one final aspect of diversity. Their heads are telling them that "diversity" means learning lots of interesting subjects. But their hearts are telling them that "diversity" also means working with different kinds of people, going different places, and maybe even wearing different kinds of clothes. In these non-bookish ways, your experience with the law may not be merely less diverse than some people

---

27. A study of Australian lawyers confirmed that lawyers are strongly influenced by the area of law in which they take their first legal job, so that there is not much movement to other types of jobs. (Roma Tomasic, "Social Organization amongst Australian Lawyers," *Australian and New Zealand Journal of Sociology*, vol. 19, Nov. 1983, pg. 471.)

28. "As the workers increase in number, more specialized castes are added." (E. Royte, "The Ant Man," *New York Times Magazine*, July 22, 1990, pg. 21.)

29. Note that the *Official Guide* changes every year or two. Your copy may not contain exactly this quote. But the things I quote were said recently enough that you can't help wondering how reliable the *Official Guide* is on these topics. Anyway, I'll let you know the next time I see a written apology by the authors of the *Official Guide* for a previous year's wrongheaded statement.

promised. It may not be diverse at all.

2. Money

Lawyers also praise the law for giving them a way of making a lot of loot. As the saying goes, money is the root of all wealth.[30] But here, too, the news is not all good.

If you like to dream, you can look at Wall Street's salaries, ignore your living expenses, working hours, and risks, and simply assume that you'll eventually become a partner at a top firm and find yourself showered with wealth.

If you face reality, though, you consider a few more variables. Such as: What if I don't do so well in law school? As one of my classmates put it, "The thing about a place like Columbia is that they attract 300 of the brightest people in the country each year, and then convince 250 of them that they're stupid."[31] You're up against valedictorians from all over the place. You genuinely cannot count on being Top Gun.

Or another variable: What if you don't get that cutting-edge job? Maybe you're strange. Maybe your feet stink. The competition is fierce, and if you wear weird ties to your interviews, you could be history.

Or what if you finish the three years of law school and decide you don't even want that kind of big-firm job? Then you have to recalculate, using the salary structure, not of Wall Street, but of your new law job in Podunk.[32]

Or, on the job: What if you can't stand it, and instead of staying around for the big money, you bail out after a couple of years and become a pianist? There's not usually a lot of money in pianism. Your grand plans may be washed up.

Or maybe you hang in there for eight years, and then they tell you to go fly a kite. It's not rare, you know, for that to happen, and opportunities for young lawyers to make partner are shrinking.[33] You'll have to leave — or, if you're working for a more enlightened firm and you haven't made major

---

30. I got this from a T-shirt I saw the other day.
31. This is from the woman with the Ph.D. in astrophysics. (See pg. 73.) She included herself in the "feeling stupid" category. Remember how I said going to law school was like joining the Marines?
32. See text starting at pg. 186 for statistics on these points.
33. Thomas F. Gibbons, "Law Practice in 2001," *ABA Journal*, vol. 76, Jan. 1990, pp. 69-71.

enemies, maybe they'll offer you a 7-percent raise and a chance to continue, forever, in purgatory, also known as "senior associateship," which means you'll always be a mere salaried employee.

Or even suppose you get the brass ring. You "make partner" — that is, they make you a partner. Even at this point, all kinds of strange things can happen. They may require you to invest a portion of your income back in the firm. You may not get a very big piece of the pie for years.[34] You'll work long hours. You can be sued now, and you'll worry about that, despite your expensive malpractice insurance — not only because of the malpractice claims, but also because of the possibility of spectacular lawsuits by former partners who decide they hate you.[35]

And this is what can happen to those who make partner at top firms! How about the many attorneys who start at salaries of less than $30,000?[36] How about those who make more, but whose working hours are so long that they'd have earned more, on an hourly basis, as word processing operators?

Even on Wall Street, an income of $90,000 a year, with federal, state, and local taxes of, say, 25 percent, and with 2,700 working (not billable) hours, comes out to $25 an hour, which is probably less than the income of your average New York electrician.[37] The limo drivers who used to take me home from the office made that much. And your net hourly income figure drops way off if you don't like to think that you went through all that hard work in law school for free, and

---

34. Or, as one junior partner confided to me, in describing his relationship to a senior partner, "I like to think I work *with* Joe, not *for* him." Nowadays, partners do get demoted from partnership if they don't work hard enough. (See Stephen Gillers of NYU Law School, as quoted by Stephanie B. Goldberg, "Then and Now: 75 Years of Change," *ABA Journal*, vol. 76, Jan. 1990, pg. 59.)

35. Malpractice insurance is no cure-all. It often covers the date of the suit, rather than when the malpractice occurred, so you can imagine the discomfort of partners at those firms that now cannot obtain coverage for their past sins. An example: firms that might be held liable for the failures of banks or savings and loan companies. (Harlan Christ and Wade Lambert, "Malpractice Insurers Worry Over Legal Work for Banks," *Wall Street Journal*, Nov. 29, 1990, pg. B-7, col. 1.)

36. The median income of all attorneys in 1988 was $32,750. (ABA Public Education Division, *Law As a Career*, (Chicago: ABA, 1989), pg. 6.) In 1990, starting attorneys at almost all governmental and public interest law jobs earned less than that. Even at law firms, the average was $43,000 or less in every city except Chicago, Cleveland, D.C., L.A., and New York. (See "The 16th Annual Salary Survey," *Student Lawyer*, Nov. 1990, pp. 30, 34.)

37. Up to $136,000 a year. See "Including Overtime, A City Electrician Outearns the Mayor," *New York Times*, May 6, 1990, pg. A-19, col. 1.

start counting those school hours and costs against your first five or 10 years' worth of income.[38]

As a general rule, your expenses keep pace with your income, even for lawyers who earn very good money.[39] You can hope to save a lot. But reality has a way of fouling that up. You might get married or, even more expensive, divorced. As they say, two can live as cheaply as one, for half as long. You might feel entitled to indulge yourself in expensive restaurants and vacations. You'll have high expectations from three years among your money-oriented law school classmates. You may have substantial student loans to pay back. The fact is, many other young attorneys before you have found themselves in deep debt despite nice incomes.

In short, going to law school to afford a nicer lifestyle over the long haul may make sense, especially if you marry someone who also has a decent income. Going in hopes of reaching financial security within a few years probably doesn't.

So here's a theory: If you're smart enough to get into law school, and if money is what motivates you, maybe you could have found a way of making money without law school. And if you're more motivated by your interests than by making money, you'll probably go back to fun and interesting things eventually anyway, even with your law degree, and find yourself somewhere near the level of financial security or poverty you'd have reached without law school.

Of course, you don't have a non-law-school alter ego, so there is no way of testing this theory. That's what makes it one of my favorites.

In case you don't believe it, though, here's a contrary

---

38. See David L. Chambers, "Educational Debts and the Worsening Position of Small-Firm, Government, and Legal-Services Lawyers," *Journal of Legal Education*, vol. 39, no. 5, 1989, pp. 714-18: For many, "the amounts devoted to debt repayment will ... seem extremely onerous ...." "Even if the first-year lawyer [who graduates with large student debts] obtains one of the most lucrative job offers in New York ..., debt repayment within a ten-year period would prove difficult." (Kramer, "Will Legal Education Remain Affordable, By Whom, and How?" *Duke Law Journal*, vol. 1987, April 1987, pg. 263.) Large student debts can now be consolidated into packages to be repaid over *20 to 25 years*. (Kramer, pg. 265.) The *average* debt per student for the Harvard class of 1990 was $41,500 per student, with some as high as $80,000. (Ken Myers, "Administrators Are Worrying About Graduates' Growing Debt," *National Law Journal*, vol. 13, May 20, 1991, pg. 4, col. 4.)

39. See Deirdre Fanning, "New York Lawyer Leaves Fast Lane for Good Life Jackson, Wyo.-Style," *Denver Post*, Mar. 25, 1990, pg. 3-G.

theory. According to this one, your decision to go into law really does have an impact on your chances of becoming wealthy; unfortunately, it can go either way. I know people who would have made lousy lawyers but who've done quite well in business. And I know proud attorneys, trained to avc:d risks, who've watched, rotting and festering in envy, while motivated youngsters without law degrees go out and start their own legitimate, successful businesses.

It's easier for those upstarts. They have nothing to lose. They haven't been taught that they must do nothing because doing almost anything means risking a lawsuit. They haven't piled up student loans that need to be paid off, and their egos have not been stroked by a prestigious law school to the point that they could never imagine themselves doing something as down-and-dirty as running a hardware store. Instead, these kids just go out and do it, and some of them make a lot of money from their little businesses, and maybe some of my law school classmates could have had the same kind of fortune, if only they hadn't gone into the stultifying practice of law.

There is indeed money in law. Some lawyers become very wealthy. But, generally, a lawyer is someone who works for a living. Maybe becoming wealthy from law is just like becoming wealthy from business — it takes hard work, ability, and luck.

Let's step back, now, and review. I've suggested that there are two sides to (a) the thought that the law is an extremely diverse profession and (b) the claim that you can make a lot of money at it. I don't altogether deny the claims to either diversity or money. I only say that you have to be careful about the ways in which you make those claims.

Unfortunately, that's not what happens. As far as I recall, no law school ever gave me the kind of detailed look at money that I just gave you. Maybe this is what happens when the law school invites prelaw students to listen only to those alumni who have distinguished records of service to the law. They get a bunch of cheerleaders. I don't rue those alumni's successes. But I do regret the perpetuation of beliefs that will work only for a portion of the students who hear them.

3. Excitement

I applied to law school because I wanted to make money and have diverse options. But once I was satisfied that those two elements were there, I began to think about other things. I especially liked the claim that law is exciting.

Some attorneys spend a lot of time dealing with clients, victims, judges, and opposing counsel. Examples include public defenders, assistant district attorneys, and Legal Aid lawyers. If your definition of excitement features lots of standing on your feet and thinking, these jobs may be for you.

For others, excitement means being intellectually engrossed. Personally, I enjoy legal research. Many lawyers sneer at it, but I find it fascinating to try to trace back through the history of an idea's expression in the law, so as to understand how the law came to its present form. It's especially exciting when I drink too much coffee, get wired, and find myself utterly absorbed in some trivial point that otherwise would have bored me silly.

But there are real limits on all these kinds of excitement. The assistant district attorneys, public defenders, and others who spend long hours on their feet or on the phone do not often handle issues of the greatest importance. People at the sophisticated[40] law firms tend to look down their noses at these attorneys and wouldn't willingly trade places with them.

Legal research may be interesting when you get to choose the topic, but it goes downhill rapidly when you've been spending weeks at it, trying to learn how to handle the paperwork in a trivial (but big-money) case. It can be exciting to get involved with a case on the cutting edge of the law, but you can't expect to fill your day with that kind of work unless you're someone like Melvin Belli.

As a junior associate at a large firm, you might be assigned to handle some of the grunt work on a few important cases. And you'll find that exciting, for a while. But you can be tempted to consider it more important than it really is. I remember running a copy machine at a printing store during

---

40. When I use the word "sophisticated" in this book, I don't usually mean to describe people who dress well or talk with a stuck-up accent. I'm referring, rather, to people who are very skilled in the area in which they work.

college and feeling personally involved with some of the important papers I was photocopying. When that thrill wears off, though, you eventually realize that great cases, like great people, look very different from the bottom.

Even the thrill of combat isn't what it used to be. The vast majority of cases settle out of court, after a period of pushing paper back and forth.[41] More and more cases are handled by arbitration rather than trial. You may get to argue some relatively narrow, technical points in court, such as whether the other guy is required to give you certain documents that you seek. It's OK, and you can get engrossed in it. But glamorous it ain't.

Even if you work in a legal speciality that particularly interests you, you can be surprised to see yourself getting sick of the run-of-the-mill cases that fall within that area. As our college professors taught us, overkill can turn the scintillating into the surpassingly tedious.

Finally, how about the thought that law is intellectually exciting because it's so creative? Calling something "creative" makes it sound intelligent. Lawyers pride themselves on their intelligence, so of course they want to think law is creative. Unfortunately, in explaining what's creative about it, they describe not only the ability to come up with genuine solutions, but also the skill to manipulate, to deceive, and to confuse.

When you get away from such perverse kinds of creativity, you may find that lawyers — including you, if you hang in there long enough — are really *not* very creative.[42] And this is not surprising. The law is a conservative enterprise. Traditions and precedents are important. Too much experimentation can get you into hot water.

---

41. E.g., 15% of cases went through trial in the federal district courts in 1940, but only 6.5% in 1980. (Marc Galanter, "Reading the Landscape of Disputes: What We Know and Don't Know (and Think We Know) About Our Allegedly Contentious and Litigious Society," *U.C.L.A. Law Review*, vol. 31, Oct. 1983, pg. 44.)

42. "In contrast to non-lawyers, [lawyers] attach less importance to originality and creativity ...." (S. Warkov and J. Zelan, *Lawyers in the Making* (Chicago: Aldine Publishing Co., 1965), as reprinted in *Law Schools and Professional Education: Report and Recommendations of the Special Committee for a Study of Legal Education of the ABA* (Chicago: ABA, 1980), pg. 30.)

4. Opportunity to Make a Difference

I had one other primary motive for applying to law school. Everything I've said so far had to do with wanting to improve my own life. But how about the idea that a person should try to improve the lives of others?

It seemed to me that there were two ways to fix the world's problems. You could be a star, and simply sweep in and move the masses, or you could work behind the scenes, proceeding step by methodical step.

Let's think, first, about people who become stars. Some are in music or in TV and film. Others make it by non-entertainment routes, particularly politics and religious broadcasting. Although most people seek stardom for selfish reasons, many who reach the top do become interested in trying to get the public's support for various good causes.

Lawyers don't use all those avenues. In particular, you don't see many lawyers becoming TV preachers or movie stars. Most lawyers who reach stardom do so through politics.

You often hear two comments about lawyers in the world of politics. One is that you need lawyers in politics, because much of politics concentrates on lawmaking. And the other is that law must be a good way to get into politics, because so many politicians are lawyers.

I now think, however, that those notions deserve a closer look. Accountants, realtors, and other businesspeople have long since shown that you don't need to be a lawyer to understand the laws that matter to you, and I'm sure the same is true of our non-lawyer senators.[43] What's surprising is not that many lawmakers are attorneys, but that so many are *not*.

By the same token, I don't think law school will make you into a politician if you aren't already. The lawyers who become politicians might have done so even if they hadn't gone to law school. Many of those lawyers who go into politics get involved in student government during college and law school, and many enter politics not long after graduation. This suggests that they already had a plan before they started law

---

43. See Heinz Eulau and John D. Sprague, *Lawyers in Politics: A Study in Professional Convergence* (Bobbs-Merrill, 1964, reprinted by Greenwood Press, Westport, Conn., 1984), pg. 144.

school, and that perhaps they wanted the law degree merely to appear more attractive to voters.

I don't know whether law school can help you get into politics. There's some risk that it'll turn you into a hopeless geek, or that you'll be a mediocre law student and that your opponents will use that against you in the election.

But if you do get into politics, the next question is whether your law school experience will have made you the kind of person, in the kind of position, who will do good for other people. And there's room for doubt on that point.[44] Will law school teach you more about honesty? What about the evidence that, during law school, law students gradually become less interested in such things as making the world a better place or going into public interest law — isn't there a risk that law school will sidetrack you altogether?[45] You want to believe that you'll have the strength to stick with your vision, but, then again, you're fooling with your entire career here, and you don't want to be a chump about it.

Does law school develop your political skills? It's not so clear. Consider, for example, two groups of political leaders in the English-speaking world during the past 50 years, namely, our most famous lawyer and non-lawyer politicians.

Aside from the unusual circumstances of someone like Bobby Kennedy, it's tough to come up with an impressive list of leading lawyer-politicians. You've got Richard Nixon and, well, I don't even know where you'd look to find another successful lawyer who became a famous politician. Gary Hart? Ed Meese? Aside from Nixon, the only U.S. President in the last 50 years who ever practiced law was Franklin Roosevelt, and he didn't seem terribly interested in it.

Anyway, whoever the lawyers are, compare them against the famous non-lawyer political leaders, like Winston Churchill, the Rev. Martin Luther King, Jr., and Ronald Reagan.

---

44. One guy who runs a seminar entitled, "Let Me Talk You Out of Going to Law School" says, "One-half of the people who attend the seminar are sent by their friends, lovers or families. They can't stand the thought that a nice person will even consider becoming an attorney." (Ed Sherman, quoted by Deborah L. Arron, "Running from the Law," *Legal Economics*, vol. 14, Sept. 1988, pg. 46.)

45. Since the 1970s, the percentage of graduates of prestigious law schools going into private practice has jumped from 70% to 90% or more, and of those, more are going into the largest firms. (Chambers, fn. 38, pg. 720. See also Lawrence Dubin, "The Role of Law School in Balancing a Lawyer's Personal and Professional Life," *Journal of Psychiatry & Law*, vol. 10, spring 1982, pg. 63.)

Churchill was a mediocre student. King's fame did not come from his scholarship. And Reagan certainly was no rocket scientist.

But could those guys appeal to the collective imagination, or what? Despite his impressive legal skills, Nixon in his wildest dreams never had either the eloquence of Churchill and King or the popularity of Reagan.

So let's hesitate at the notion that a lawyer who wants to do good things must start out by becoming a star. If you know lawyers and the way they operate, you know that you're much more likely to see them working behind the scenes, in government and in nonprofit organizations, handling issues and solving problems that their political bosses simply don't have the time, interest, or training to comprehend. Without these attorneys, from Legal Aid to the Securities and Exchange Commission (SEC), our lives would be less bearable.

This, by the way, is a perfectly valid way to make a difference. It does not do as much for the ego as being elected president, maybe, but it's still important.

I want to warn you, however, against making too much of it. Budgets, laws, and politics impose real limits that keep young lawyers from making a noticeable difference in government and other organizations. As a result, one's idealism can easily turn to frustration.[46]

And on this avenue, too, law school can sidetrack you. Public-interest organizations, unlike private law firms, may not be able to afford to send interviewers to your law school. They also won't necessarily know, a year in advance, how many lawyers to hire for next year. This presents even the best-intentioned law student with a difficult choice: Accept a job offer from a private law firm in September of your third year in law school, and have all your job worries taken care of long before you graduate, or else "go naked" while your classmates are lining up their jobs, and hope that someone in public-interest law will offer you a job next April.

---

46. "'There are a million ways for recalcitrant Federal agencies to vitiate a law,' said Representative Ron Wyden, Democrat of Oregon. 'It is extraordinarily frustrating. ... Passing legislation today is just the very first step. After that, you have to run through a veritable gauntlet of administrative ... procedures to get the law carried out.'" (Robert Pear, "U.S. Laws Delayed by Complex Rules and Partisanship," *New York Times*, March 31, 1991, pg. 1, col. 6.)

Your law school classmates may not understand how you could turn your back on the money (and, they'll say, the top-quality training) that you'd get if you went with a law firm instead of this public-interest stuff. They'll tell you that the law firm will look better on your résumé. They'll say that the improved résumé, and the superior training you'll get at that firm, will make it possible for you to get a much more important public service legal position after a few years, if you still want it at that point. And how about enjoying a little of the good life, and being able to pay off those student loans?

If that weren't enough temptation, big law firms make a point of announcing that their attorneys can pursue *pro bono*[47] work while employed at the firm. (Once the firms have you, of course, they often behave as though your *pro bono* work had better not interfere with your regular duties, nor with the number of hours you bill. I didn't see a lot of *pro bono* work during my years around law firms.[48])

In short, despite your most saintly dreams, it may not be too wise to just fly off to law school with a vague notion that you're going to become a happy, important do-gooder some-how. Different career plans require different approaches, and your idealism may not necessarily benefit from law school.

5. What Makes Others Go to Law School

The things that motivated me to want to go to law school — including diversity, money, excitement, and the opportunity to do good — are not unusual. In one study, more than 500 Chicago attorneys checked off the items that described why they went to law school. Here are the answers they gave:[49]

---

47. "When attorneys take on cases without compensation to advance a social cause, they are ... representing the party 'pro bono publico.'" (Steven H. Gifis, *Law Dictionary* (Woodbury, NY: Barron's Educational Series, 1975), pg. 163.)

48. *Pro bono* work does not ordinarily include having sex with one's clients. For specific rules on that issue, we must look, of course, to California. (See Richard B. Schmitt, "Stated Simply, It'll Be Hands Off For Those Long Arms of the Law," *Wall Street Journal*, Nov. 13, 1990, pg. B-1, col. 1.)

49. Frances Kahn Zemans and Victor G. Rosenblum, *The Making of a Public Profession* (Chicago: ABF, 1981), pg. 28.) Respondents could select multiple answers. I added the asterisks. Arguably, one asterisk indicates an answer that says nothing positive about the law itself, two asterisks indicate something to do with law that would also apply to other careers, and three indicate suggests something unique to law.

Interest in the subject matter	48%	***
Wanted to practice law	40	***
Good background for other occupational goals	32	*
Prestige of the profession	28	**
Influence of family	23	*
Prospects of above-average income	19	**
Opportunity to be helpful to others and/or useful to society	18	**
Uncertainty about future plans	16	*
Opportunity to work with people rather than things	10	**
Stable secure future expected	9	**
Relative freedom from supervision by others	9	**
Influence of friend or teacher	9	*
Like to argue and debate	6	**
Opportunity to have an influence on the settlement of legal questions	4	***
Wanted to postpone military service	3	*

I'm not saying there's anything conclusive about this study. The factors listed here may be much more important for some law schools, for lawyers who are older or younger, etc. The main thing is to understand your own goals and decide whether law matches them.

C. In Brief: Applying to Law School

I have been negative here because I've wanted to provide a counterpoint to the overwhelming popular beliefs about being a lawyer. Everyone knows the upside: Among other things, you make lots of money and do work that's more interesting than working as a cashier at the supermarket. I've considered it important to point out some things that lawyers and law schools don't always tell you.

I wasn't aware of the objections I just raised for you when I, myself, was applying to law school. I was sold a dream, created by a complex chorus of praises sung all around me, about this profession called the law. I have to admit, I find it refreshing to read one lawyer's description of law school admissions officers as "salespersons" who produce "significant misconceptions" in the minds of people who are applying to law schools.[50]   But I guess I should have known.   You don't go to the Tourist Information Center and ask why the city is so ugly and mean.

My dream inspired me to work very hard to prepare for and take the LSAT and then file my applications for law schools.   I was quite eager to be accepted by those schools. And when I was accepted, my future looked bright.   The months between acceptance and enrollment passed quickly, and then I was a Columbia Law School student.

50. Anthony J. Scanlon, "Ethics and Law School Admission," *Catholic Lawyer*, 1988, vol. 32, pp. 152ff.

§ 2. Your Success in Getting There

As I was applying to law schools, I began to imagine myself as a future Wall Street lawyer, a real wheeler and dealer. Once that self-image took hold, I went with it in a big way, and applied not only to law schools, but to business schools as well. Ultimately, I enrolled in the joint JD/MBA program between Columbia Law School and the Columbia Graduate School of Business. As it turned out, that joint program affected my view, not only of my future, but also of my present, of what I was experiencing as a student.

My courses at the business school taught me how to use computers and statistics. With those tools, and my interest in administration, it seemed natural to get involved in law school student government and to look into the way in which the law school was run.

I started with my own situation. Here I was, in a law school that got 6,000 applications each year, but actually enrolled only 300 of those students. I wondered what had made me and my classmates so worthy in the eyes of the admissions people. Were we really so special? And were we going to be able to live up to their faith in us?

A. The GPA and the LSAT

I had assumed that the law school admissions people must have tons of data printouts and statistical reports, not to mention studies from all kinds of behavioral experts. I was sure they had lots of tricky ways to analyze the things we put on our applications from perspectives that we would never have imagined. After all, I knew that if Columbia Law School wanted to keep on producing top-quality attorneys, it would have to start by selecting the very best applicants.

I took this assumption, along with my business-school numbers-and-computers attitude, to the dean of admissions at the law school. I was very surprised to learn how simple the Columbia approach really was. There were no advanced computer programs and statistical analyses. Instead, the admissions people relied very heavily upon our scores on the LSAT and our GPAs, glancing briefly at other things from our applications.

I hadn't wanted to believe that, even though everyone had told me that this was how it worked. But there it was. And Columbia probably wasn't alone in that. For example, Harvard has been accused of rejecting several thousand applicants each year on the basis of those numbers alone, without even glancing at anything else in their applications.[51]

If you don't think about it too much, it seems sensible to concentrate heavily on LSAT and GPA numbers. You want your law students to be people who get good grades, because law school requires a lot of studying. And you want those who can show their smarts on a test like the LSAT.

But ponder, if you will, the applicant's grades. I knew lots of people in college who specialized in finding the easiest courses and the highest-grading professors. I can't tell you how many times I heard someone say that they were not going to take a particular course because of the risk that they'd get a B in it and would thereby damage their GPAs and their chances of getting into law school.

I've been told that law school admissions committees are skilled at figuring out which students have always taken the easiest classes and professors. But I doubt it. If the college senior's transcript reflects an average of five courses per semester for three years, and if each line on the transcript contains three relevant data items,[52] then a law school that

---

51. R. Klitgard, *Choosing Elites* (1985), cited by Scanlon, fn. 50, pg. 154.
52. Namely, the date of the course, so that they can see how you're progressing; the name of the course; and the grade you got.

receives 6,000 applications would have to review a total of more than a half-million data items if they were really going to examine the details on all those transcripts.

It might help the admissions people if they had the time to enter all that data into a computer and analyze it. But they don't. It would also help if all applicants came from the same college, because then the law schools could begin to figure out which professors were tough graders. As it is, there's no knowing whether an A in literature at College No. 1 is comparable to an A in literature at College No. 2.

So when someone tells me that the admissions people have a good feel for what your transcript means, I have to say that I don't think so. I think they look at the GPA, and that, in most cases, that's about all they get from your transcript.

There's a lot that you can't tell from the cumulative GPA, and even from the transcript's course-by-course details. For example, during my college years, I once skipped a final exam in protest, because I thought the professor had done such a bad job. In another course, I chose a thesis topic that interested me, even though I knew it irritated the professor. I awoke late another morning, and arrived at a final exam 45 minutes after it had started, because I had stayed up very late the night before, reading a lot of stuff that I knew probably wouldn't be on the exam but that interested me anyway. On some exams, I avenged truly stupid questions by scribbling discourses on unrelated subjects.

My professors penalized me for most of those escapades. I guess I'll never know for sure, but I often console myself with the thought that the grades I got for misbehaving in these courses were the only thing that kept me out of Harvard Law School, and then I feel better.

My transcript says nothing about all those experiences. It also ignores those that went the other way. I still remember the professor who apologized to me for the inferior quality of the other students in his course. I was amazed, and pleased, that he would say that. I didn't ask him for that opinion, and I didn't necessarily even share it. He gave me an A. That was the best he could do, short of giving me a medal, which wouldn't have appeared on the transcript either.

We all hear the standard comment that, "Well, the GPA is just a rough measure, but it is often a helpful one." I think we should shorten that comment thus: "Yes, the GPA is just a rough measure. Period."

And then there's the LSAT, that other primary determinant of your law school future. According to the people who created it, the LSAT is designed to give some measure of your aptitude for the work that you'll have to do in the first year of law school. This notion leads to an odd result.

It works like this. You take the LSAT and do extremely well. This gets you into an excellent law school. The LSAT is usually a pretty good predictor; sure enough, you do well in that school. People tend to like the things they do well, and, as the saying goes, if you love to study law, you'll hate to practice it. So you graduate from law school, go to work, and discover that you were really much happier back in school.

So you return to law school as a law professor, where you join other people who went through a similar process. As professors, you and your peers decide on the curriculum. The people who write the LSAT take a look at what you and your buddies are requiring of first-year law students, and they design the LSAT accordingly. This completes the circle, which I describe thus:

> **in·breed·ing** ... *2.a.: confinement to a narrow range of intellectual and cultural resources issuing chiefly from a limited field of specialization. b: employment in an institution ... of an excessive number of people who received their training there.*[53]

The LSAT does not ask whether you have what it takes to be a good lawyer. It just wants to know whether you'll quickly pick up the attitudes and methods that you'll need to succeed in law school. If law school is closely linked with real-life lawyering, then the LSAT will be a good guide as to who should become a lawyer. And if law school is off in its own world, then the LSAT might have nothing at all to do with finding the best future lawyers.

---

53. *Webster's Third New International Dictionary* (1961). It may not be the same law school, but since law schools are so similar, it comes to the same thing.

B. A Note on the LSAT and Being Smart

It's important to understand, at this point, that the LSAT does not necessarily try to find people who are smart.

There's a good reason for that. "Smart" is not a simple concept. For instance, I recently saw this idiot-savant[54] on TV. He's barely able to talk. But he has an incredibly quick ability to create complex sculptures. When they ask him how he does it, he points at his head and says, "I'm smart." I may be sitting here laughing at him, thinking that he's dumb as a stick, but then watch me try to reproduce his sculpting feat. Clearly, there's more than one way to be brilliant.

You might think of lawyers as "savant-idiots" — that is, as a reverse of that idiot-savant. They're brilliant in many ways, except where they're stupid. But where they're stupid, it's like they fell through a hole in the floor, and you suddenly get this weird feeling that there's nobody home inside their heads.

For example, the LSAT does not require nearly the same math abilities as, say, the GMAT, which you take as part of your application to business schools. Of course, you don't need to know as much math to practice law as you do to be a businessperson — if only because the legal system was cooked up, and has been maintained, by people who like to work with words more than numbers. Numbers matter in the real world, but not much in law school, and therefore not much on the LSAT.

In fact, after three years of law school and another seven years of working with lawyers, I can say that a lot of them actually fear numbers. I've heard stuttering and I've seen nervousness in the eyes of influential attorneys when they've had to deal, under pressure, with a simple, but unfamiliar, math problem. I've watched managing partners spend thousands on consultants, apparently believing that some kind of black magic was involved, when those consultants' studies could have been assembled by any self-respecting MBA at a fraction of the cost. And I've had to keep my silence at times

---

54. An "idiot-savant" scores very low on standard tests of intelligence — but, in one particular way, is gifted. See *Webster's*.

when partners, ignorant of the ways in which a computer could have aided them, have advised clients by guess and by golly.

I wouldn't say that math is beyond the grasp of those attorneys who fear it. I assume that most of them could pick it up. The problem is that they don't. They remain ignorant of quantitative procedures, and tend to forget even the math they used to know. But that doesn't stop them from thinking that they're brilliant, nor from handling highly numeric problems when perhaps they shouldn't.

The fact is, that's how they're trained: to approach all problems aggressively. Consider, for example, the findings of one study of what lawyers promised and what they actually delivered:

> *[L]awyers are overconfident of their chances of winning lawsuits, especially in cases in which they had been highly confident of winning to begin with. This affects the decisions they make about whether and how to settle or litigate cases.*[55]

You can talk to me about who's smart and who's stupid, but at some point I have to say that a brilliant person who doesn't know when s/he is skating on thin ice is more dangerous and, practically speaking, more stupid than people who get lower scores on the LSAT but who can tell when they're in over their heads.

The problem goes well beyond the subject of mathematics. In remarkable sympathy with the attitude of many of today's lawyers, Plato (a philosopher) observed about philosophers that

> *Until philosophers are kings ... cities will never have rest from their evils — no, nor the human race, as I believe — and then only will this our State have a possibility of life and behold the light of day.*[56]

Refreshingly, another great philosopher responded with the

---

55. Elizabeth F. Loftus and Willem A. Wagenaar, "Lawyers' Predictions of Success," *Jurimetrics Journal*, vol. 28, summer 1988, pg. 437.
56. John Bartlett, *Familiar Quotations*, 15th ed. (New York: Little, Brown & Co., 1980), pg. 84.

observation that "One cannot conceive anything so strange and so implausible that it has not already been said by one philosopher or another."[57]

For philosophy, the bloom is off the rose. Philosophy has ceded most of its old territory to the sciences. You don't philosophize, anymore, when you want to know something about the real world. Most of the time, you're better off finding, or becoming, a scientist.

If you're as non-scientific as the most muddled philosopher, and if you don't want scientists telling you to butt out because you don't know what you're talking about, my advice is this: Don't go into philosophy. Go, instead, into law. Law is perhaps the last refuge in our world for those who, knowing nothing, wish to assume that they know more than enough. Nowhere except the courtroom do you find people making arguments and arriving at far-reaching decisions about the most important problems of our society without ever having taken so much as a single college course in the subjects they address. As one judge put it,

> *Judges ... are handicapped not merely by lack of information but by the narrowness of their training .... No one ... can become an instant authority on psychiatry, lung diseases, computers, accounting, reconstructive dentistry, aviation, structural engineering, and hospital management — to name only a few of the problems that I have had to rule upon in the past few years.*[58]

Attorneys pride themselves on their ability to think critically, and yet their egos and their training often forbid them to be self-critical and admit that they are not competent to solve certain kinds of problems. The fact is, law school's training makes you smarter in some ways, but it definitely makes you more stupid in others.[59]

You find the same thing in attorneys' social skills. As

57. René Descartes, as quoted in Bartlett, fn. 56, pg. 272.
58. Judge Lois G. Forer, *Money and Justice: Who Owns the Courts?* (New York: W.W. Norton & Co., 1984), pg. 216.
59. Mark H. McCormack, *What I Should Have Learned at Yale Law School* New York: Avon, 1987), pp. 18-20.

you'll learn, many lack even the most basic notions of courtesy.[60] And I'll leave it to you to decide how well they have absorbed such helpful, productive attitudes as optimism and cooperation.

I don't need to say that all attorneys, or even a significant minority of them, have problems with numbers, social graces, or attitudes. All I need to say is that the LSAT does not test for these other ways in which one can be "smart."[61]

In any event, the brightest person is not always the best person for the job. I've seen bright people screw up the simplest task, either because they were bored or because they thought they knew it all and couldn't bear to take directions from someone else. Unfortunately, in the words of one legal administrator, "there is work floating around the hallways of the most prestigious law firms that could be done by a cadre of trained chimpanzees"[62] — posing the very real risk that the lawyers will be too smart, and frustrated, for the job.

Since lawyers pride themselves on their precision, we might reasonably ask them to say, in the future, not that they are simply the best and the brightest — because, for many purposes, they aren't — but, rather, that they are the best and brightest, as measured by the LSAT, for the specific purpose of excelling in the first year of law school.[63] There are other kinds of brilliance, and there may even be other kinds of brilliance that would be valuable in the practice of law, but the LSAT does not recognize them, and therefore the law school admissions committees do not get a comparably objective measurement of them.

My criticism of lawyers may sound harsh. It's not meant to be. Many of my friends — or perhaps I should now say *former* friends — are lawyers. I understand that it may be

---

60. How about the attorney who sneezes into his hand just before shaking yours? (See Sol Stein, *A Feast for Lawyers* (New York: M. Evans & Co., 1989), pg. 161.)

61. Consider, for example, the comment by Patti Hulvershorn, a career consultant: "A satisfied lawyer has good analytical thinking skills, an aptitude for handling masses of detailed paperwork, and a good vocabulary (not a great vocabulary, a good one) and scores low in many other aptitudes." ("A Talent for Torts: Is Law for You?" in *Full Disclosure*, fn. 13, pg. 133.)

62. Arnold B. Kanter, *Kanter on Hiring: A Lawyer's Guide to Lawyer Hiring* (Chicago: LawLetters, 1983), pg. 36.

63. See Donald E. Powers, "Long-Term Predictive and Construct Validity of Two Traditional Predictors of Law School Performance," *Journal of Educational Psychology*, vol. 74, Aug. 1982, pp. 568-76.

difficult for some of them to admit that they are not, in all ways, simply amazing. But it's important to say so. I'd hate to see someone go into the practice of law merely because nothing else makes him/her feel quite as intelligent.

C. How Little the Admissions Committee Really Knows About You

The LSAT, of course, can't measure all of the skills that you'll need in your first year of law school. For example, it won't tell us whether you can sit and read the same old stuff for a long time without getting bored, or how you'll react when you do get bored, or whether you can do good research or defend yourself in front of 150 classmates.[64]

"That's fine," the admissions committee might say. "We don't need to learn those things from the LSAT. We have the entire application of this student here on the table in front of us. It gives us everything we need with which to decide whether the applicant has those abilities."

That, however, is nonsense. The application period runs for about five months, from September through January or so. At a top school, 6,000 applications in five months means 1,200 per month, or 45 per day, six days a week. Each application includes grade transcripts, the applicant's essays, and at least two recommendations from professors or former employers.

Every applicant is different, and so is every school. But if you assume that the transcripts, essays, and recommendations take 10 pages in a typical application, then the dean of admissions at a top school has to review about 450 pages of material every day, six days a week, for five solid months.

The law schools do not advise you that they may take one look and toss your application into the trash. On the contrary, in their *Official Guide to Law Schools*, they claim to review, not only your GPA and your LSAT, but also

your undergraduate course of study — especially its difficulty and depth; the quality of the college you

---

64. A word to the wise: Learn to speak in public. It's essential for any career in which you may take a leadership position. You'll find attorneys joining your local Toastmasters group (listed in the phone book).

attended; improvement in your grades and grade distribution; your college activities, both curricular and extracurricular; your ethnic background; your moral character and personality; your letters of recommendation; your personal interview and/or written essay; significant activities since you graduated from college, such as work experience; your state of residency; your motivation to study and reasons for deciding to study law; and, finally, anything else from your file that might make the admissions committee sit up and take notice.[65]

So, OK, let's take them at their word. If they're going to look at all the materials in every serious application, how well are they going to get to know you?

Let's assume, for starters, that the college seniors who apply to law school are bright, and that they do a good job with their paperwork. Besides, they don't want to waste their application fees of $30 to $50. So, at most, maybe 10 percent of the applications are in such poor shape that the dean of admissions can safely reject them out of hand, without even reading them.

That leaves 400 pages of text to review every day. So the dean, being a sensible person, hires three assistants. Unless the dean wants to pay them to sit around for seven months out of the year, they'll have to be willing to take a five-month job and then get laid off. So they probably aren't exactly your career-track kinds of people. Also, they won't be formally trained,[66] but that's OK. The dean can train them, and then give them the power to screen out 75 percent of the material. That still leaves the dean with 100 pages of highly individualized, personal writing to read each day.

I have never received 100 pages of letters from close friends on any single day of my life. But I can tell you that if I did, I'd be awfully tired a long time before I got through all of them. And I'd much rather read letters from close friends than the numbingly redundant essays and recommendations in

---

65. *Official Guide*, fn. 2, pg. 6.
66. Scanlon, fn. 50, pg. 158.

a bunch of law school applications.

The dean will have other distractions, of course. Besides the bureaucratic hassles of life as a law school administrator, s/he will have to keep checking up on the assistants, to make sure they don't go haywire, and will also have to look at those applications that the assistants have singled out for special attention. There will always be a few turkeys who insist on a personal interview, and there will be occasional crises.[67]

I think you begin to see that something, somewhere, has gotta give.

Let's come at the problem from the other side of the table. Let's say you're applying to law school. The essay you write as part of your application will be your best chance to explain yourself to the admissions committee. Will that tell them enough to permit an informed decision on your application? A few comparisons may be instructive.

First, let me tell you that I recently visited a video dating service. Here's how it works. They videotape you for 10 minutes, while you chat with one of their employees and pretend to be normal. They ask lots of specific questions, and they make you write an essay about yourself. People of the opposite sex can look at these materials and then decide whether they're interested in you.

This is not a simple process. The list price for a year's membership is more than $1,700. It's also much more sophisticated than the process that the dean of admissions uses. For one thing, it's harder to hide phoniness, bad attitudes, or physical problems from this video club's camera. Also, you're being examined by potential lovers, who probably have a lot of experience with the long-term dangers of knowing someone like you. It's unlikely that the dean of admissions reviews your application materials with anxieties and hopes that are anywhere near as intense as those of the people who examine your dating/mating videotape.

Even so, the video dating service gets mixed results. Most

---

67. At some schools (e.g., Yale), faculty members read the applications. (See *1979-80 Prelaw Handbook* (AALS/LSAC, 1980), pg. 381.) But faculty members presumably have limited time for this exercise, and may not be experts at choosing future lawyers. Consider, too, schools like Georgetown, which was once accused of having only two full-time admissions officers to screen 7,000 applications. (Philip M. Stern, *Lawyers on Trial* (New York: Time Books, 1980), pg. 176.)

people sign up for a three-year membership ($2,300) rather than betting that they'll hit the mark in only one year of dating. Most members apparently go out on lots of dates, which suggests that even though the video and the other materials give them a general impression of you, it's not enough, and they still need to meet you in person to appraise you properly.

That's one example of a technique for selecting the right person from among many applicants. For a more advanced approach, you might think about what happens in a headhunter's office. For example, the elite personnel agencies that try to find just the right lawyer for a major national law firm may be paid 20 percent of that attorney's annual salary for their effort. It can take months, and it can require scores of interviews. The headhunter earns his/her fee.[68]

These examples — the video dating service and the headhunter — show how far you *can* go if you care about the quality of the person you're looking for. There's quite a contrast between these examples and the $30 fee you pay for the privilege of having a one-shot, two-minute review by a dean of admissions whose momentary whim will affect your entire career.

The fact is, there are real limits on what the dean can do. If you come in with bad grades or bad LSAT scores, you're sunk. It's not just that you will appear unable to do the work in law school. It's also that there are books that publish the LSAT and GPA numbers of those students who are admitted to the law schools. If a school accepts a lot of low-scorers, it will look like they couldn't get better applicants, and the school's reputation will suffer.[69]

Of course, accepting *no* losers will discourage losers from applying and will therefore cut off a large source of funds. If people knew more about the application process, maybe only the 500 or 1,000 applicants who are likely to be admitted would apply to a school like Columbia. The other 5,000 would apply elsewhere instead, and the school would lose up

---

68. Consider my own experience as a headhunter, starting at pg. 196.
69. This kind of disclosure probably affects law schools' willingness to publish statistics about themselves. (Council of the ABA Section on Legal Education and Admissions to the Bar, *Long-Range Planning for Legal Education in the United States* (Chicago: ABA, 1987), pg. 20.)

to a quarter million a year in application fees.[70]

D. So Where Does That Leave You?

We've already seen that the law schools aren't exactly humble about their limitations in the application process. They claim to review all kinds of things, and to get to know you really well. This leads to the next claim, which *The Official Guide to Law Schools* puts this way:

> *Nowadays, almost everyone admitted to law school survives to graduate. In fact, on average, less than 5 percent of law students drop out of school for academic reasons, so the admissions people must be rather accomplished at admitting academically qualified students.*[71]

I can think of two theories that may explain why the dropout rate would be only 5 percent. One is that law school is still as difficult, and the professors still try to drive away those who aren't cut out for it, but the dean of admissions, all by him/herself, has become exceedingly skilled at choosing just the right people. The other theory is that the dean of admissions gets no credit, because the law schools have made it easier for students to survive.

Perhaps the key phrase in that quote is "for *academic* reasons." The law schools probably keep track of the reasons that people give for dropping out of law school. We can assume that people always give accurate reasons — that, for example, the proud college valedictorian who doesn't understand the law isn't playing make-believe when s/he uses "family needs" as an excuse to bail out.

But I don't think that's so believable. I went to school with some pretty egotistical characters, and I'd be amazed to hear many of them say that they were having academic difficulty. The better approach here is, I think, not to rely on the self-description offered by these students as they run away;

---

70. Law schools are big business. In 1987, the combined budgets of the ABA-approved schools were already over $4 billion a year. (*Long-Range Planning*, fn. 69, pg. 8.)
    71. *Official Guide*, fn. 2, pg. 6.

it is to look, instead, at the logic of the situation.[72] The fact is that law schools have very good reasons not to push their luck. If they overdo it, they'll wind up with a bunch of underemployed professors commanding half-empty classrooms. As one model of legal statesmanship puts it,

> *The economic realities of providing a quality legal education ... has mandated that schools accept qualified candidates who will continue through the three or four year program. The first year of law school is no longer a contest where only the fittest survive. The wimps, nerds and jerk-offs will also survive.*[73]

Let me tell you a story. One semester, I was taking a course called "Corporate Taxation." I took it because I thought it would be useful in my future job. But, if you want to know the truth, I hated corporate taxation. I despised it. It was boring. It was for accountants. I didn't know what it was for, except that I knew it wasn't for me.

Halfway through the semester, I went to the academic dean and told her that I was going to drop the course. She said, "You can't do that." I said, "Why not?" She said, "Because then you'll have too few credits for the semester, and it won't count as a full-time 'semester in residence,' as required by university rules. If you drop that course, you'll have to stay here another semester after your classmates have graduated."

Well, I went home, and I thought about it, and I said, "What the heck, I've got to hang around for another semester after law school anyway to finish my MBA. Maybe I can work out something between the law school and the business school. At worst, maybe it'd be just as well to stay that extra semester and take some courses I'd miss otherwise." I had spent six years getting my college degree, and had enjoyed it, so this seemed OK. It wasn't my first choice, but it would do.

I was so sick of corporate taxation I was green. I don't know why I disliked it so badly, other than possibly the fact that I was about five miles behind the rest of the class. But I

---

72. And, for that matter, at the statistics. See pp. 186ff.
73. William D. Henslee, *How to Survive the First Year of Law School* (Chicago: ABA Law Student Division, 1986), pg. 3.

was determined to bail out, come what may, so I went ahead and dropped the course.

When the academic dean found out, she summoned me to her office. "Now you've done it, haven't you?" she said. "I see only one way out."

Hope fluttered in my breast. "I have a way out?" I asked. "Indeed you do," she replied. "You will have to take three extra units next semester, and I will have to 'deem' those three units to apply to this current semester, as though you were taking them now, so that you will get residence credit for both semesters."

Needless to say, this approach had all kinds of possibilities. During college, I had discovered that taking 20 or 25 credits in a semester made me get the most out of every minute. During those semesters, my grades actually improved. So now that I saw how much freedom the academic dean had, I was powerfully tempted to ask her if it would be OK to take a double load in the autumn semester and then spend the spring in Fort Lauderdale.

More to the point, this experience told me that Columbia was going to see to it that I got through, one way or another, in my allotted three years. I had been thinking it was me versus them — the professors, the administration, and the maintenance men — but now it was turning out that they were all secretly rooting for me, even if I was sort of a screwup.[74]

Here's how I see it. When you're a good child, you have a horrendous fear of what they'll do to you if you ever do something bad. And then, when you actually do something bad, you're surprised at how mild the punishment turns out to be. I mean, even if they wallop you, the pain is soon gone, but the joy of the forbidden lingers.

So here I'd gone into the dean's office, cringing with fear, only to emerge with a head full of new ideas. It seemed to me that there must be a whole subgroup of law students like me, and that some of them had medical problems and some had psychological problems and some just didn't like school all that much anymore, and yet most of them managed, with the dean's

---

74. "Remember, the faculty and the administration is [*sic*] there to help you. They mean well despite themselves." (Henslee, fn. 73, pg. 4.)

help, to graduate on time and in good standing. I'm not saying that she showed me a list of such rogues. It's just that the ease with which she handled my case made me think that it wasn't all that unusual.

Nor am I complaining. But after this experience, it's funny for me to read this stuff, in *The Official Guide to Law Schools*, about how the admissions people are so skilled at choosing academic winners. The fact is that, as one of my friends put it, even the best law schools have unselfish individuals who are willing to serve at the bottom of the class, so as to make "the average" more attainable for their peers.

E. Getting In: A Summary

After reviewing the evidence, I came to the conclusions that my classmates and I were almost guaranteed to survive law school if we just kept punching the clock, and that we had gotten in, in the first place, because of a couple of very simple items of data, namely, our LSAT scores and our GPAs.

In a way, this was depressing. You'd really rather believe that the admissions committee examined your life and your personality in great detail and reached the well-considered judgment that, from all the evidence, you are an obviously superior person; and that, once admitted, you survived against difficult odds. Being shooed on through merely because we had come out ahead by a few points on a standardized exam just didn't offer the same sense of self-importance.

It might have been to my advantage, though, that it worked this way. If they'd examined the other factors, I might not have gotten in at all. I hadn't been too focused on career goals in high school or college. I did not suffer the teenage experience common to my rich-kid classmates, in which "You feel like if you make one mistake, your future is gone."[75] Some of my unfortunate peers had gone through decades of parental pressure, expensive prep schools,[76] deep anxieties, therapy — you name it — and here I, this hick, managed to wind up in the same prestigious law school as they.

---

75. "Could Suicide Be Contagious?" *Time*, Feb. 24, 1986, pg. 59.
76. Law students come from higher social and economic levels than other college graduates. (Warkov & Zelan, fn. 42, as cited by Dubin, fn. 45, pg. 61.)

You can imagine how I felt when one of these poor bastards spent 15 minutes telling me how he really did not belong at Columbia and how he and his parents could not believe that Harvard had made the obvious mistake of rejecting him. I didn't mention that my mother, by contrast, had sent me a card, congratulating me on my college graduation, a year before I was actually graduating. She'd simply lost track.

§ 3. The Study of the Law: Myth and Reality

No matter why I went to law school or how I got in, I was finally there, and the games were about to begin. I had a lot to learn — about everything — and so will you.

A. The First Year: The Moment of Truth

Law school lasts three years. In the first year, you're just taking a bunch of basic required courses. Your legal education may not really take off until the second and third year. But that first year can make or break your career.

1. Why It's Important

When you look in from the outside, you might think law school is just like any other kind of school. You put in your time, and then one day you're finished and you graduate.

But it's not like that. The first year is everything. You need to plan for law jobs from the very start. The clock starts ticking immediately.

Let's say you start law school in September of Year Zero. You'll finish your first year of law school in May of Year One, which is when your "first summer" begins. You go back to school for your second year of law school that September, and that school year ends in May of Year Two, followed by your "second summer." Finally, you graduate in May of Year Three, take the bar exam in your "third summer," and start work at your permanent job in September of Year Three.

So here's how the interviewing schedule works. In the autumn of Year Zero, you'll already start to look for first-summer jobs. In August of Year One, the formal interviewing season begins for second-summer jobs. And in August of Year Two, you'll start interviewing for your permanent job.

At each stage of the process, grades are very important. Employers ask about them, and so does the Law Review.[77] Only the best students make it onto the Law Review, and the only grades the Law Review considers are first-year grades.[78] If you get invited to join the Law Review, you'll probably find that employers *drool* over you — not literally, we hope — and that your classmates are exceedingly jealous.[79]

2. The Struggle to Excel

You need good grades to get on Law Review and land the best jobs. You want good grades because they make you feel good about yourself. And you're used to getting good grades, because you were a top performer in college.

The process of getting good grades in law school is not like that of getting good grades in college, though, and for that reason it's humorous, to me, that deans of admissions should choose law students according to their undergraduate GPAs. To do well in law school, unlike college, you have to be able to adapt quickly to an entirely new learning environment.

I, for one, was no good at that. I'm like a locomotive. Get me cranked up and point me in the right direction, and there's no stopping me. But don't ask me to adjust to a whole new world at once. For all I know, Columbia would have been wiser to replace me with someone who had a lower GPA but who could have adapted more easily.

---

77. Most law schools have a Law Review. For example, "The Harvard Law Review ... is a general legal periodical that serves ... the legal profession as a whole, while training its members in legal research and writing. Membership is limited to second- and third-year students and is determined by grades and the results of a writing competition. ... Student editors write and publish their own work in several forms, including notes, case comments and book reviews. We also edit pieces ... for substance, organization and style." (*Student Organizations 1989-90* (Cambridge: Harvard Law School, 1989), pg. 24.)

78. Many law schools have other journals besides the Law Review; often, though, their prestige depends on the grades of the students they accept.

79. "[A]n excessive focus on the employment dimension and misinterpretations of ... grades ... often turn law schools into grim and inhumane institutions that are much less conducive to learning." (Philip C. Kissam, "Law School Examinations," *Vanderbilt Law Review*, vol. 42, Mar. 1989, pg. 483.)

As an example, I rebelled against the "Socratic method" in which many classes were taught. The method is named for Socrates, who supposedly never made statements, but just kept on asking questions.[80] So in law school, your professors ask, and you answer, until they stump you. At that point, you may finally be ready to listen and learn.

I grant that, as compared to a lecture, it's more entertaining to watch some poor jerk squirm under the professor's relentless badgering. But when you move beyond sadism and start to ask how much you're learning, you have to wonder. It always seemed moronic, to me, to use a question-and-answer format in a class of 150 students. You can't hear what the students are saying, you can't believe they're saying something that stupid (or that complicated), you can't stand a particular student who likes to dominate the debate, etc.

In most of those large classes, no one is assigned to the row of seats in back of the big classrooms, near the exits. As the semester grinds on, you see a growing fringe of students sitting back there, where the lights don't shine too well. These are obviously not their assigned seats, and you realize that this is a form of truce. They'll attend class, even though they don't understand what's going on, as long as the professor pretends they're not there and doesn't call on them.

By semester's end, many students have lost track of what's happening in the intimate little chat that goes on between the professor and the few students who are still on his/her wavelength. Does a student's love of the Socratic method have anything to do with his/her ability to practice law? No. Is it a better way of teaching than the one they use in, say, engineering school? No. But the Socratic method will arbitrarily help to determine whether the student understands the professor, earns a higher grade, and gets a better job. When I ran head-on into this teaching method, I had no patience for it. And, of course, it had no patience for me either.

My inflexibility hurt me in another way. I didn't like the books that were supposed to be guiding me.

In college, if you can't grasp what's happening in the

---

80. No parallel is intended to the other Socratic method, namely, using hemlock as a reality antidote.

classroom, you go home and read your textbook. Even when you do understand the subject, you try to keep looking ahead in the book, to get a picture of how it all fits together. Textbooks usually follow a helpful, sensible scheme of organization that proceeds from step A to step B.

In law school, it's not like that. You work out of a "casebook." As the name implies, this book contains reprints of bits and pieces from important cases that judges have decided down through the years. The cases are often difficult to understand, not only because the law is complex, but also because the judges who wrote them talk in circles.

Half the time, when you've finished reading a case, you say to yourself, "Now what the hell was *that* all about?" You look at the notes after the case, hoping for answers, but all you see are a bunch of questions or, at best, some comments that seem to be moving forward, as though you were itching for more. You turn the page, and they're starting a new case. You're baffled. You turn some more pages, and you discover that this goes on, case and notes, case and notes, for 50 or 100 pages. And then it's a new chapter, and you're *still* utterly confused.

Sometimes you learn, long afterwards, that the only reason you were forced to read all those cases, and their incomprehensible notes, was so that you would appreciate why the Supreme Court or Congress eventually changed the law and made all those cases irrelevant. At other times, they make you read a lot of cases just so you'll understand that Congress and the Supreme Court have *not* made any big decisions, which means that, like you, the law in this area is still messed up.

I was pleased to be one of the first people in my law school class to discover that companies like Gilbert's publish outlines that cover most of the important issues in your law courses. These outlines won't put you at the head of the class, but they'll preserve your sanity. Ultimately, you just want to know what's going on.[81]

Students respond in different ways to these problems with the law school teaching method. Some, who are doing poorly for perhaps the first time in their lives, will rebel at that and

---

81. Dubin, fn. 45, pg. 65.

either drop out or pretend to understand. Meanwhile, in a true indication of how nasty the situation can get, some of those who think they are *not* doing well really are.[82]

The more you learn about legal education, the less surprised you'll be to hear that *The Official Guide to Law Schools* responds to this situation by implying that there's something wrong with those students who wish the whole teaching process made more sense. Here's what it says:

> *People who especially value structure, authority, and order are often attracted to law school. ... But the study of law does not involve the kind of certainty such students are seeking.[83]*

Obviously, law schools prefer students who *dislike* order and structure. This explains why the anarchists among us were overjoyed when they got to law school.[84]

After reading that quote from *The Official Guide*, I found it interesting to review Scott Turow's view that students at Harvard Law "are men and women drawn to the study of rules, people with a native taste for order."[85] I also looked again at the words of a shrink who has spent more than 20 years with law students and who finds, in them, a "greater than average concern for orderliness."[86] According to the ABA itself, a lawyer's job includes "putting entangled affairs in order."[87]

The fact is, law students seek to understand. *The Official Guide* may make snide remarks about their love of order, as though they were closet fascists, but the point remains: The legal educational process really is goofy.

Well, if I liked the casebooks and the classroom method, I knew I would just *love* the exams. And I was right. They

---

82. Edwin H. Greenebaum, "Law Firms and Clients as Groups: Loyalty, Rationality, and Representation," *Journal of the Legal Profession*, vol. 13, 1988, pg. 224.
83. *Official Guide*, fn. 2, pg. 19.
84. I'm being sarcastic.
85. Turow, fn. 10, pg. 275.
86. Andrew Watson, professor in the law and medical schools of the University of Michigan, "The Quest for Professional Competence: Psychological Aspects of Legal Education," *University of Cincinnati Law Review*, vol. 37, summer 1968, pg. 91, as cited by Dubin, fn. 45, pg. 63.
87. "Law As a Career," fn. 36, pg. 3.

were off the wall.

In one of my first-semester classes, the prof hinted that parts of this year's exam would be similar to exams from previous years. We thought this meant that he'd be asking questions on the same topics. Those old exams, and their model answers, were on reserve in the library. Some of us reviewed them there in the library, and others spent the money and time to make photocopies of all those exams, which we added to the stack of outlines and notes and books we were studying.

On the morning of the open-book exam, some of us didn't take along those photocopies, even if we had them. Maybe we believed that it would be more confusing than helpful to have too many materials available during the exam, or maybe we had opted to type the exam and had to lug our typewriters. It seemed sufficient, or necessary, to restrict ourselves to only those few books and outlines that pulled it all together.

Bad mistake. One major question on our exam was practically identical to a question from a preceding year, and others were very similar. Those who brought along the old exams more or less copied the old answers directly into their test books, even if they didn't understand what they were writing. Many students had brought along those old materials, so the competition was really intense. Under the professor's grading curve, a loss of only a few points meant a drop from an A to a C for the semester.

To me, this stunk. Call me sour grapes, if you wish, because I didn't take along those model answers. But I really didn't mind getting a C, under the circumstances. As far as I'm concerned, if the exam is intended to test your knowledge, rather than your ability to carry paper around, then that's what it should do. That exam affected the careers of law students who had worked their tails off and had performed brilliantly all semester long. I considered that obscene.[88]

At Columbia, and no doubt at many other schools, they throw in an added twist. Your first-semester exams don't start

---

88. I appreciate the professor who says that the typical law school exam "results in poor education," "is too reductionist and too fragmentary to serve the varied intellectual demands of most legal practices," and "is distorted towards ... memorization." (Kissam, fn. 79, pp. 433, 436-37, 487.)

until after New Year's Day. This means that you can go home to your family and friends in Pittsburgh or Omaha, study constantly through the holidays, and then return to your slumlike dorm room on the edge of Harlem just in time for a blizzard and the commencement of exam season.

By the time it's all over, you can feel like a ghost. I drank far too much coffee, and it caught up with me on the night before my last exam. I couldn't get to sleep until 2 a.m., and then awoke at 6. I was extremely tired, so I started in on the coffee again. That made me shake so badly that I feared I wouldn't be able to write, so I drank a half-pint of peppermint schnapps to calm me down. Just to be safe, I packed a flask of bourbon and a quart of coffee to the exam, in case I went off the deep end in either direction. A note to our viewers: We are trained professionals. Do not attempt this at home.

I was not the only one who freaked out at exams. One classmate stayed awake almost continuously for several days, in a desperate bid to catch up. Another one, a bright Texan who had been engaging the professors in debate all semester, got as far as the middle of his first law school exam during that New York City winter, and then got up, went out to the restroom, kept right on going to the airport, and never came back. At the end of the exam, his books were still sitting there where he'd left them. We never saw him again.

3. What the Pressure Does to You

Perhaps you've had the experience of dealing with people who've been working 80 or 100 hours a week for months on end. At times, they're irrational. Their moods swing with the wind. They have no patience. This experience is not limited to law students.

But there's something special about law school. It goes beyond the quantity of work and the pressure to get it done. Law school is the door into a hard new world. It brings you face-to-face with a different, less friendly kind of person, and eventually that's what you become too.

I sometimes wonder whether it's anything like what people feel in the moments before their first act of cannibalism. In law school, people seem to hope that you'll fail, and you find yourself thinking the same way in return. Some classmates may share your unhappiness with this, but others seem eager to say, "Hey, if you don't like it, go somewhere else. It'll be one less body for me to climb over."

Sometimes, the tension was impressive. One law student punched out a clerk at a copy center when the clerk told him that his photocopies would be delayed. During an otherwise relaxed pick-up game of volleyball, one of my fiercely competitive classmates, a top-flight athlete, could not resist spiking hammer-blow shots at the two out-of-shape women on the opposing team. I cut my roommate's telephone cord, in the middle of a phone conversation, when he wouldn't stop talking right outside my door and disturbing my study. And I remember, one night in the Third Phase bar, being reduced to tears, when I didn't even think that was possible anymore, by a vicious verbal attack from a classmate whom I had considered one of my better buddies.

Scott Turow, describing his experience as a Harvard 1L (i.e., first-year student), put it this way:

> *I know of at least one suicide attempt in my class, and there were more people than I can count who confided that they'd been driven through the door of the psychiatrist's office for the first time in their lives by the experience of being a Harvard 1L. ...*
>
> *[He quotes one of his professors as saying that] men who fought in World War II or Korea or Vietnam ... never felt as scared or oppressed as they did when they were law students at Harvard ....*[89]

Supporting that, studies comparing law students to medical students and other graduate students have found far more depression, anger, stress, and hostility, and much less contentment and feeling of friendliness, in the law students.[90]

I can complain about my situation, but I have to mention that it was apparently even worse for female students. There

---

89. Turow, fn. 10, pg. 154.
90. Robert Kellner et al., "Distress in Medical and Law Students," *Comprehensive Psychiatry*, May-June 1986, vol. 27, pp. 220-223; Marilyn Heins et al., "Perceived Stress in Medical, Law, and Graduate Students," *Journal of Medical Education*, vol. 59, Mar. 1984, pg. 178.

are more women in law school, and in the practice of law, now than ever before. They have made important advances in the practice, and they find it a lot easier now to be taken as seriously as men. But they remain separate. In law school, according to Columbia dean Barbara Black, "The aspirations and expectations of male and female students are still quite different."[91] Even the language of law school exams "ignores the more distinctively feminine patterns of ... thinking and caring about complex relations ... among persons, ideas, and situations."[92] Women experience significantly more stress in law school than men,[93] they have noticeably different career goals,[94] and their personal relationships suffer much more during the process.[95]

I'm not a woman, so I can't describe my firsthand experience on these points. Likewise, I'm not a member of what you might consider a minority group, so I can't tell you about the personal experiences that others might have had. But I can read, and on that basis I can tell you that legal education has very different results for different kinds of people.

Consider, for example, these findings: that Protestant, Jewish, and Catholic lawyers tend to go into very different kinds of practice;[96] that, of those who had taken the California bar exam in 1985, the pass rates of whites, Asians, Hispanics, and blacks differed dramatically;[97] and that a college student's likelihood of considering a career in law will depend on the extent to which s/he is familiar with corporate

---

91. Goldberg, fn. 34, pg. 58.
92. Kissam, fn. 79, pp. 456-57.
93. Kellner et al., fn. 90, pp. 220-223.
94. Forer, fn. 58, pg. 72.
95. In a study of medical and law students, professional training resulted in noticeably more strain upon the personal relationships of female students than upon those of male students; the women received more stress from their partners; proportionately more women than men reported that their personal relationships had ended during those periods of stress; and, among the married subjects, 31% of the men, but only 19% of the women, described their spouses as moderately or very supportive. (Elizabeth J. Clark and Patricia P. Rieker, "Gender Differences in Relationships and Stress of Medical and Law Students," *Journal of Medical Education*, vol. 61, Jan. 1986, pp. 32-40.)
96. E.g., one study found Catholic lawyers to be three times more likely than Protestants or Jews to become prosecutors, mainstream Protestants five times more likely than Catholics or Jews to be doing securities or antitrust defense work, and Jews more than twice as likely as Catholics, and very much more likely than mainstream Protestants, to be doing divorce work. (John H. Heinz and Edward O. Lauman, *Chicago Lawyers: The Social Structure of the Bar*, pp. 327-32, reprinted in Hazard & Rhode, fn. 282, pp. 57-58.)
97. See fn. 360.

America.[98] I, personally, can tell you that it's not so easy to come from a lower-middle-income background and compete successfully, right out of the box, against kids whose parents have been grooming them for years.

Now, not everyone agrees that law school is terrible, or that it favors those who arrive there with a certain set of attitudes. The ABA, for example, does not want the law schools, its pride and joy, to be accused of doing evil things to people. So in *Law Schools and Professional Education*, they comment that, in one important study,

> *[T]he ... students entered with highly positive estimations of legal practice and the justice system. Over the first year their views became less positive .... But it requires some considerable invention to conclude that the first year at ... law school instilled cynical views. A more appropriate interpretation is that first year students began with naïvely positive views of the legal profession and of the justice system but during the year came to perceive greater ambiguity, complexity, and human frailty. That seems to be both appropriate and healthy. ... Further research is clearly appropriate.*[99]

But let's think about that for a minute. Reasonable dictionaries may differ, but, according to *The Oxford English Dictionary*, cynical means "disposed to disbelieve in human sincerity or goodness; sneering."[100] So let me ask this: Do these law students lose their belief in sincerity or integrity? If so, I'd forgive them if they sneer sometimes.

The ABA seems to say, "No, it's not that first-year law students come to doubt other people's sincerity. They just learn that people are ambiguous, complex, and frail."

But I say, come off it. Are we talking about priests, or what? These law students aren't saying to themselves, "Gee, I feel sorry for this complex, frail individual who, unfortunate-

---

98. See, e.g., J. Clay Smith, Jr., "The Role of Primary and Secondary School Teachers in the Motivation of Black Youth to Become Lawyers," *Journal of Negro Education*, vol. 52, 1983, pg. 308.

99. *Professional Education*, fn. 42, pp. 76-77 (my emphasis).

100. *Oxford English Dictionary*, 2d ed.

ly, took advantage of his fellow man in this lawsuit." They're reading bad stories and saying, "Sheesh! What a screwing!" They see themselves involved in these cases someday, and it's an anxious thought. Paranoia becomes a virtue, because it helps them and their clients avoid similar disasters. Do they come to disbelieve in other people's sincerity? You betcha.[101]

Erwin Griswold, former Dean of Harvard Law School, has been quoted as saying,

> *For some years now, I have been concerned about the effect of our legal education on the idealism of our students. ... They bring to this school a large measure of idealism. Do they leave with less? ... If they do, what is the cause? What do we do to them that makes them turn the other way?[102]*

To which you want to respond, "Hey, buddy, wake up and smell the coffee." What do you expect — to make an ideal house pet out of a rat that's just been released from a cage where it was fighting for its life?

B. The Upperclass Years

I've described the stresses because they're an important part of your first-year law school experience. I think they made us harder, more competitive, and more paranoid.

But we did not cease to be human. Even during the first year, there was humor in the classroom. For instance, one exceptionally self-assured student actually had the nerve to interrupt the professor, in the middle of a 150-student class, to tell jokes. The amazing thing is that they were really funny, and everyone laughed.

In some classes, you could play Bingo. You create the Bingo card by using the names of the turkeys who are constantly speaking up in class. You put John in this corner, instead of B13, and you put Susan down here, instead of G8,

---

101. According to that study of Australian lawyers, the most common binding ideology among the attorneys studied was not that of service to the community, but rather cynical realism. (Tomasic, fn. 27, pg. 473.)
   102. Stern, fn. 67, pg. 169.

etc. Each time John or Susan or one of the others pipes up in class, you fill in the corresponding square on your Bingo card. When you get a complete row, you have to raise your hand, respond to something the professor said, and, well, you might say, "Yes, Professor Berger, the defendant was negligent, and — Bingo! — they slapped him with a lawsuit." Everyone knows the game, so you're guaranteed a round of applause when you win at Bingo.

And you get silly sometimes. This is what happens when you force 1,000 nerds to stay in the same building for all those hours. What's the translation of the Latin phrase, *sic transit gloria mundi*? It's "How does Gloria get to work on Mondays?"[103] For those who joined the Army to pay their tuition, hoping for wealth from private practice just as soon as they were discharged, ROTC means "Rich Off The Corps." In my international maritime law class, it wasn't the size of the ship, it was the motion re: the ocean. Female students need to learn how to get into an adversary's briefs. It takes a tough man to make a tender offer. Lawyers are always appealing. Etc.

Some humor requires guerrilla tactics. At the start of the semester, the professors post blank seating charts in the hallway. You're supposed to put your name down in a seat, and be in that seat, and respond when called upon. The trick is to put false names in some of the blanks, so that you get a laugh when the professor looks at the chart and then calls out, "Mr. Navark? Joe Navark?" or "Mr. Tannik? Ty Tannik? Is Arthur Itic here today? Brock O'Lee?"[104] You can deride your professors in hilarious, anonymous poems on the school bulletin board. Or you can distribute a rambling, stupid memorandum in which you pretend to be a particular universally despised professor and apologize for your incompetence.

I have to admit, not all of my classmates really got the hang of this concept called "fun." Perhaps this quote will give you a feel for what I'm saying:

---

103. It actually is from Thomas à Kempis, *Imitation of Christ*, written about 600 years ago, as quoted in Bartlett, fn. 56, pg. 148, and means "So passes away the glory of this world." The man obviously lacked a sense of humor.

104. If you're reading this note, I'm afraid you're one of those people who'll have to say these names out loud to yourself to get the point.

> *During my first year ..., we had a Halloween party, a "Spring Fling" barbecue and dance, a law week, intramural sports competitions, and a theatrical production called "Assault and Flattery" in which students and faculty members parodied themselves and each other. The somewhat underground "Kamikaze Law Student Association" also held a party with the student spoof law firm of Saliva and Sloth, P.C. Now that was a bash. However, back to the pressure, hard work, and tedium.[105]*

Outside the classroom, not everyone utterly subordinated their personal lives to their studies. Lawyers like to talk about their endless days of toil in law school. But for some of us, the senior year in college had been an opportunity, finally, to have a good time. The habit had become ingrained during that year, and now, 12 months later, not even law school could entirely break us of it. From the very start, I, personally, was a proud member of a pioneering group of law students who tacitly agreed that only a fool would ignore the charms of New York City during the three years of law school.

In the second year, as other students came to share my group's attitudes toward law school, our numbers and energy grew. And that seems proper. After all, we were only observing the spirit, if not the letter, of this rah-rah advice from two Fordham professors:

> *If you become a participant in the school's social life, you will likely describe your school as a warm, friendly, caring place where you spent some of the finest years of your life. Join a school-based organization or study group. It is in the warmth of such groups of mutually supportive friends that one finds the recollection, years after graduation, that law school was a warm and caring place.[106]*

We took that recommendation. Our study group met on

---

105. *Full Disclosure*, fn. 13, pp. 17-18.
106. John D. Calamari and Joseph M. Perillo, *How to Thrive in Law School* (Pelham Manor, NY: Hook Mountain Press, 1984), pp. 2, 4 (paraphrased).

Friday nights at about 10 p.m. at an East Side bar called The Sugar Mill. I was in the company of people whose idea of a good time was to dance until the clubs closed at 4 a.m., pull out a previously concealed bottle, drink until sunrise, and then have breakfast.

The partying was perfect. The dean of admissions had weeded out all those sick puppies who, as college students, would get too drunk and get arrested or set fire to the frat house. The only ones left, by the time we got to law school, were those who knew how to get positioned, carefully and intensely, before partying themselves into oblivion.

The motto by which some of us passed our second and third years of law school was this: Live now — there's plenty of time to be dead later. So we went out to clubs, to museums and concerts, playing video games at Times Square and rollerskating and bicycling all over town, not to mention spending hours in the scroungy old West End Cafe, the Marlin, and the other horrible bars in the Columbia area. We made ourselves more respectable by founding a local chapter of a legal fraternity and using it as a legitimate excuse to hold parties in the law school itself.

It was helpful that my friend Alice had become a sort of informal party chairperson. One February, she came up with a beach party in the corridors — "Law Beach," we dubbed it — complete with beach chairs and sand strewn across the floor.[107] Another time, she declared a Hat Party. It got crashed by some huge guys from the Columbia rugby team. They started by grabbing everyone else's hats, although it took them a minute to unwire my buddy David's electric halo. Then they stacked all those hats on their heads and paraded around in a tight circle, one behind the other, singing tunes about ... well, about the kinds of things you'd expect guys from the Columbia rugby team to sing about.

Not all law students were lighthearted. But even the most serious ones turned their attention to extracurricular pursuits in their upperclass years. For the better students, there were the demands of the Law Review and of other legal journals. Some devoted their hours to clinical programs, going to court on

---

107. I hope the maintenance men understood.

behalf of the poor, as I probably should have done. One classmate would step out of classes every now and then to call his broker and buy or sell gold futures. Another one arranged an impossible schedule in which she took her law school classes in the morning, worked at a law firm in the afternoon, and taught two classes at a community college at night, while commuting from Staten Island and devoting weekends to her dachshund and her doctoral work in astrophysics. Seriously.

My own extracurricular activities included getting elected to the student senate and starting a war with an authority on grammar at *Student Lawyer*, the ABA's magazine for law students. We were fighting over, would you believe, the proper use of the word "only." That's right. There's this word, the word "only," and the question is whether you can put it after, rather than before, the word it modifies. I mean ... never mind.

It started with a letter from me to this grammar authority, and quickly reached the point where she was writing articles, for every law student in the U.S. to see, in which she said things like, "Woodcock ... so muddles facts and logic that only a full-scale response will do," and "This is one of the many fine distinctions Woodcock managed to miss."[108] I got in a good last word, though,[109] in which I said she was losing her grip and implied that the magazine's editor had to be asleep at the wheel to let her publish this crap. I wrote a letter about it to William Safire, the language columnist but, judging from his reaction, he may have thought that I was on drugs.

I don't know. Hey, this battle soaked up some time I would otherwise have wasted on Corporate Taxation or something, and it made me temporarily famous. A lot of my friends mentioned it. One classmate — the type who liked to hang out in the jurisprudence section of the library — even seemed proud of me.

Even without such extracurricular interests during your upperclass years, you'd naturally lose interest in the nonsense

---

108. Flora Johnson, "Verbatim," *Student Lawyer*, vol. 10, Dec. 1981, pp. 53, 55. My initial letter, and her initial response, are on pg. 4 of the Sept. 1981 issue, and my second letter is on pg. 6 of the Nov. 1981 issue.
109. *Student Lawyer*, vol. 10, Feb. 1982, pg. 4.

of the Socratic method and that daily classroom grind.[110]
Having survived the first year, you know the shortcuts, and
you know you can make it. In the words of one professor who
mourns his loss of power over students,

> *the irregular attendance, poor preparation level, and
> disinclination to participate in class discussion demon-
> strated by so many third year students are the subject
> of constant complaint.*[111]

As an upperclassman, when the prof asks, "How many fingers
am I holding up?" you're tempted to reply, not with a number,
but with another question, such as, "Up what?"

Those last two years are not really a time of leisure. You
still have to work. And that's not entirely bad. I, and others
who had resisted some of the craziness of first year, found
that, during these upperclass years, we were able to take
elective courses that interested us more, and our most harshly
competitive classmates bothered us less.

Other aspects of the situation were worse, however, and
perhaps that's why we partied so intensely. In the first year,
you're working hard, but you haven't yet been proved to be
second-best. In the third year, by contrast, your mediocrity is
established. And at the same time, you now have to grapple
with how you'll fit into the cold, cruel world, which is
approaching you at an altogether unpleasant speed.

There was the definite feeling that, as one law professor
puts it, those who do the best on exams adopt an air of
"presumptuous self-importance," while the more average
students frequently feel worthless, isolated, and detached.[112]
Despite the partying and escapism, or perhaps ultimately
because of it, the little-known fact is that there's significantly

---

110. There is, as you'd expect, a link between students' motivation to study
in law school and their belief that they're involved in a rational program of study
that uses sensible teaching methods. (*Professional Education*, fn. 42, pp. 37-38.)
Besides, law school is expensive enough that a lot of people just don't have any
option but to work part-time during their upperclass years, and sometimes even
during their first years in law school. (See Kramer, fn. 38, pg. 275.)

111. James W. Ely, Jr., "Through a Crystal Ball: Legal Education — Its
Relation to the Bench, Bar, and University Community," *Tulsa Law Journal*, vol.
21, summer 1986, pg. 658.

112. Kissam, fn. 79, pp. 433, 481-83.

more stress in third-year law students than in first-year students.[113]

C. The Purpose of Those Three Years of Study

I got used to law school, but I never did believe that the Socratic method and the weird casebooks were a sensible way to teach people. What really killed my motivation, however, was the fact that there seemed to be no good reason for making me go through this three-year program before I could become a lawyer. I heard lots of different theories on why it was necessary, but they didn't hold much water.

1. To Help You Choose Your Legal Specialty?

I don't doubt for a minute that spending three years in law school can introduce you to different areas of the law. But it's a limited introduction. You won't get much of a feel for real-life legal practice from your law professors, many of whom have no such experience.[114] Studying geology does not make you a coal miner, and the study of law doesn't seriously initiate you into legal practice.

You do get some experience from your brief summer jobs. It's a start, but it's probably not enough to tell you for sure whether you'll even like being a lawyer, much less which kind of lawyer you might be. This is why many law firms rotate you through different areas of the firm during your first year of practice, letting you sample each of them before you decide where you're going to settle down.

Law schools certainly can claim that, during those three years, they increase your understanding of the law. But the fact is, three years of *anything* will make you more knowledgeable about law than you were before you started. You could be a pig farmer for three years and learn as much about the real-world legal profession as you'll know after law school.

---

113. Kellner et al., fn. 90, pp. 220-223. Late spring is the worst time: Depression levels rise to 32% at that point in the first year and to 40% at that point in the third year. (G. Andrew H. Benjamin et al., "The Prevalence of Depression, Alcohol Abuse, and Cocaine Abuse Among United States Lawyers," *International Journal of Law and Psychiatry*, vol. 13, 1990, pg. 234.)

114. See Forer, fn. 58, pp. 176, 209, for an account of one who tried it and made a fool of himself.

You'd get up in the morning, slop the hogs, and then spend a couple of hours each afternoon going to different courts, doing paralegal work for various kinds of lawyers, and reading things that directly answered your questions. I'm not exaggerating. It's possible to be very uncertain about your place in the legal system after three years of law school.[115] There's no substitute for hands-on experience.

In short, if law school is intended to help you plan your future, it's not exactly an outstanding success.

2. To Help Employers Determine Who's Worth Hiring?

If the LSAT is designed to predict your performance in the first year of law school, and if legal employers choose you on the basis of that first year, why not skip law school altogether and cut out the middleman? It seems like the LSAT people could cook up an exam that would tell employers the same thing that the first year of law school tells them. Law professors might say that their classes provide a better "screen" of your ability to practice law than any standardized test can, but it's not true, and anyway, if it were, I'd have to ask, then, why we need a standardized bar exam.

There are real problems with placing much faith in the screening value of law school grades:

> *What firm has not regularly bemoaned that law school does not prepare students for the practice of law? Yet we are willing to take [law school grades] as strong evidence of how they will perform in practice. Am I missing something, or does that not make a whole hell of a lot of sense? And who is making these evaluations for us? By and large, professors who ... are likely to have little appreciation of what it takes to be a successful practitioner.*[116]

Law firms and other employers definitely do use law

---

115. Whether we're talking about formal or informal education imparted through law school, "far too frequently our graduates enter practice with impractical and sometimes quixotic notions about what they'll encounter." (Letter from Columbia's placement dean to Columbia Law alumni, Feb. 22, 1991.)
116. Kanter, fn. 62, pp. 35-37.

school grades as an indicator of your abilities. And there's probably some merit to that. But it doesn't take three years to detect aptitude and motivation.

I suspect that a lot of the emphasis on grades comes from a basic desire, on the part of the attorneys who do the hiring, to cover their rear ends. If they hire someone with great grades, they can't be easily criticized if that new lawyer turns out to be a bozo, whereas if they take a chance on someone who was mediocre in law school, and that person does poorly, all the blame will come back to the lawyer who made the hiring recommendation. It's a long stretch from there, however, to the assertion that your law school grades will give employers a reliable indicator of your ability to practice law.

3. To Prepare You for the Bar Exam?

I can tell you right off that there's nothing to this theory. The ABA rules for law schools used to say explicitly that "The law school may not offer to its students, for academic credit or as a condition to graduation, instruction that is designed as a bar examination review course."[117]

That rule did not prevent the law school from teaching subjects that appear on the bar exam. The bar covers so many subjects that there'd hardly be anything left for law schools to do if that were the case. Instead, the rule meant just that law schools must concentrate on teaching the subjects without regard to how you might use what you learn.

That rule does not appear in the revised ABA rules for law schools. But its spirit lives on. Since those rules were revised in 1983, professional bar review courses have not exactly suffered a serious decline in enrollment as law schools raced to become more bar-oriented. *Plus ça change, plus c'est la même chose.*[118]

The underlying principle here is that it's low-class for a law school to concentrate on the bar exam. Thus, the "national" law schools like Harvard, Yale, and Columbia emphasize that they're training students who can practice law anywhere,

---

117. *Approval of Law Schools: ABA Standards and Rules of Procedure* (Chicago: ABA, 1973), rule 302(b).
118. "The more things change, the more they remain the same." (Alphonse Kerr, as quoted in Bartlett, fn. 56, pg. 514.

and not just in the states in which those schools are located.

In fact, the prestigious law schools seem to take perverse pride in the thought that their graduates might *not* perform as well on the bar exam as those who graduate from a "local" school. It seemed to be commonly accepted at Columbia, for example, that Brooklyn Law graduates were a step ahead:

> *"At the New York bar review course," goes the joke, "all the Harvard and Columbia students run after the Brooklyn and St. John's students yelling, 'Hey, what's the New York law on torts?' All the Yale students run after the Harvard and Columbia students yelling, 'Hey, what's a tort?'"*[119]

This state of affairs keeps the big-name schools from having to compete head-to-head against the supposedly lowbrow schools. You can't get statistics on how many graduates of each school pass the bar exam,[120] but even if you could, and even if Brooklyn Law had a higher pass rate, schools like Columbia could look down their noses and say, "Well, thank God Brooklyn Law School does *something* well."

Practically everyone wants to go to one of the big-name schools. By ignoring the fact that those schools are not particularly concerned with the bar exam, these students essentially admit that the bar exam is not a big concern to them.[121] And no matter which school they attend, many will study securities law, international law, and other areas that hardly appear on the exam, while ignoring subjects that will be tested heavily. Given this, it's no surprise that even the ABA's

---

119. Carol Eisen Rinzler, "Torts & Torture: On the Way to the Bar Exam," *Savvy*, Dec. 1980, pg. 55. A "tort" is a wrong that doesn't involve breach of contract, or anything like that, and doesn't get handled by the prosecutor as a crime, but is instead something that you have to sue for yourself. Examples include libel, assault, and malpractice. (See Gifis, fn. 47, pg. 210.)

120. Law schools freak out at the thought that someone will actually discover this information: *"No data will be published in a form which could be reasonably foreseen as permitting a determination of the bar passage rate for graduates of a specific law school. ... All data submitted in support of the bar study will be protected by security measures above and beyond even these security procedures,"* which involve sheltering data "in a secure building under guard twenty-four hours a day." (Henry Ramsey, Jr., "Law Graduates, Law Schools and Bar Passages Rates," *Bar Examiner*, vol. 60., Feb. 1991, pp. 25-26 (*his* emphasis), on the LSAC study described in fn. 123.)

121. See Zemans & Rosenblum, fn. 49, pg. 57.

Section on Legal Education has suggested that law school programs and bar exams are out of kilter with one another.[122]

4. To Teach You What You Need to Know to Practice Law?

If the bar exam tests your readiness to practice law, then law schools that don't prepare their graduates for the bar exam are shortchanging them. On the other hand, if law schools feel comfortable ignoring the bar exam, then they must think that it *doesn't* test what you need for a legal career.[123]

Something's gotta give. For the moment, though, let's assume that, no matter what's on the bar exam, law schools are keeping their eye on this question: What should we teach our students to make them good attorneys? Of course, we'll have to ignore these contradictory statements by legal experts:

> *[T]he function of law school is to teach a trade.*[124]

versus:

> *If a legal education is designed solely to prepare the student to pass a bar examination, to know the rules (whatever that may mean), and to learn "the tricks of the trade," then the law school does* not *belong in the modern university.*[125]

Or, on the bar exam specifically:

> *If the bar exams became the sole criteria [sic], law schools [might] teach toward the bar exam, instead of better, deeper teaching. ... Yale doesn't teach toward*

---

122. *Long-Range Planning*, fn. 69, pg. 31.
123. Don't worry too much about these contradictions. A major study is now underway by the LSAC "to explore the relationship between law school admission credentials, the law school experience, and performance on the bar examination." They hope to be able to distribute this study soon — no later than 1998. I'm not kidding. (Ramsey, fn. 120, pp. 21-22.)
124. Lawrence M. Friedman, "The Law and Society Movement," *Stanford Law Review*, vol. 38, Feb. 1986, pg. 776.
125. John Cribbet, "The Changeless, Ever-Changing University: The Role of the Law School," *Arizona Law Review*, vol. 26, 1984, pg. 250 (his emphasis).

> *the bar exam .... [A] lesser institution might have a better bar exam pass rate. But to choose [a lesser institution] over Yale is absolutely crazy.*[126]

as opposed to:

> *Almost all of the 60,000 people who take the Multistate exam every year must take a bar review course to pass the exam. Are these bar review companies doing something that the law schools should be doing?*[127]

Or, on the long-term future:

> *There is not a single lawyer with whom I went to law school who feels that his legal education adequately prepared him for the practice of law (or anything else for that matter).*[128]

versus:

> *There will be a dangerous tendency to impose narrowly-professional courses on law schools. These may be of immediate value to employers, but of dubious long-range benefit to students. If anything, law schools should give more attention to ... courses which seek to broaden the perspective of law students.*[129]

Or, on what subject matter they're trying to teach:

> *[I]t is neither possible nor desirable to teach the contents of the great body of statutory law, judicial opinion, and agency ruling that exists in the United States ....*[130]

---

126. Sherman Cohn of Georgetown, quoted by Margaret Fisk, "Bar Examiners Taking a Look at Lawyering Skills," *National Law Journal*, Oct. 1989, pg. 9.
127. Fisk, fn. 126, pg. 8, quoting Douglas Roche, chairman, Multistate bar exam committee, National Conference of Bar Examiners (NCBE) (paraphrased).
128. Paul N. Savoy, "Toward a New Politics of Legal Education," *Yale Law Journal*, vol. 79, Jan. 1970, pg. 444.
129. Ely, fn. 111, pp. 656-57.
130. *Official Guide*, fn. 2, pg. 19.

versus:

> *[This casebook on securities law] has been pre-*
> *pared primarily for law school use, but we have been*
> *heartened that securities lawyers and Judges have also*
> *found it valuable as a reference work.*[131]

Again, let's ignore these contradictions, and simply assume
that law schools are trying to teach their students what they'll
need to be good lawyers. That's a tall order. It includes a
couple of different elements, and I'll break them out under
separate headings now to keep things clear.

When I started law school, I expected to have an opportunity to take courses that would give me *knowledge* of the law.
But I also thought I'd be learning academic *skills*, especially
research and writing, and that there would be a great need for
the study of *practical*, non-academic matters. I don't remember which practical issues concerned me at the time, but
nowadays I see magazines, seminars, books, and other devices
to help lawyers deal with such managerial-type topics as how
to avoid malpractice suits, how to market your services, and
how to set up the books and records for your own law office.

a. Courses in Law Practice and Academic Skills

I was partly right. Law school did offer many academic
courses. But I saw very few practical courses, or courses
designed to develop our skills in research and writing.

It's not that those topics are somehow unimportant. On the
contrary, attorneys who have good interpersonal skills, for
example, have been shown to appear more trustworthy and
capable to nonlegal observers.[132] If you graduate from law
school without practical skills, you can forget about hanging
out a shingle, and you'll be embarrassed to discover that you
don't know how to handle ordinary legal problems for your

---

131. Richard W. Jennings and Harold Marsh, Jr., *Securities Regulation: Cases
and Materials*, 4th ed. (Mineola, NY: Foundation Press, 1977), pg. xvii. That is,
it's a highly detailed casebook, taking pride in teaching much of "the contents of
the great body" of law on the subject of securities.
132. Stephen Feldman and Kent Wilson, "The Value of Interpersonal Skills in
Lawyering," *Law & Human Behavior*, vol. 5, 1981, pg. 320.

family and friends. Frankly, you won't even be as useful as the "Be Your Own Lawyer" collection in your local public library, or the neighbor who has already gone through a particular kind of legal problem firsthand.

Studies indicate that practicing lawyers wish their law schools had focused more on such academic skills as legal writing and research.[133] In one study, 84 percent of attorneys said that their law school educations were "only fair" or "poor" in giving them "the ability to conduct a law practice on a businesslike basis." Only 40 percent said that law school had been "good" or "excellent" in teaching them "to diagnose clients' problems and needs and to provide counsel."[134]

When discussing the place of skills training and practical courses in legal education, researchers typically make comments like these:

> *The skills rated [by questionnaire respondents] as the <u>most</u> important to the practice of law were apparently learned <u>outside</u> law school. ...*

> *[T]here was substantial criticism of law schools' failure even to make their students <u>aware</u> of the importance of some of these competencies to the actual practice of law. ...[135]*

I guess that leaves one possible goal for law school: to give you academic *knowledge.* We've skipped a lot, but, thank God, at least we've finally figured out what you're supposed to be getting out of law school. Armed with that insight, we must try to believe that there is so much academic knowledge to teach, and the goals of that academic teaching are so clear and so important, that it was worthwhile and even necessary to ignore the practical side.

---

133. See *Professional Education*, fn. 42, pp. 50-51.
134. "LawPoll: Learning and Licensing: Law School and Bar Exams," *American Bar Association Journal*, vol. 68, May 1982, pg. 544.
135. Zemans & Rosenblum, fn. 49, pp. 137, 141-43 (their emphasis).

b. Mainstream Academic Courses

Before we start to talk about the academic knowledge you get from law school, it's important to realize the limits. The best law libraries have millions of volumes. Legal scholars produce many careful books of new thought each year. You can't expect law school to do more than skate across the surface of the law's academic depths.

It's tough to know how to narrow it down. You can't just teach federal law. There are often 1,000 pages in a volume of federal court decisions, and thousands of those volumes on the shelves. Nor can you simply teach the law of a particular state. Even in minor states, the books of laws and cases can take more than 100 feet of shelf space.

It's hard to teach even an introduction to subject areas in the law. A casebook in constitutional law, for example, might contain as many words as the Bible, and will be much tougher reading. People spend years learning their Bibles, but a two-semester, six-unit course covering that casebook will give you the equivalent of a mere six weeks of full-time study.

The simple fact is that law school could go for two years or 20 years, and unless you organized it well, you'd still be getting a mere introduction. You can't just sit down in the law library and start reading. You have to have a goal. So here's the question: What academic knowledge is law school trying to impart?

(1) What You'll Need in the Long Run?

Law schools sometimes say that they're teaching you things you won't appreciate for many years, but that someday you'll look back and thank them. You doubted your parents when they said this kind of thing to you, though, and there's at least as much room to doubt the law schools.

Personally, I think it's a crock. Look at lawyers. What entitles them all to be called "lawyers"? Certainly not something that they experience only after long years of labor. The thing that makes them all part of the same profession is that they all *started* the same way, with law school and the bar exam. After sharing those early experiences, they all go in separate directions. Law schools never could, and never will, have the vaguest idea of what will be useful to all those varieties of attorneys 20 or 40 years from now.

And anyway, if law school doesn't do a good job of training you in the skills you'll need during your early years of practice, the long-term training will be irrelevant. You'll never last that long. Your incompetence will ruin you long before you reach any silver anniversary.

Well, if the 20- to 40-year horizon makes no sense, how about the notion that law schools are really trying to teach you the things you'll need to be a good attorney five or 10 years after graduation?

I ask you to consider two options. In the first one, law school plants a time bomb in your brain. You graduate from law school, you enter your first job, and you feel like you've had a lobotomy. You know nothing, you remember nothing. You survive the first five years by sheer luck.

And then, after five years, shazam! Suddenly the time bomb goes off. You smack yourself and say, "Wow! Now I understand what they were telling me in law school!"

It's possible, right? Not too likely, but possible.

Maybe it does happen once in a while. But my classmates and I are now in the middle of that five-to-10-year stretch, and I don't see too many of us getting zonked with long-submerged insights. Chances are, if you haven't used it for five years, you're not going to remember it when you need it.

Besides, during those five years, while law school was becoming a fading memory, you were spending every day working with lawyers and learning all kinds of things about the law. It's asking a lot, I think, to expect a long-lost bit of knowledge from law school to suddenly arise and make itself seem half as relevant as the nitty-gritty of your daily struggle.

As far as I can tell, the only way in which law school can give you meaningful preparation is to start you out on the right foot and teach you enough to keep you going in the proper direction. If you find that things have begun to make sense after five or 10 years of practice, surely it's because you've been a good boy or girl, learning and doing like you're supposed to, and not because your ancient law school lore has miraculously sprung to life.

In short, it sounds suspicious to talk about how law school gives you long-term career training. Lawyers, of all people, know better than to talk about the distant future while neglecting immediate needs.

(2) What You'll Need in Your First Job?

When you squelch law schools from talking about the 10-year horizon and ask, instead, how well you're being prepared for the job that starts next month or next year, it's a different ballgame. Suddenly it's much easier to see whether you're getting the training you paid for. If your education doesn't match your employer's needs, you just won't fit.

Now, remember, we already noted that law school doesn't even try to give you practical training. So if you eat like a pig during a sensitive business luncheon, or don't know when to shut up, or if you alienate everyone in the office, or can't get the hang of writing a simple memo for the files, it's just your employer's tough luck. Law school is an *academic* matter.

So how do attorneys feel about the academic subjects that drove them to despair during the first year of law school? Well, according to that study of lawyers in Chicago, the only law school course endorsed by more than 25 percent of the attorneys as being "particularly helpful" to their practice of law was contracts. Torts? Only 24 percent. Constitutional law? Only 16 percent. Trusts and estates? Ten percent.[136]

Ah, but there's a response. This thing of academic learning is not just limited to academic *subjects*. When people begin to complain that their academic courses are irrelevant to their future careers, law schools quickly offer another concept, as suggested by these words:

> *[Years ago,] the law schools turned inward and came to regard their educational responsibilities as complete upon imparting to the neophyte the basic education of learning to "think like a lawyer" ....*[137]

And there you have it: my first mention of the famous, mystical concept of "thinking like a lawyer." The basic idea

---

136. Zemans & Rosenblum, fn. 49, pg. 146.
137. Robert MacCrate, "What Shapes the Profession: Money, Morals, Social Obligation?" *ABA Journal*, vol. 74, Mar. 1988, pg. 10.

seems to be that your time in law school will give you this intangible mental quality you lacked before.

To teach you to "think like a lawyer," law school has to give you two things. First, they must teach you some academic law, so that you'll have something to think about. Not much of it, because you don't know a lot of details (other than possibly in one area of specialization) when you graduate. And the academic law won't necessarily be in the same subjects as your classmates might study, except for those few courses that everyone has to take. Thus, one classmate of mine could concentrate on tax law, and another could concentrate on the law of China, and as long as they both passed the bar exam and were admitted to practice, we'd have to call them both lawyers.

And second, law school must give you a perspective, or a set of attitudes, that help you talk to other lawyers in a way that's not so easy with non-lawyers. An example of such an attitude: the ability to accept that lawyers sometimes take positions without necessarily believing in them personally. Another example: the view that it's good for lawyers to do so. A third example: the belief that questions of emotion must not be permitted to overrule conclusions of logic. I'm not saying that any of these attitudes are bad. I'm only saying that you'll see how important they are when, as a lawyer, you find yourself glancing at your watch while talking to an upset client about a legal problem that's ruining his/her life.

There are a lot of those attitudes.[138]   But not all lawyers accept all of them, any more than all lawyers study all the same areas of law. Nobody bothers to do an inventory on you, to see whether you've swallowed the right ones before you'll be allowed to practice. They just take the easy way out. If

---

138. Other examples: the belief that it's sometimes more important to put an end to disputes (even if one side gets a raw deal) than it is to set things right; that courts can't really get into the business of going out into the world and making people do things, which means that, in most cases, people must be satisfied with awards of money when something goes wrong; that the time of the court is more precious than the time of the people who come into court, so that you can't go in there with just any little complaint, and when you do go in there, you'd best make it snappy; that courts can't make a habit of giving their opinions on problems until someone has actually been damaged and has gone to the trouble of bringing a lawsuit; and, perhaps, that people are essentially bad, so that you can't rely on them, and instead you need an adversary system in which everyone is working their hardest to make their opponents seem terrible.

you go through three years of law school, they figure that, in most cases, you'll have accepted enough of the basics to function as a normal lawyer.

And that's about all there is to it, on the subject of learning to "think like a lawyer." Except for a smattering of legal ethics, there's no required course in "legal attitudes." The attitudes tend to filter in while you're studying other subjects. In terms of what's explicit, the major emphasis of law school is, by far, on the substance of the law that you're studying, even if nobody really knows for sure what the hell it might have to do with your future. That substance deserves a closer look, and I will turn to it now.

§ 4. The Law You Study: End of the Fantasy

Earlier, I said that law students get stress from a number of sources. But I left out perhaps the most important one. When you finally understand what you're studying in law school, you sometimes can't help rebelling against it.

A. Order in the Court

If you go into a law library, you'll find sets of books devoted to the laws that are passed by legislators, and other sets of books that contain the decisions of judges around the country. Scholars write about those laws and decisions, and other scholars collect all of the important laws and decisions into volumes that are dedicated to explaining every aspect of the law. The whole thing is very organized.

By taking certain steps, you can find out what the law is on any subject. Special books and computer programs help you find what you are looking for, if it exists. And when there's nothing precisely "on point," certain techniques can help you figure out what a judge is most likely to say if the case should arise in the future. There are always gray areas, but at least you can get a feel for why people disagree.

When you apply what you've learned in the library, you find that the formal procedures for prosecuting or defending a lawsuit based on your research are just as organized. The rules tell you when you may take any particular step and what you must include in your effort to accomplish your goal.

B. The Other Half of the Story

Unfortunately, not all of us have the luxury of being legal scholars or having cautious, well-thought-out law practices. Many lawyers are out in the storm, rocking and reeling from the more miserable aspects of our legal system. And that does not begin to describe what happens to the clients.

It is possible to characterize the situation less charitably than I did a moment ago. In practice, the case decisions you find in your legal research often contradict one another. Judges invent reasons to ignore what they're supposed to do, so that they can do what they want. And cagey adversaries quickly learn how to manipulate the rules so as to reduce the grand, smooth machinery of procedure to a clunky wreck that usually operates in ragged fits and starts.

1. This Is Substance?

In law school, you struggle to understand the law you're being taught. And then, when you do understand it, you can hardly believe it half the time. The law, in its infinite wisdom, gives Jim Bakker 45 years in prison for being a religious crook; and nails a former U.S. Olympic diver with a 17-year sentence for killing two people while driving drunk, after he kindly drops his not-guilty defense to make it easier for his victims' families to collect from his insurance company; but you can murder the mayor of a major city and be out in less than five years.[139] And I strongly suspected that many of my law school classmates would have found it more suspicious for me to have been arrested for shoplifting when I was 15 than they would if I went on to become a big-time corporate lawyer who would screw innocent stockholders out of millions.

A jury might give you $31 million just for getting

---

139. See, e.g., the story of Dan White, who murdered the mayor of San Francisco, "Disputed Parole Kindles Anger in San Francisco," Jan. 5, 1984, pg. A-18, col. 5, and compare "Jim Bakker's Startling Sentence," Oct. 29, 1989, sec. 4, pg. 22, col. 1; Peter Applebone, "Bakker Sentenced to 45 Years for Fraud in His TV Ministry," Oct. 25, 1989, pg. A-1, col. 4; and "Kimball Gets 17 Years in Accident that Killed 2," Jan. 31, 1989, pg. B-7, col. 4, all from *New York Times*. Fortunately, Bakker had enough fame or money to hire Alan Dershowitz to appeal that sentence and get it dropped on Feb. 12, 1991.

fired.[140]   The jury can award $125 million to Pinto drivers whose gas tanks explode, and perhaps that's appropriate.[141] But it's troubling that the jury doesn't get to consider the question of what a $125 million payout would do to Ford's ability to produce cars and employ people.   And it's *really* troubling that no jury will even be called when you're looking for someone who'll pay one-thousandth as much to help your sweet wife put her life back together if she gets slashed and raped.

As a law student, you learn not to worry too much about those kinds of cases.   First of all, they're too dramatic, and that's bad for anyone who considers him/herself a professional. Professionals are paid to control their emotions and understand the reasoning behind a situation.   For the lawyers, there's usually either a bit of logic that explains it all (although it'll never satisfy the victims), or else there's no logic and you can stand back with everyone else and shake your head at the crazy judge and jury who made such oddball decisions.   Either way, the phrase that fits is, "What can I say?"

a. A Shortage of Logic

Once I mastered the art of professional cool, the things that I found more disturbing than the emotionally extreme cases, as a law student, were the rules that controlled the more mundane ones — that is, the cases that many ordinary people experience every day.

In contract law, for example, I couldn't understand why a guy had to go through a lawsuit to enforce a minor contract, when he was the good guy all along, doing everything that the contract required him to do.[142]   And then, I could not understand why the courts wouldn't award attorneys' fees to him if he did bother to sue, and won.   It seemed to me that nobody with any sense would ever hire an attorney for any contract

---

140. Amy Dockser Marcus, "Juries Rule Against 'Tort Reform' With Huge Awards," *Wall Street Journal*, Feb. 9, 1990, pg. B-1, col. 3.

141. See Peter W. Huber, *Liability* (New York: Basic Books, 1988), pg. 115.

142. Not to mention the could-be-productive companies that get bled white by legal expenses of $250,000 merely to defend themselves against other companies with bigger resources. (See Peter H. Lewis, "When Computing Power Is Generated By the Lawyers," *New York Times*, July 22, 1990, business section, pg. 4, col. 2.)

that was worth less than literally thousands of dollars — and even then, it seemed that the plaintiffs[143] would have to write off their own time investment in the case as a total waste.

It appeared that the only option, if your complaint doesn't involve a huge amount, is to master your nerves, summon your hardest face, and go into small claims court. It's a hassle. Weeks may pass before your day in court. When the day arrives, you have to sit there and wait your turn while others get up and argue in front of the judge. Your adversary may be experienced in manipulating small claims court to his/her advantage. And if you're not a tough person, you may not present your case very well, and you may lose anyway. To put it bluntly, small claims court is often a failure.[144]

After trying small claims court once or twice, you're not apt to fool with it for anything less than hundreds of dollars. But what good is that? You don't go paying that kind of cash every day. Most people's typical expenses are under $100 each. For such "petty" complaints, it seemed to me, as a law student, that the courts had a simple message: Get lost.

In short, I found contract law frustrating. Not for its careful rules in their narrow theoretical world, but for the real-life implications that seemed so much more important to ordinary people. In contrast to the quiet precision I found in the law library, the real working of the legal world was like a free-for-all brawl.

I don't mean to overstate. Even in the worst cases, the law does not operate in total chaos. If you file your complaint in the courthouse, you'll eventually wind up in court, whereas if you file your complaint in the men's toilet, no court date will be set. But I didn't have to be a fortune teller to see a serious problem of missed connections, between what the library promised and what the courthouse delivered.

I had a different kind of problem with criminal law. I

---

143. A "plaintiff" is the person who brings a civil lawsuit, i.e., the one who has the com*plaint*.

144. Frank E.A. Sander, "Varieties of Dispute Processing," *Federal Rules Decisions*, vol. 70, Apr. 7-9, 1976, pg. 124: "[T]he evidence now seems overwhelming that the Small Claims Court has failed its original purpose; that the individuals for whom it was designed have turned out to be its victims." See also Forer, fn. 58, pg. 104: "The cases are repetitious and ... boring .... Understandably, not many judges of small claims court are learned, patient, and considerate and the litigants appearing before them often do not receive either equal justice or due process of law."

learned that New York State recognized one form of first-degree murder, three forms of second-degree murder, three forms of first-degree manslaughter, three forms of second-degree manslaughter, and one form of criminally negligent homicide, for a total of 11 different ways to characterize the fact that someone was recklessly or intentionally killed.

I understood the differences among those classes of homicide, and I realized that the degree of the crime would determine the maximum possible penalty. But New York had no death penalty, and judges did not usually sentence criminals to maximum prison terms, because the prisons were too crowded. The lines got even fuzzier when I tried to explain to myself exactly why the courts would give a guy a break because he attempted, but failed, to kill someone.[145]

Beyond that, God did not hand down those maximum sentences on Mount Sinai. I suspected that they would have been different if, for example, there had been a rash of murders during the month before the legislature voted those criminal penalties into law. And I didn't like the thought that all this was much too confusing for any would-be murderer to understand and reckon with, nor the fact that, as far as I could tell, no one had done a really serious cost-benefit analysis of the whole thing.

I grant that I might feel differently about it if I were the defendant. I would probably not care to spend needless extra years in prison if I were guilty of it. Then again, I'm not, I never will be, and if I were, my opinion wouldn't be the first one you'd want to listen to anyway.

As I learned, homicide was hardly the only spot of spaghetti complexity in the criminal law. There were eight different ways to commit larceny, and I still am not clear on the differences between them. If I take something from you, is that larceny by trespassory taking? I don't think so. I think it must be larceny by trick. Unless, of course, it's larceny by false promise, which we must distinguish from the crime of

---

145. That is, why consider the success or failure in choosing the category of crime, but not when deciding on the punishment? (Douglas N. Husak, *Philosophy of Criminal Law* (Totowa, NJ: Rowman & Littlefield, 1987), pg. 44.

obtaining property by false pretenses.[146]

I don't want to oversimplify the situation, but the defendant took something, he knows he took something, he knows (or should know) that it was wrong, and they aren't even going to make him say he's sorry. Hammer him, I say.

That's not how it works, though. Instead, what we've got to do is require judges and lawyers to spend their lives concentrating on him and others like him. These judges and lawyers are some of our society's most brilliant people. Many of them scored in the top 10 percent of all of the bright, highly motivated students who took the LSAT. And there they are. What I wanted to know, in law school, was whether anyone had ever really thought about replacing these complex laws and procedures with something much simpler that would accomplish the same goals without wasting so much of these brilliant, could-be-useful people's precious time.[147]

Oh, I know, it's nice to think that these judges and lawyers are diligently guarding our civil liberties. And when there's a trial, they are, truly. But have you ever sat in a criminal courtroom and watched what goes on most of the time? Plea bargaining, sentencing hearings, all kinds of stuff that's awfully time-consuming and terribly far from the grand picture we have, in our minds, of those defenders of the American way. I had to believe that there was a better approach.

OK. Next. After our judges are through spending time on the defendant, if he's guilty, we've got to put him into a prison that costs a fortune to run, and take good care of him, while perfectly decent people who've lost their jobs are wandering around the streets in winter without a home.[148] By this

---

146. Some of this complexity has been reduced in these areas. Other areas, meanwhile, become worse. Next year's example may be different, but there will still be a useful example next year.

147. As an example, I recently sat in on a plea bargain hearing — not a trial, just a formal hearing to record the defendant's plea — in which 10 people (judge, judge's clerk, judge's secretary, bailiff and another guard, defendant, defendant's attorney, defendant's attorney's assistant, prosecutor, and translator) spent an hour in court (and who knows how many hours in preparation for court), just to address the fact that the defendant was going to plead guilty to a criminal charge.

148. I don't mean to push a political point of view. I'd be much happier, even with a decision to continue doing things exactly as we're doing them now, if only that decision could be reached after an assessment of how much we're spending and how much we want to spend, in my example, on the homeless versus the criminals. My problem, in law school and now, has been that the question is not being approached from that kind of allocation-of-scarce-resources perspective.

point, I'm crying. Cost-benefit analysis, please. Yo!

I'm here to say that I found frustrations in criminal law as well as in contract law. And then, to take one more example, there's tort law.

In torts, it got to a point where courts would award negligence damages against doctors who made mistakes when they stopped to help the victims of auto accidents. So doctors quit trying to help, and the states had to pass Good Samaritan laws to protect them against this kind of liability. The number of doctors in certain medical specialties has plummeted. The whole situation has reached the point where patients and doctors fear and sometimes even hate each other.[149]

Similarly, drug companies can't afford to defend themselves all the time, and instead simply stop developing new vaccines and birth control methods. As *Time* noted, "The U.S. is the only country other than Iran in which the birth-control clock has been set backward."[150] A lot of businesses and civic activities that could improve our lives don't even operate anymore because they can't get insurance.[151]

And by what logic? Peter Huber sketched it out in his excellent book *Liability*:

> *Accidents are socially costly, these legal experts pointed out, and the law should encourage accident prevention by the most economical means. So liability began to fall on the ones who could prevent accidents at the lowest cost, namely, those who provide goods and services.*
>
> *The next step was to hold manufacturers "strictly liable" to consumers for accidents caused by a "defect*

---

149. Gina Kolata, "Wariness Is Replacing the Trust Between Physician and Patient," *New York Times*, Feb. 20, 1990, pg. 1, col. 1. Doctors who have been sued are much more likely to stop seeing certain kinds of patients, think of retiring early, and discourage their children from becoming doctors. (Sara C. Charles et al., "Sued and Nonsued Physicians' Self-Reported Reactions to Malpractice Litigation," *American Journal of Psychiatry*, vol. 142, Apr. 1985, pp. 437-40.)

150. "A Bitter Pill to Swallow," *Time*, Feb. 26, 1990, pg. 44.

151. Not to mention many other problems with tort law as we now know it, e.g., the fact that nonprofit organizations find it harder to recruit good managers to serve on their boards of directors because of the number of horror stories about lawsuits being brought against such directors. (See, e.g., Claudia H. Deutsch, "Giving Less Time to Good Causes," *New York Times*, July 15, 1990, sec. 3, part 2, pg. 23, col. 6.)

in manufacture" of their product. And then, courts began to condemn entire productions, not for a manufacturing defect in one item, but for a design defect in them all.

Before long, juries across the country were busy redesigning lawn mowers, electrical switches, and products of every other description. By the late 1970s, the technical and economic questions were triggering titanic courtroom struggles. But these struggles remained mere parodies of the actual process of real-world design. The original design of a car, drug, or appliance takes years. A jury typically has a few days, seldom more than a few weeks, to re-design it.

The legal experts easily assumed that the doers, the makers, and the providers of this world would willingly be pursued at every turn by a hound-like legal profession. But in response to the question of who would be building and fixing, treating, immunizing, and curing while the lawyers were busy assessing the fines, the answer, with growing frequency, was no one at all. Innovation was suppressed, and the consumer ended up worse off than he would have been had the legal system been slower to rush to his rescue.[152]

After torts, I could continue on down the list: the rule against perpetuities, the hearsay rule, the whole freaking tax code. As I was going through law school, wearing my cost-benefit MBA attitude like a chip on my shoulder, I was amazed at everyone's willingness to pretend that we live in a timeless world, where we can talk about legal problems forever. No one seemed to think that sometimes these efforts could cost more — in time, money, and sheer waste of valuable brainpower — than they were worth.

---

152. Huber, fn. 141, pp. 27-44, 154 (paraphrased).

b. Avoiding Knowledge

It's not that the law schools have failed to ask how law fits in with our society's needs. It's worse than that. Law professors affirmatively resist such questions. Consider, for example, this statement by one law professor who appears to wish that things were otherwise:

> *The law and society movement has been trying to shoehorn its way into law schools for more than 60 years. ... To be frank, the study of law and society, by whatever name, is something of a stepchild in the law school world.*[153]

Law professors have been prodded by Supreme Court Chief Justice William H. Rehnquist;[154] former Harvard University president Derek Bok;[155] and, decades ago, Ralph Nader,[156] among many others. And yet they continue, by and large, to ignore the functioning of the system.[157] For instance, I recently looked through the *Directory of Law Teachers* and found that, of the 88 subject areas in which America's law schools offer courses, only a handful have anything to do with the way in which the legal system is run.[158] Those areas may account for as little as 1 percent of all law classes.[159]

Legal scholars even ignore the study of law firms, despite the fact that huge numbers of law students go directly into law

153. Friedman, fn. 124, pg. 773.
154. William H. Rehnquist, "The State of the Legal Profession," *Legal Economics*, vol. 14, Mar. 1988, pg. 49.
155. Derek C. Bok, "A Flawed System," *Harvard Magazine*, May-June 1983, pp. 44-45. Reprinted in parts in *New York State Bar Journal*, vol. 55, Oct. 1983, pp. 8-16, and Nov. 1983, pp. 31-35.
156. See Bryant C. Danner, "Looking at Large Law Firms — Any Role Left for the Law Schools?" *Indiana Law Journal*, vol. 64, summer 1989, pg. 449.
157. Friedman, fn. 124, pg. 778.
158. *AALS Directory of Law Teachers 1988-89*, AALS, Washington, D.C., 1988, pg. 865. The closest topics were Judicial Administration, Law Office Management, Legal Profession, and Women and the Law.
159. Of the approximately 26,500 entries in the *Directory's* listing of all classes taught by all law professors, the four topics mentioned in the preceding note contained a total of about 1,050 entries (4%). About 2/3 were listed under Legal Profession, which does not restrict itself to the practical operation of the system. Then, too, almost all of these classes will have fewer students than mainstream classes like torts and contracts.

firms upon graduation.[160]   These are the same scholars who notice every last detail when talking about their favorite complicated, extremely specialized legal questions.   Consider this half-apology from one article in a top law review:

> *As a preliminary matter, we should perhaps justify devoting attention to so <u>arcane</u> a subject as the career patterns of young lawyers who practice in corporate law firms.*[161]

Strange as it may seem, the study of law firms is simply not considered a normal part of the law school curriculum.[162] Similarly, legal experts have declined to do much research on the value of bar admissions character reviews;[163] the use of trial court time; the effectiveness of settlements; the workings of jury trials; how many erroneous decisions are not appealed for lack of funds; and the excessive expenses of celebrity trials,[164] to give just a few examples of areas in which there would seem to be room for a lot more analysis.

There's a reason for law professors to avoid such practical questions.   They're no fools.   They can't answer these questions.   If they tried, they'd fail, and everyone would see right away that they're not suited for it:

> *[E]mpirical research is hard work, and lots of it; it is also non-library research, and many law teachers are afraid of it; it calls for skills that most law teachers do not have; if it is at all elaborate, it is team research, and law teachers are not used to this kind of effort; often it requires hustling grant money from foundations or government agencies, and law teachers simply do not know how to do that.*[165]

---

160. Robert W. Gordon, "Introduction to Symposium on the Corporate Law Firm," *Stanford Law Review*, vol. 37, 1985, pg. 272.

161. Ronald J. Gilson and Robert H. Mnookin, "Coming of Age in a Corporate Law Firm: The Economics of Associate Career Patterns," *Stanford Law Review*, vol. 41, Feb. 1989, pg. 568 (my emphasis).

162. Danner, fn. 156, pg. 449.

163. Deborah L. Rhode, "Moral Character as a Professional Credential," *Yale Law Journal*, vol. 94, Jan. 1985, pp. 493, 512, 518.

164. Forer, fn. 58, pp. 24, 25, 48, 151, 153, 173, 177, 180.

165. Friedman, fn. 124, pg. 774. We all appreciate Peter Schuck's observation that, to his knowledge, "[N]o law professor has ever empirically investigated

Law schools could hope to address these bigger questions about the legal system only by shunting scads of professors in these directions and retraining them for the job.[166]

Unfortunately, legal experts' lack of information and training in the real workings of the system does not deter them from making far-reaching recommendations based on what they *assume* the facts must be.[167] As a poignant example, one study concluded that, after 16 years of experimentation on the American public, no-fault divorce was fundamentally flawed, but that legal experts had lacked the scientific data and expertise to understand those flaws.[168] Even the Justices on the U.S. Supreme Court risk "being seriously misled in their interpretation of empirical data [because of, among other things, a lack] of training in statistics and research ...."[169]

Instead of trying to force-fit empirical studies into law schools, you may be happier if you listen, not to legal experts, but to others, outside the law. For example, the scholar who found that the Supreme Court has problems with empirical issues was not a law professor, but a professor of psychiatry.[170] Even in the law reviews, many of the articles on the management of the law are written by, or rely heavily on, nonlegal experts.[171]

It certainly is possible to find non-law schools that pursue

---

the extent to which legal scholars actually conduct empirical research." ("Why Don't Law Professors Do More Empirical Research?" *Journal of Legal Education*, vol. 39, Sept. 1989, pg. 323.) See also Barry B. Boyer and Roger C. Cramton, "American Legal Education: An Agenda for Research and Reform," *Cornell Law Review*, vol. 59, Jan. 1974, pg. 227; Rehnquist, fn. 154, pp. 45, 49.

166. Bok, fn. 155, pp. 44-45, 71.

167. Forer, fn. 58, pg. 173. This, despite studies that yield "highly counter-intuitive" conclusions. (See Donald Wittman, "Dispute Resolution, Bargaining, and Selection of Cases for Trial: A Study of the Generation of Biased and Unbiased Data," *Journal of Legal Studies*, vol. 17, June 1988, pg. 346.)

168. Lenore J. Weitzman, *The Divorce Revolution* (New York: Free Press, 1985), pp. 362-64. This conclusion was confirmed by Thomas M. Mulroy, "No-Fault Divorce," *ABA Journal*, vol. 75, Nov. 1989, pg. 80.

169. Paul S. Appelbaum, "The Empirical Jurisprudence of the United States Supreme Court," *American Journal of Law & Medicine*, vol. 13, 1987, pg. 347.

170. See Appelbaum, fn. 169, pg. 349.

171. See, e.g., Christopher Simoni et al., "Litigant and Attorney Attitudes toward Court-Annexed Arbitration: An Empirical Study," *Santa Clara Law Review*, vol. 28, summer 1988, pg. 543 (in which only one of the three authors is now working in the teaching or practice of law); E.C. Lashbrooke, Jr., "Legal Reasoning and Artificial Intelligence," *Loyola Law Review*, vol. 34, 1988 (a professor in the business department at Michigan State); Wittman, fn. 167 (an economics professor); Loftus & Wagenaar, fn. 55, pg. 437 (psychologists); see also, e.g., Lucian Arye Bebchuk, "Suing Solely to Extract a Settlement Offer," *Journal of Legal Studies*, vol. 17, June 1988, pg. 437 (relying on economists).

these subjects. To take one field, graduate business schools now offer a variety of law-related graduate studies. At Carnegie-Mellon, Wharton, and Minnesota, for instance, business professors have studied jury behavior, criminal sentencing guidelines, intrastate motor carrier regulation's impact on interstate commerce, risk assessment in environmental regulation, private treble-damage lawsuits, and the legal strategic behavior of corporations.[172] Courses in alternative dispute resolution (ADR) are becoming so important[173] that the most popular offerings at the graduate business schools at Northwestern, Virginia, and Columbia — and probably elsewhere — are courses in negotiation and ADR.[174]

Similarly, sociologists and other scientists have studied the question of which battered spouses are most and least likely to use legal restraining orders;[175] the extent to which mediation might be better than the adversarial approach in handling child protection and custody disputes[176] and divorces;[177] the process of jury decision-making in criminal trials;[178] and jury standards used in awarding damages.[179]

Lawyers aren't doing these studies. They can't now, and it appears that they won't anytime soon. So in the future, many of the answers we want about the system will have to

---

172. Drawn from a review of the schools' 1990-91 Ph.D. program bulletins.
173. See Nancy G. Neslund, "Why Teach Conflict Resolution in Business Schools?" *American Business Law Journal*, vol. 26, fall 1988, pg. 557.
174. Joel Kurtzman, "Shifting the Focus at B-Schools," *New York Times*, Dec. 31, 1989, pg. F-4, col. 6.
175. E.g., Anne L. Horton et al., "Legal Remedies for Spousal Abuse: Victim Characteristics, Expectations, and Satisfaction," *Journal of Family Violence*, vol. 2, Sept. 1987, pp. 275-78.
176. E.g., Sally E. Palmer, "Mediation in Child Protection Cases: An Alternative to the Adversary System," *Child Welfare*, vol. 68, Jan.-Feb. 1989, pp. 21-31; Robert E. Emery and Melissa M. Wyer, "Child Custody Mediation and Litigation: An Experimental Evaluation of the Experience of Parents," *Journal of Consulting and Clinical Psychology*, vol. 55, Apr. 1987, pp. 179-186; Laurence Loeb, "Fathers and Sons: Some Effects of Prolonged Custody Litigation," *Bulletin of the American Academy of Psychiatry and the Law*, vol. 14, 1986, pp. 177-183.
177. E.g., Helen R. Weingarten, "Strategic Planning for Divorce Mediation," *Social Work*, vol. 31, May-June 1986, pp. 194-200; Richard W. Evarts, "Comparative Costs and Benefits of Divorce Adjudication and Mediation," *Mediation Quarterly*, spring 1988, pp. 69-79; Sarah C. Grebe, "Mediation at Different Stages of the Divorce Process," *Family Therapy Collections*, no. 12, 1985, pp. 34-47.
178. Robert J. MacCoun, "Experimental Research on Jury Decision-Making," *Science*, vol. 244, June 1989, pp. 1046-1050.
179. Leticia Rodriguez and William R. Bogett, "Societal Considerations in Scaling Injury Severity and Effects," *Journal of Safety Research*, vol. 20, summer 1989, pp. 73-83.

come from nonlawyers who've been trained to provide them.[180] The findings of experts in computers, math, social sciences, and other technical subjects can't continue to be mere footnotes to the learned books of the law professors. We need those experts' findings much more than we need a lot of the stuff that the lawyers spend their time debating.

These shortcomings of the law schools made it hard for me to accept the whole enterprise. I failed to use my anti-empirical blinders properly; as a result, my legal vision was impaired by the glare coming from a single bright insight: that all those nice, neat cases had gotten into my law books only after a huge, rarely mentioned quantity of human suffering by clients on both sides of the battle. It has been both satisfying and depressing to see, time and time again, in psychological studies and in real life, that I was right. The contest hurts people in positions of grief[181] and trust;[182] it sometimes interferes with your ability to do the sensible thing for yourself; and it frequently triggers Litigation Response Syndrome, or LRS, in which the individual experiences difficulty in concentrating, burnout, feelings of detachment and estrangement, sleep and other physical problems, and other behaviors similar to those found in people suffering from post-traumatic stress disorder.[183]

Those human dimensions didn't interest my law professors much. So maybe it should not be surprising that law schools are often criticized for turning out lawyers who'd rather be adversarial than master "the gentler arts of reconciliation and accommodation."[184] It seems clear that when you diligently avoid areas of knowledge, you inescapably skew the educations of those who listen to you.

---

180. Despite the tremendous importance of the *Miranda* decision, the social scientists rather than the lawyers have been the ones to study its impact, and the same has been true in many other areas. (Forer, fn. 58, pp. 177-180.)
181. Paul C. Rosenblatt, "Grief and Involvement in Wrongful Death Litigation," *Law and Human Behavior*, vol. 7, Dec. 1983, pp. 356.
182. David Lewis and Andrew Weigert, "Trust as a Social Reality," *Social Forces*, vol. 63, June 1985, pp. 978-79.
183. See Paul R. Lees-Haley, "Litigation Response Syndrome," *American Journal of Forensic Psychology*, vol. 6, 1988, pp. 3-12.
184. Bok, fn. 155, pg. 45.

c. Games Professors Play

Now, law professors aren't irrational. They have the option of being more sensitive or scientific. They ignore that option, partly because their philosophy about the law tells them that a non-sensitive, non-scientific approach is best.

You can learn more about that philosophy in courses on jurisprudence. I didn't take any such courses, and I've often regretted that, thinking that maybe doing so would have helped me see what weirdness in high places was responsible for the current state of the law on the everyday level.

On the other hand, when I *have* glanced at articles on legal philosophy, I've found that either I don't understand them or that their authors are on another channel. In one article[185] I looked at recently, for example, a professor asserts that, since facts are so darned hard to figure out, a system of justice is better off if it simply avoids[186] worrying too much about the *truth*, and focuses instead on other goals. For him, "the truth and nothing but the truth" is "a myth."[187]

He doesn't trash the truth just for the fun of it, though. Rather, he says, society has other important goals that justice must consider, even if they force truth into the back seat. One such goal is "social harmony." He notes that some cultures have conflict resolution methods that restore social harmony without emphasizing truth. In a fit of anthropological fervor, he offers us these examples:

> *Turnbull says of the Pygmies of the Forest: "Disputes are generally settled with little reference to the alleged rights and wrongs of the case, but more with the sole intention of restoring peace to the community."* ...

---

185. Donald T. Weckstein, "The Purposes of Dispute Resolution: Comparative Concepts of Justice," *American Business Law Journal*, vol. 26, no. 3, fall 1988, pg. 605. I don't mean to make Weckstein a scapegoat. I'm sure he has plenty of company. I chose his article merely because it's recent and it's striking.

186. His word was "eschew" (fn. 185, pg. 607). It's defined, in the *American Heritage Dictionary*, in the way shown in the text here. His position is so hostile to truth-seeking that my translation seems fair.

187. Weckstein, fn. 185, pg. 606. I just don't understand why nobody has gotten around to changing the oath that you take to testify in court. I hate to say it, but I probably would have flunked this law professor's course in justice.

> *The Eskimo song duel involves parties pouring out*
> *abuse in song at one another, sometimes combined*
> *with head and rear buffeting, before a village assem-*
> *bly.*[188]

So there you are. You've got your basic Eskimos clubbing each other on the ass, and this professor tells us that this has a lot to do with the way justice should function in America. What can you say to something like this? Thanks for noticing the 4,000 years of Western jurisprudence, pal.

It's not that I think the Eskimos have it all wrong. I don't see *them* writing a book, like the one you're now reading, that's full of bitching and moaning about their legal training. All I'm trying to say is that the Eskimos' way of handling things does not necessarily mean a lot for American law. Apparently unlike the Eskimos, we think the truth is terribly important. As the Declaration of Independence puts it, "We hold these *truths* to be self-evident ...."[189]

What can I tell you? The professor evidently got into the wrong end of the donkey costume. The rest of us are trying to go in the other direction, toward a *more* truthful system.[190] (He's not really that much worse off, though, than the legal theorists who insist that they can define their terms any way they want, so that it makes sense to them to say that a failure to act is an act too. Not that it's *like* an act. For them, it *is* an act.[191] I mean, where are we?)

Like I say, when I look at this stuff, I quickly lose much of my regret for neglecting to take my complaints about criminal law and the tax code to a more philosophical level. In an undergrad philosophy course, I once spent six weeks trying to understand what we mean when we say, "The cat is on the mat." Pursuing that kind of inquiry with the law would have driven me bats.

---

188. Weckstein, fn. 185, pp. 608-609.
189. Or, as they say in the Evidence law casebook that I used in law school: "The rules represent a pragmatic attempt to come as reasonably close to *the truth* as the law's resources permit." (Jack M. Maguire et al., *Cases and Materials on Evidence* (Mineola, NY: Foundation Press, 1973), pg. 1 (my emphasis).)
190. Forer, fn. 58, pg. 105; Marvin E. Frankel, "The Search for Truth: An Umpireal View," *University of Pennsylvania Law Review*, vol. 123, May 1975, pg. 1035 (citing Justice David W. Peck).
191. See the discussion in Husak, fn. 145, pp. 83ff.

In the end, you'll find difficulties all along the spectrum of legal substance, from theory to data, intuition to induction, top to bottom. As long as you exercise your tunnel vision, you might make it through and learn to concentrate only on what the judges say. But the minute you widen your perspective and ask bigger questions, you're going to see that you've been standing in deep doo-doo. The only thing that could be worse would be if you let yourself go beyond *thinking* about the law, and started to *feel* what your clients are going to be feeling — a point to which I turn now.

2. This Is Procedure?

As you're going through law school, you begin to hear things. Sure, you heard them before, but you were able to ignore them in your eagerness to get into this exciting new career. Now, however, when you can settle down and realize that yes, you really are going to be a lawyer, some of these things slowly seep through to your consciousness. You, personally, are going to be involved in — indeed, you may be worsening — a situation that authorities abhor. For example:

> *The system is ready to crash. It's ready to fall apart without relief. People get frustrated with the system. They blame the lawyers, they blame the courts. You can't get justice when you have to wait five years[192] ....*

That is from Los Angeles County Bar Association President Larry Feldman, explaining why the LACBA had filed suit against the State of California, demanding the appointment of more state court judges.[193] Derek Bok, the president of Harvard University, said this:

---

192. Court gridlock now prevents American patent developers from defending themselves against foreign infringers. (Christopher J. Steffen, "Protecting Creativity in a Global Market," *New York Times*, Aug. 26, 1990, business section, pg. 13, col. 2.) A civil case in some major cities frequently takes five years or more to get to a jury trial. Cases rarely move routinely to trial within a year. (ABA Action Commission to Reduce Court Costs and Delay, *Attacking Litigation Costs and Delay: Final Report* (Chicago: ABA, 1984), pg. 7.)

193. "L.A. County Bar Sues California," *ABA Journal*, vol. 74, Feb. 1988, pg. 28.

Access to the courts may be open in principle. In practice, however, most people find their legal rights severely compromised by the cost of legal services, the baffling complications ..., and the long, frustrating delays .... [T]his nation, which prides itself on ... justice, has developed a legal system that is the most expensive in the world, yet cannot manage to protect the rights of most of its citizens.[194]

But I think the situation becomes clearest when you consider the words of one very famous lawyer:

We must not doubt the serious dissatisfaction with courts and lack of respect for law which exists in the United States today. Our adversary system turns objective witnesses into partisans who hope one side defeats the other. It leads to sensational cross-examinations.

Our system of justice is archaic. Uncertainty, delay and expense have created a deep-seated desire to keep out of court, right or wrong, on the part of every sensible businessman in the community.

Now, I wish I could tell you that those words were written last year, or at least during the last decade. But I can't. They're from a man who's been dead for many years. He read them aloud at a meeting of the ABA on Aug. 29, 1906.[195]

The basic principle is this: Lawyers are trained to focus on doing what they have to do before their clients will pay them. That does not mean they have the clients' best interests at heart, and it certainly doesn't mean that they give a hoot about whether the legal system itself continues to function well. In the big picture, it goes like this: If you let your United States go on for a couple of centuries with lawyers who rarely lift a finger to improve the system, it's not surprising that the

---

194. Bok, fn. 155, pp. 38ff.
195. Roscoe Pound, "The Causes of Popular Dissatisfaction with the Administration of Justice," *American Law Review*, vol. 40, Sept.-Oct. 1906, pp. 730, 739, 742 (first paragraph paraphrased).

system begins to show some signs of neglect.

It's like a taxicab in which you, the lawyer, are always going where your clients demand, at whatever speed they say, without ever stopping for maintenance. At first, you lose a few functions. You run out of windshield wiper fluid; the radio stops working. If you keep it up, more important systems fail you, like the clutch and the brakes. And then, one fine day, the machine won't start or, worse, it won't stop.

Our legal system has now reached a point where, if you're a client, your basic expectations of justice are so far off track that attorneys will sometimes laugh at you for expressing them. It's not necessarily that the attorneys don't wish they could do something for you; it's just that the functions you would like to use are, like the cab's radio, kaput.

I'll try to make it a bit clearer. Let's suppose you go out, today, and sue someone. You don't realize it yet, but you're about to begin working with judges and attorneys who, when they speak of "justice," do not mean the same thing as you. What they mean is "the justice that this legal system will produce." What you mean, by contrast, is "the justice that God would render if He were in charge of this case." You may not know that that's what you mean, but you'll find out.

And here's how you'll find out. You'll slowly see that what you get from the legal system is not at all what you'd get in heaven, or even in some far-away country where attitudes may be different. And that will frustrate you. But, as you'll learn, it's silly, in the eyes of lawyers and judges, for you to act as though there's some kind of alternative, perfect justice system to which you can easily refer if you don't like this one.[196] This is the only one we've got; it's the best we could do; and it's all you're gonna get. For your purposes, Sir or Madam, this *is* justice.

It's mistaken to think that the justice system is concerned with the things you want it to be concerned with. It happens to be a system of justice, rather than a system of religion, or a system of finance, or a system of partying and good times.

---

196. See William M. O'Barr and John M. Conley, "Lay Expectations of the Civil Justice System," *Law and Society Review*, vol. 22, Apr. 1988, pp. 159-60. It speaks volumes that HALT ("Help Abolish Legal Tyranny," 1319 F Street N.W., Washington, DC 20004) now has over 150,000 irritated members.

But it is, first and foremost, a system. It may have looked like more at the outset, but appearances are deceiving, to say nothing of the people involved.

So you take your number and you wait in line. We're used to complaints about the service. If you aren't happy, chances are that the problem is in your head. The system is doing what it's supposed to do, or at least it's doing all that it's capable of anymore. We lawyers realize that there will be imperfections, and since we have no alternative, we accept them (except when clients will pay us to challenge them, or, more rarely,[197] when we have time to devote, as volunteers, toward reforming them). Our justice system is just a system, not to be confused with a just system.

I wish I could give you better news. I'm not even asking you to believe me. Go out and talk to some attorneys. Talk to some people who've been through lawsuits. If you ask the right questions about whether justice was done and how much it cost, in dollars and in tears, you'll almost certainly find yourself engaged, not only intellectually, but also emotionally, with the problems of the legal system.

In law school, I was introduced to the head and heart of the law, and I found it disturbing. I couldn't begin to get personally attached to it. And I think I wasn't alone. It seemed to me that few of my classmates *believed* in what they were doing. We all just wanted to get jobs and make money, without trying to make sense of the bigger picture.

C. The Pit: Legal Ethics

As a law student, you may do well in constitutional law and poorly in evidence, or you may have a gift for oral argument or a real problem with legal research. And that's fine. You'll just have to steer your career toward your strong areas. But there's one subject in law school that permeates and overrides everything else, and if you're not able to grasp it, you don't belong in law school.

That subject is legal ethics. And before I describe why it's

---

197. See Judge Forer, fn. 58, pg. 73: "I see many lawyers. Most are competent and conscientious. A few are brilliant. But too many are not interested in their clients. [Few] have the opportunity to engage in law reform."

so important, I'll explain briefly what it is.

1. The Problem

The term "legal ethics" does not refer to a philosophical theory with which some attorneys agree and others disagree. It's not a matter of one's beliefs. Legal ethics are specific, printed rules, adopted by each state, and usually based on the ABA's Model Code of Professional Ethics and Model Rules of Professional Ethics.[198] Attorneys who get caught breaking them are supposed to be punished for it.[199] These are rules of *ethics*, not *morals*: written compromises that their authors reached, not on the basis of their own views of good and evil, but because of political decisions about what was necessary to preserve freedom under our system of government.

Among the many ethical rules, one in particular gave me problems. It is expressed in Canon[200] No. 7 of the ABA Model Code, which says, "A lawyer should represent a client zealously within the bounds of the law." This canon means that you have to work toward your client's objectives, as long as they're legal, even if they're sleazy.[201] You're not permitted to sit in moral judgment on your client.[202]

Now, if you're a client, you could really appreciate this rule. It would be bad news if your attorney could back away just because s/he didn't like what you were trying to accomplish. It'd be like hiring a mechanic who wanted to keep his/her hands clean.

---

198. I see no substantive difference, for my purposes, between the Model Code and the Model Rules. The next few footnotes discuss the Code, since it was what they were teaching me when I was grappling with this subject in law school, but for purposes of comparison see the discussion of Model Rule 1.3 on pg. 37 of the ABA *Annotated Model Rules of Professional Conduct* (1984).

199. The punishment can even include disbarment, which permanently prohibits the attorney from practicing law. In some states, a disbarred attorney can apply for reinstatement after being "rehabilitated." Other punishments include suspension (i.e., a temporary revocation of the right to practice), and reproval (i.e., formal censure, which can hurt your ability to attract clients). See Gifis, fn. 47.

200. A "canon" is a "rule" or a "standard." (*American Heritage Dictionary*.)

201. Disciplinary Rule ("DR") 7-101(A)(1), explaining that Canon, says, "A lawyer shall not intentionally fail to seek the lawful objectives of his client through reasonably available means permitted by law and the Disciplinary Rules ...."

202. You do have the option of asking your client if they will let you do the honest thing, but that's about as far as you can go in obeying your own moral feelings. See, e.g., Doris Del Tosto Brogan, "Responding to Client Perjury under the New Pennsylvania Rules of Professional Conduct: The Lawyer's Continuing Dilemma," *Villanova Law Review*, vol. 34, 1989, pg. 89.

But I wasn't the client. I was training to be the lawyer, and I was supposed to be looking forward to the dirty work. That bothered me. I wasn't eager to be a bad guy, if badness was what it took to help my client win.

I don't deny the power of this canon's approach. I have personally had the experience of starting into a case, not believing what the client was saying, but doing my best to build a good case for him/her anyway, and then discovering, as I went along, that, hey, maybe there really *is* something to this argument I've been concocting. That process never would have taken place, and perhaps that best defense of my client would not have been made, if I'd been sitting back, appraising everything like a judge.

Still, a person can have a philosophical problem with this canon. Even though my clients may have benefited in the particular cases I just mentioned, I can't guarantee you that their benefit outweighed the social cost of all the other cases in which clients honestly have no leg to stand on, but are allowed to go into court and yank the other guy around for a while — and maybe even win, wrongly.

Everyone has to choose his/her own reckoning ground, when it comes to this duty to serve the client's lawful goals zealously. But a question from the field of religion may show one useful way of thinking about the problem.

The question is this: Have you ever run into a Moonie? (Or, if you're a Moonie, have you ever run into a Jehovah's Witness?) There is this experience of trying to talk sense with people who, no matter what you say, have an answer for you. You spend a couple of hours dealing with objections, exceptions, and explanations, and by the time you're through, either you want to strangle them or else you're signing on the dotted line. If their logic doesn't draw you in, it'll drive you nuts.

Perhaps the best solution, in that kind of situation, is to go back to the very first nonsensical thing they said and start over. You stick with what you believe on that point, and although you listen to what they have to say, you don't move off that point until they've totally convinced you that your former views were wrong.

We have an adversarial legal system. The theory is that, by teaching the attorneys on both sides to confuse and deceive, you arrive at the facts. And now that you've considered the

Moonie problem, you know the proper response: "No way! Prove to me that two liars will produce the truth!"

To be sure, I don't want to irritate the litigators among us. So I will buttress my accusation of lying. Here is a close paraphrasing from a booklet that the New Jersey bar association gives to people who pass the state's bar exam, as part of their preparation to practice law in that state:

> *If your adversary is an exhaustive cross-examiner, call your strongest witnesses early in your case. After your opponent bores the jury with a repetitive cross-examination in which s/he will fail to discredit these strong witnesses, you can then <u>sneak</u> <u>in</u> your worse witnesses. The jury will be much less attentive.*

> *If you ask questions carelessly, <u>the answers of a bright</u> or <u>honest witness may be devastating</u>.*

> *Unless there is a particular reason for <u>obfuscating</u> the issues, it is most important that the jurors understand all of the salient points of an interrogation.*

> *A truthful and intelligent opposing witness can be deadly. A good peripheral examination of that witness, however, will give you arguments that you can make to the jury at the close of the case, <u>regardless</u> of the answers given by the witness.*[203]

Ultimately, I had to conclude that this wonderful notion, the adversary system, is just another complicated gadget that should have been replaced, long ago, by something simpler and more suited to the task at hand, and that as long as we continue to use it, we'll get all kinds of weird side effects.

For example, you wonder what happens when you take 36,000[204] of the brightest people in the country each year,

---

203. Philip G. Auerbach, *Try It*, New Jersey Institute for Continuing Legal Education, Newark, 1976, pp. 38, 69, 71, 73, 75 (my emphasis).
204. Average annual graduates in recent years. (*A Review of Legal Education in the United States, Fall, 1990: Law School and Bar Admission Requirements* (Chicago: ABA, 1991), pg. 66.) If you include those who absorbed adversarial atitudes before dropping out of law school, the figure might be as high as 41,300.

send them to law school, and teach them to excel in the arts of confusing the issue, hiding the truth, defending the useless, and damning the valuable. Is this, indeed, the most productive use of their talents? Or are they, instead, being taught to destroy the society they were supposed to help?

There is an answer to that question, and as I was going through law school, I realized — perhaps from comparing the attitudes I found in my contemporaneous business school classes — that it was not what my law professors wanted me to believe. As far as I could see, no matter what the grand principles might be, it was a mistake to persuade your brightest people that they must master these dirty skills.

In 1920, we had 122,519 lawyers, or one for every 863 people. But by the year 2000, we will have one million[205] extremely intelligent, highly influential people who will have been trained, by law schools, to be lawyers — that is, to concentrate on learning how to strip as much as possible from one person, without regard to the virtues of the case, and grant it to the other person, just because that other person happens to be the client. At least one out of every 290 Americans will be a lawyer, trained to speak eloquently, work diligently, and become public figures, so that they may teach the rest of us these bitter ways of dealing with one another.

As much as I'd been taught never to use the word "obviously," because nothing is truly obvious, I had to make an exception in this case. There was something obviously wrong here, and I was becoming a part of it.

(Using 12.8% attrition rate. See text at fns. 346 and 350. See also fn. 362.)
(Note: I refer to the *Review* frequently in the following footnotes. It is an annual publication. Most of my data comes from the Fall 1990 issue.)

205. Gibbons, fn. 33, pg. 71. After removing duplicates, there were 655,191 lawyers in the U.S. in 1985 (*Statistical Abstract of the U.S., 1990* (Washington: GPO, 1990), pg. 182, based on ABF statistics) and, preliminarily, 755,694 in 1990 (call to spokesperson from ABF on July 12, 1991), for a net average annual increase of 20,101 between 1985 and 1990, as compared to, on average, 35,841 new law graduates during those years (see *Review of Legal Education*, fn. 204, pg. 66). Perhaps 84% of all law school graduates become lawyers (see text at fn. 361). This produced about 30,000 new lawyers (84% of 35,841) per year in the late 1980s, before deaths and other departures; at the midpoint of that period, the net annual increase in lawyers was 2.85%. (Note an inconsistency in the data: In the conversation mentioned in fn. 380, I was told that mortalities were already about 15,000 in 1980. The 30,000, less 15,000, less inactives and retirements, would make the net addition of 20,000 per year impossible, no?)

2. How Other Attorneys Handle It

Not everyone has problems with this, of course, or we wouldn't have many lawyers. The fact is, attorneys have a couple of ways of learning to put up with legal ethics.

a. Option 1: Sheer Crooks

Some attorneys are simply dishonest. They like the money, or the feeling of power, that they get from cheating someone else, and they don't seem to suffer from the guilt that might deter a good person. It helps them, too, to see that other attorneys and clients share their attitudes.

In law school and law practice, I sometimes cooperated with dishonest attorneys, while at other times I insisted on honesty. In the latter case, I would flatter myself for being so noble. It was fun to stand on a pedestal and sling bad names at crooked lawyers. But when I got tired of that, I wanted to understand why honesty seemed better. As far as I could tell, it came down to a question of competition.

Competition can be fun. But it can also be a pain. In law, as in sports, it's sometimes tough to know where to draw the line and say that someone has gone too far.[206]

The rules for competition need to be liberal, so that people will want to come up with successful new ideas. But the rules can't let you win for an irrelevant reason. You're supposed to win because you're skilled or because you have a winning position. People sometimes call this "sporting" or "gentleman-ly" competition. The idea is that you compete as hard as you can, but you stay within the rules, even if it means losing.

That can sound wimpy to those who want to win no matter what, even (indeed, for some people, *preferably*) if it involves cheating. For these people, winning is the only thing that counts, and the only people talking about fair competition are those who can't hack it when the fight gets fierce.

For those who do cheat, cheating pays. Not always, but often enough to persuade them to do it. It may carry some

---

206. For contrast, you might consider Alfie Kohn, *The Case Against Competition* (Boston: Houghton Mifflin, 1986), pp. 46-47: "Do we perform better when we are trying to beat others than when we are working with them or alone? ... [T]he evidence is so overwhelmingly clear and consistent that the answer to this question already can be reported: *almost never.*"

long-term drawbacks — such as always having to look over your shoulder, always feeling dirty, not having real friends, etc. — but those are easy to ignore now and regret later, especially if the immediate payoff is rich enough.

Cheating does no good for the rest of us, though. If we hadn't believed in those rules for the courtroom or the baseball diamond, we wouldn't have set them up in the first place. We wanted them to show us who's the best. People who avoid them simply wipe out the whole purpose of the competition. For example, in the business world, ignoring the rules gives us shoddy goods and services. Your product can be inferior, and yet, with the Mafia behind you, or with the right advertising budget or the right attorneys, you can chase your competitors out of the market.

That's one drawback of playing to win. There's another drawback, namely, that sporting competition is much more fun. Winning is everything to the winner, but it's only part of why all those other people showed up to participate in the competition, knowing as they did that the odds were against them. The fact is, the contest wouldn't be the same without the enjoyment that those others are having, win or lose.

It's not surprising to see cheating occur so frequently in the practice of law. Law is not like a footrace, where there's a direct link between what you're doing and what you're trying to accomplish. In running, you win the race, not because of your juggling skills or how many pancakes you can eat, but simply because you are the fastest runner.

But in law, you use one kind of means to get to another kind of end. For example, most authorities say that you're in court to find the truth, and yet they let attorneys mislead people. As another example, courts are supposed to add to social peace. If you have an argument with someone, they're supposed to help you resolve it. But, instead, they add fuel to the flame.[207] You learn that it helps your case to think of more and more reasons why you — and the judge — should hate the other guy.

---

207. Many lawyers and judges criticize the adversary process. See, e.g., former Supreme Court Chief Justice Warren E. Burger, "The State of Justice," *American Bar Association Journal*, Apr. 1984, vol. 70, pg. 66; Bok, fn. 155, pg. 42; Arron, fn. 44, pg. 47.

This hurts those who come to the system sincerely, willing to compete fairly, on the merits of the specific problem that brought them there. It helps those who, for the sake of winning, will cheat, play games with the truth, and trot out irrelevant stuff to make the other guy look bad.[208]

Of course, what one person can do, the other can do as well. Clients get tougher. And what used to be considered outrageous becomes standard. Indeed, as this process goes on, attorneys who *aren't* dirty fighters risk being held liable for malpractice, for not trying hard enough.[209]

I found this prospect discouraging. I tried to believe that winning was always a good test of whether you and your client were in the right. But even that way of thinking of it put me at a disadvantage against those who, right or wrong, wanted to win at all costs.

b. Option 2: Conform and Compromise

Not all attorneys are cold-blooded sharks. In my experience, most are human beings who feel some degree of responsibility to do the right thing. Starting in law school, their lives have been a matter of balancing their personal integrity against the demands of their legal careers.

That compromise does not always require great dishonesty. Some attorneys practice in legal specialties in which they simply don't come across many challenging moral questions. A few others are able to distinguish themselves from the crowd as, for example, "Honest Abe Lincoln."

Also, in a lot of places, there aren't that many attorneys. It's a small world, and reputations get around. You can fight dirty for a while, but it may come back to haunt you. I've even heard of attorneys teaming up against the newcomer who gets too aggressive. Thus, in a bit of fatherly advice, one lawyer urged,

---

208. I speculate: A legal system that emphasizes fierce competition instead of cooperation is one that cannot help shifting so that tort law overrides contract law. See Huber's chapter on "Death of Contract," fn. 141, pp. 19ff.

209. See, e.g., Richard E. Crouch, "The Matter of Bombers: Unfair Tactics and the Problem of Defining Unethical Behavior in Divorce Litigation," *Family Law Quarterly*, vol. 20, fall 1986, pp. 413-14.

> *[G]et to know as many lawyers as you can. ...
> Why? Because [they] will send you business, they will
> give you advice, they will serve as a sounding board
> and a foil for your ideas, and ... as role models,
> mentors and an emotional support system.*[210]

In that pleasant spirit, too, many attorneys nudge their
clients in the direction of honesty:

> *Clients ... usually look to their lawyer for cues as
> to what they can and should expect from the legal
> system and their lawyer. Give them the proper mes-
> sage, raise the ethical issues with them, and you will
> find it relatively infrequent that a client persists in
> asking something that you are uncomfortable do-
> ing.*[211]

But having said those nice things, I'm poised to attack.
There's something wrong with the quotes I just offered.

First, not all attorneys share this urge to make the world
a more honest place. Even the honest ones might be indignant
at the suggestion that they're supposed to act as moral police-
men for their clients. "Business is business," they'll say, "and
my job is to help my client win. That's where my paycheck
comes from, and that's what I promised to do when I became
an attorney." Sometimes you'll appreciate it, and sometimes
you won't, but the bottom line is that, under our system of
justice, your adversary's lawyer has a job to do.[212]

Second, let's not flatter ourselves on our ability to sway
the client. Clients may be flexible in Utah, but when you're
in New York, they expect you to fight like a cornered were-
wolf. Too many of them, anyway.

Third, that incentive to be "one of the guys" may soften

---

210. Sam F. Fowler, Jr., "Dear Uncle John: Advice on Beginning Solo
Practice," *Legal Economics*, vol. 12, Jan. 1986, pg. 25 (his emphasis).
211. Michael D. Zimmerman, "Professional Standards Versus Personal Ethics:
The Lawyer's Dilemma," *Utah Law Review*, vol. 1, 1989, pg. 8.
212. Consider, e.g., the finding that adversarial lawyers are more effective
than conciliatory lawyers at preventing post-separation abuse of women in divorce
cases. (Desmond Ellis, "Post-Separation Woman Abuse: The Contribution of
Lawyers as "Barracudas," "Advocates," and "Counsellors," *International Journal
of Law and Psychiatry*, vol. 10, 1987, pg. 403.)

your aggression, but it can also mellow out your ethical conscience. For example, one article, foolishly entitled "Lawyers Are Serious About Professional Responsibility," noted that 58 percent of the attorneys who have witnessed misconduct by judges have decided not to report it; at least 33 percent of the attorneys polled said they would find it difficult to object (and remember, they're talking about themselves, so the percentages are probably higher) if a partner in their firms asked them to do something unethical; 76 percent say they occasionally or often encounter dishonest opposing lawyers; and one-third can't say that they believe the legal profession should police itself.[213]

I had one additional problem when I was dealing with this notion of ethical compromise. It will take a moment to explain the underlying concept, but it's important to do so, because I'll be using it again later.

I don't know whether you've ever had the experience of talking about something you don't understand. I have. And when I do, I tend to go on and on about the things I do understand, and talk as though this blank spot in my knowledge is just a minor annoyance. But then, when I get to know the subject better, I realize that there are whole dimensions, of which I never dreamed, within that little blank spot.

Attorneys do this sometimes, and it's a peculiar sight. After all, they're normally the first to focus on the details. Somehow, though, lawyers who can think for hours about how a staircase was designed will not hesitate for a moment when they face huge gaps in their understanding of who they are and what they're doing. Instead, they flit right across, as though there's nothing to talk about. I call this phenomenon the "Lawyer's Black Hole of Confident Ignorance."[214]

Those Black Holes pop up all over. And there's one right here. Look again, if you will, at the last quote I gave you. Is it OK to do something that makes you "uncomfortable" if you only have to do it on a "relatively infrequent" basis? Like murder — maybe if I keep it down to one a month, nobody will mind? The author of that quote didn't seem to have any

---

213. Lauren Rubenstein Reskin, *ABA Journal*, vol. 71, Dec. 1985, pg. 41.
214. See also the mention of attorneys' overconfidence on pg. 47.

urge to dwell on the ambiguities in it. And how do you feel about a law professor who refers, almost contemptuously, to people whose sense of honesty follows "the 'rural God-fearing standard,' so exacting and tedious that it often excludes the use of lawyers."[215] He makes it sound like a headache, right? It's easy to dismiss these things when they don't interest you.

I'm sorry, folks. To me, "moderation in all things" is a pain in the neck, and particularly when we're talking about ethical behavior. I don't feel like a better person for going out and deliberately ignoring my principles once in a while. Who invented this notion that compromise and flexibility can take care of the lawyer's ethical concerns?

I repeat, there are all kinds of lawyers, and many of them are genuinely honest people who struggle with difficult issues of right and wrong. But the foregoing attitudes came up far too often for my taste in law school, and I heard far too few people, among faculty or students, daring to defend the *moral* against the *ethical*.

Needless to say, by this point I had a real problem with law school. My stubbornness turned these ethical questions into solid barriers for me. I was never able to form an attachment to the study of law, perhaps because I think I really did love the underlying principles that it claimed to serve.

I was far from the only one who felt this way. Some dropped out because of their feelings. Others stayed in, as I did, and survived law school. For us, the end of that three-year period marked the end of our formal classroom education. It certainly did not complete the task of turning us into lawyers.

---

215. Geoffrey C. Hazard, Jr., "The Lawyer's Obligation to Be Trustworthy When Dealing With Opposing Parties," *South Carolina Law Review*, vol. 33, 1981, pg. 193.

PART II

ENTERING
THE LAWYER'S WORLD

Non-lawyers sometimes seem confused as to whether a certain person is a lawyer. If someone finished law school but did not pass the bar exam, is that person a lawyer? What if s/he passed the bar exam but never practiced law? How about practicing law and then quitting — are you still a lawyer?

The formal answer is that law school graduation, by itself, usually isn't enough. You're not really a lawyer until you're admitted to practice law — and that process usually requires a bar exam and some other things that I'm about to describe.

But the informal answer is that being a lawyer, for all practical purposes, requires an introduction to the real world of legal practice. That introduction can be entirely as foreign and stressful as law school was. And although "the real world of law practice" lies several years away from the person who is only now applying to law school, it nevertheless forms a very real part of legal education. As such, it's something that the future lawyer should understand before taking the first step toward a future in law.

To tell the story properly, I need to back up and describe how life as a practicing lawyer begins for you while you're still in law school.

§ 5. Bar Admission:
The Arrival of Knowledge

I finished law school in the requisite three years. The bar exam promised to take only a few months from my schedule. In return for being shorter, the bar exam period was more intensely painful.

A. The Bar Exam

In case you're wondering, attorneys are called "the bar" because they have the privilege of entering beyond the wooden railing that separates the general courtroom audience from the judge's bench;[216] thus the word "barrister" as a name for an attorney in Britain.[217]

The term "organized bar" refers to those attorneys who belong to a bar organization. It comes up most often in references to the ABA, which fights for the interests of attorneys, offers annual conventions (for which attorneys can get a tax writeoff) in places like San Francisco and Hawaii, and researches questions pertaining to the legal system.[218]

Besides the ABA, there are city and county bar associations, associations of trial attorneys, etc. Each state has a bar association that handles issues having to do with the practice of law there; that association, or else the state's supreme court,

---

216. Gifis, fn. 47, pg. 20.
217. *American Heritage Dictionary*.
218. See, for example, how many of the citations in this book come from ABA-sponsored activities.

sets the requirements for admission to the practice of law in the state. With few exceptions,[219] practically everyone has to take a bar exam before they can practice law.

In law school, all I knew about the bar exam was that it was given twice a year. Nobody talked much about it. It just kinda stayed out there in never-never land until graduation day. But things changed quickly after graduation.

1. The Exam Itself

As I soon discovered, one day of the two-day bar exam is devoted to the Multistate Bar Examination (also referred to as the Multistate or simply the MBE). It covers six subjects that most states and territories consider basic to the practice of law, namely, contracts, torts, constitutional law, criminal law, real property, and evidence. Most of us hadn't even looked at those subjects since the first year of law school.

On the other day of the exam, you don't take a standardized national test. Instead, you answer questions posed by the state's bar examiners. The questions might require essays, or even a brief in which you tell an imaginary judge why your hypothetical client should win.

The examiners also reserve the right to cover a lot of different topics on the state portion. Here is what they told me about the New York exam that I was going to take:

> *In addition to the six subjects covered by the MBE, the New York section may also deal with Administrative Law, Agency, Bankruptcy, Carriers, [Ethics], Conflict of Laws, Corporations, Damages, Domestic Relations, Equity, Federal Jurisdiction, Insurance, Labor Law, Municipal Corporations, Negotiable Instruments, New York Constitutional Law, New York Practice and Procedure, Partnership, Personal Property, Sales, Suretyship, Taxation and Trusts and Estates. More than one subject may [appear] in a*

---

219. I am told that Wisconsin considers your legal education at one of the in-state ABA-approved law schools to be good enough, so that no exam is required. I think Wisconsin is unique in this.

single question.[220]

This was scary. I had worked in a law firm during my second summer. After that, I had decided to spend my third year of law school studying corporate law rather than preparing for the bar exam, so that I'd be ready for the demands of the job when I started work after graduation.

Besides, as a "national" school, Columbia didn't even offer courses in some of the New York bar exam subjects. New York Civil Procedure, for example, was a nightmare of more than 120 legal-sized pages in my bar review book, and I'd never seen any of it before.

Thus, after three years in law school, I hadn't studied even half of the 23 non-Multistate subjects on which New York planned to test me. I had to learn or review them all in the two months between graduation and the July bar exam.

2. Morale, Crisis In, Explained

You start your bar review preparation intelligently. You don't waste a minute pretending that you know the law. The exam wants you to memorize the rules and spit out the right answers, not to sit there and theorize. For this, your three years of open-book exams in law school leave you unprepared.

The first step is to sign up for a bar review course. You pay up to $1,000[221] and attend classes five days a week for those two months. My course was BAR/BRI, for which I'd been an on-campus representative (and therefore got a free ride). At our daily class meetings, when we weren't taking notes, we gossiped about a competing course called Peiper. They supposedly charged a premium price, admitted only the best students, and had a very high pass rate. No doubt the people over at Peiper were meanwhile gossiping anxiously about yet another course.

You're a fool if you don't sign up for one of these courses.

---

220. Taken from the "Notice to Candidates for Admission to the Bar" published by the New York State Board of Bar Examiners and sent to those who had signed up for the July 1982 bar exam.

221. More, if, like one student who failed 10 times, you hire a tutor for $5,000 who finally, blessedly, helps you to pass. (Cheryl Lavin, "Bar Exams Are Not Easier the Second Time Around," *Denver Post*, June 21, 1990, pg. 2-F, col. 1.) Pity the poor sucker who failed 16 times. (*Bar Examiner*, May 1991, pg. 36.)

I already told you how big the law library is. I have no idea where you'd start if you wanted to do it on your own. There really are patterns to the bar exam's questions, and these review courses can detect them. They also give you mnemonic devices and shortcuts to cram your memory full of the trivia on which you're likely to be tested. With their assistance and a lot of devoted effort, you can make it.

You can, that is, if you don't defeat yourself, as I did. I got married on the day before I graduated from law school. It was grand to drink champagne on my European honeymoon. Upon returning, I found it difficult to drop my happy-newly-wed attitude in favor of the desperation and fear that is essential if you're to study as hard as you must for this exam. Besides, I was distracted by two business school classes that I had to take that summer in order to finish my MBA.

I also kept thinking that this was a stupid exam. I didn't want to practice all those different areas of law. I had no interest in spending weeks learning stuff I knew I'd never use. It didn't help that, every summer, *The New York Times* runs an editorial that points out how the bar exam is so irrelevant and how much time and money it wastes. Who would willingly dedicate themselves to such a dumb project?[222]

3. Behind the Curtain

As if my personal situation weren't debilitating enough, I couldn't help wondering what happened to my bar exam when they were grading it behind closed doors. On what basis did they set the pass-fail line? What was their goal? Did they do a fair, competent job of grading my exam?

The answers are not reassuring. The scores from each year's exams are published each May in a magazine called *The Bar Examiner*, and, boy, are they silly.

The first problem is that these guys don't understand arithmetic. Here are a few of their many miscalculations:

They mess up the percentages on first-timers. In 1988, Montana did not know how many people were taking its February bar exam for the first time. This is understand-

---

222. If you'll pardon my antisesquipedalian floccinaucinihilipilification.

able. The statisticians in Helena must have been over-
whelmed by the data that flooded in from the 25 people
who took that exam. And it is an improvement, because
they had tried to count the number of first-timers the
previous year, but had gotten it wrong.[223]

Maybe they aren't really sure what a "percentage" is.
In Nevada in 1987, 169 percent of first-timers passed the
July exam. The overall 1980 pass rate was either 67
percent or 87 percent — we just don't know which. In
Idaho in 1990, 147 out of 179 passed, for a total of ... 90
percent?[224]

They can't count. In 1988, the total number of people
taking the exam was 67,888, and the total number passing
was 45,054; and then the total number taking was 45,054,
and the total number passing was 34,876. Of those
people, a whopping 1,193 came from ABA law schools.
In North Carolina in 1990, there were 94 first-timers and
58 repeaters, yielding a total of — you guessed it — 234.

There are dozens of such errors in *The Bar Examiner* each
year. For instance, the first-timer figures fail to work with the
totals in as many as half[225] of the jurisdictions.[226]
The bar examiners do mean well, however. In 1989, they
produced an "Errata" sheet to correct the errors that had
"occured" [*sic*] in their first try. This sheet was terrific. Such
ambition! It changed the data for a whopping *eight* jurisdic-

---

223. The information supplied, in the format takers/passrate/exam-try, is: for
February 1987, 42/74%/1st, 4/50%/repeat; and for July 1987, 83/96%/1st,
7/57%/repeat. This yields 117, not 120, passers.

224. And they're sneaky. For instance, you might be tempted to divide their
total for the number of first-timers in, say, 1990, into their total for the number
of all exam-takers that year, to get the passing percentage of first-timers. But
don't do it, because the first-timer total is not complete. It leaves out data on a
half-dozen jurisdictions that are nevertheless represented in the overall total.

225. E.g., in 1990, miscalculations appear for AR, CO, DC, GA, ID, IN, KS,
KY, MA, MO, MT, NM, NC, OK, OR, PA, PR, RI, SC, SD, TN, UT, VT, and VA.
I have corrected them, using estimates conservatively where necessary, to arrive
at certain other figures in this book. See also the worksheets on pg. 218.

226. A "jurisdiction" is, more or less, the area over which someone or
something has authority. The U.S. Supreme Court has jurisdiction over the whole
United States, whereas the Ho-Ho-Kus Municipal Court has jurisdiction over the
burb of Ho-Ho-Kus only. In this bar exam context, a "jurisdiction" is a state or
territory. (And yes, there really is a town in New Jersey called Ho-Ho-Kus.)

tions. Unfortunately, after those changes, the other numbers for at least two of the "fixed" jurisdictions no longer added up.

Small wonder that they say, each year, that "The National Conference leaves the interpretation of the following statistics to the reader." All hope abandon, ye who enter here.[227] And to think that these people were calculating the number of right answers on my bar exam.

Besides bad math, you can get suspicious about bad intentions. Did they want more lawyers or fewer? It's not clear. From 1982 to 1988, a number of jurisdictions cut their pass-rate percentages, on top of the fact that they were getting *fewer* applicants for the bar.[228] Meanwhile, others had a different idea: Pass rates stayed about the same or even increased, despite the fact that those states were getting significantly *more* applications.[229] Nor is it a geographical phenomenon. Neighboring states go in opposite directions,[230] as do states containing some of our biggest cities.[231]

One explanation is that state bar examiners are doing their level best to find out who's capable of practicing law in their states. The other is that it's a hoax, and their real goal, to the great pain of law schools, law students, and clients, is simply to control the number of attorneys who are permitted to enter the practice of law in their states each year. Limitation is the severest form of flattery: As they know, once you're admitted, you'll be taking business away from other attorneys.

If you believe that the examiners are sincere, you have to conclude that they don't even know for sure what it means to be a "competent" attorney. Although the bar exam questions are becoming more similar from one state to another, the pass

---

227. Dante Alighieri, *The Inferno*, ca. 1320, as quoted in Bartlett's, fn. 56.
228. E.g., Colorado, Iowa, Oregon, Utah, Wisconsin, Wyoming.
229. In Connecticut and New Jersey, for example, the number of test-takers roughly doubled from 935 and 2,241, respectively, in 1982, to 1,961 and 4,132 in 1988, and yet pass rates stayed right in the range of 66-72%. Other examples: Kansas, Montana, Maine, New Hampshire, Pennsylvania, and Rhode Island.
230. For example, in 1988, New Mexico had one of the highest pass rates, at more than 82%, while its neighbor, Arizona, had one of the lowest, at 63%. Nebraska's pass rate was nearly 85%, while that of its neighbor, South Dakota, was another one of the lowest. Between 1982 and 1988, Alabama tested 8% fewer law school graduates, and yet, despite that drop, 38% *more* people passed in 1982 than in 1988. Meanwhile, its neighbor, Mississippi, tested 142% more people in 1988 than in 1982, and yet its pass rate hardly changed at all.
231. Only 19% failed in Illinois in 1988, while 40% failed in New York.

rates continue to diverge.[232]   It was no surprise to hear former Stanford Law School Dean Charles Meyers quoted as saying that the bar's claim that its exam insures a high quality of entering lawyers is based on "an act of faith."[233]

None of this helped me, of course. By mid-July, I had pretty much relaxed. I knew I could not pass this damned thing. I continued to study several hours a day, and took the exam, but only because I hoped that, by going through the motions, I'd get psyched up for the next one, in February.

B. The Bar Exam Revisited

It takes them a long time to grade those July exams. I devoted the autumn to the last four classes I needed at the B-school for my MBA. Around Thanksgiving, I received the bad news. I applied again and began to think about studying for the February exam.

1. Getting Geared Up

Failing was not the worst possible experience. The bar examiners informed one of my friends that his examination had been, would you believe, lost. A pessimist, he thought there was a good chance he'd failed, so he put in two months studying all over again before they found his exam, graded it, and told him that he had passed after all.

Some failed multiple times. The classmate who had been proud of me in my battle with *Student Lawyer* over the use of the word "only" rode with me on the subway to the July exam. He insisted on getting off at 59th Street and running the remaining blocks to work off tension. He had done well in law school, but, last I heard, he never did pass the New York bar exam, even after trying three or four times, and despite taking months to study before a couple of those tries.[234]

---

232. Tamar Lewin, "More Bar Questions Are the Same But Scores Still Vary State by State," *New York Times*, Jan. 1, 1988, pg. A-38, col. 3. Overall, pass rates, as reported by *The Bar Examiner*, have been remarkably consistent, at about 2/3 of all exam-takers, every year over the past decade — although, within each year, February rates are usually much lower than July rates.

233. Doug Bandow, "Assaulting the Barriers to Legal Practice: A Brazen System of Self-Enrichment," *New York Times*, March 15, 1987, bus. sec., pg. 2.

234. There really is a perma-flunk contingent, and as far as I know, there's no test you can take in advance to predict whether you'll be in it. See fn. 360.

Another classmate's firm dumped him when he failed. He couldn't find another job, so he eventually got depressed and gave up. Several years later, a TV reporter did a story on the people who were living in the New York City subway tunnels, and they found this classmate taking shelter in the dirt under Grand Central Station.

In most things, as they say, the best approach is: If at first you don't succeed, try again, then quit. No sense being a damned fool about it. In this case, having already invested so much, not to mention looking forward to life on Wall Street, I felt that I had to pass, no matter what. I would indeed give it one more try, but it would be a *real* try.

That determination forced me to make some tough decisions. First, I decided that I'd have to fake it on the business school final exams that December. Second, I decided that my early months at the law firm, beginning in January, would feature lots of days when I avoided work and tried to leave by 5 p.m. to study, even though that would almost certainly give a bad initial impression to people at the firm who expected me to be available. And third, I knew I had to accept the necessary consequences in my personal life.

2. Extreme Effort

I began my full-time studies for the bar exam in early December. "Full-time" meant 14 to 18 hours a day, seven days a week during that month. I continued to devote every spare minute to study, as planned, in January, and took two weeks off in February, before the exam, to wrap things up.

I decided to go it alone instead of returning to a review course. I had the books that they had given us during the summer, and felt that I'd be better off not getting beaten down by the group panic that pervaded the bar review classes.

I learned that I could not study at home, because my wife was a distraction. Even on the days when I did not have business school classes, then, I found myself commuting to Columbia from our marital home in Passaic, New Jersey.

I saw that sitting in the library at Columbia was not going to be stimulating enough. So I broke down the major subjects into thousands of questions and answers, and then typed them out on Columbia's computer. The questions on the law of contracts, alone, filled 200 single-spaced pages.[235]

Then I found a computer nerd who stayed up until 2 a.m. one night, writing a program for me. This program was great. It would pop a question on the screen. I'd try to think of the answer. Then I'd punch a button, and the answer would appear. If I felt that I got it right, I'd hit the Plus key, and if not, the Minus key. Wrongly answered questions would go back into the stack and circulate up again at random.

When I wasn't at Columbia, I attacked the subjects that I was not putting into the computer. For these, I went through and underlined the key sentences in the review books. Then my wife and I went back through with tape recorders and read all of the underlined stuff into the recorder. I'd listen to those tapes on my way to work.[236]

I have never studied as hard, without stopping, as I did for that re-try at the New York bar exam.

3. Side Effects

They say there's nothing more stressful than the first year of law school. The drummer to whom I was marching during that year, however, appeared to have been experimenting with a kazoo. Besides, I had friends going through that first year with me, and big, naive dreams about what it would do for my future. In all these ways, my second shot at the bar exam was very different and much harsher, and it had some side effects.

The first had to do with coffee. When I'm sitting around studying, it gives me a real jolt. Or, more precisely, it revives my interest in, say, the doctrines of *stare decisis* and *res judicata*. A little coffee made a big difference.

Then again, I did not have "a little" coffee. They started brewing an amazing new brand at the Columbia student union. I gave myself up to it and found my life transformed. By February, I was buying exotic blends at Balducci's and getting a buzz at home too. I bought two thermoses, a quart each, and on each day of the bar exam, I carried them with me, brim full, refilled them both at noon, and took them home empty.

---

235. It required a lot of typing to set this up. But I type fast. I also copied questions over and over, changing just one phrase, so that I could test myself on different wrinkles in the same basic fact situation.
236. It seems ironic that this was how I studied matrimonial law.

All fun has its price, of course.[237] I was often nauseous from the coffee.[238] Sometimes I'd shake, get dizzy, and even

---

237. I've always believed that those people on Law Review were able to do the things they do — such as writing pages on which, would you believe, there are more footnotes than text — because they drink too much coffee and lose all sense of proportion.

238. In "A Survey of Drug Use and Attitudes toward Drugs among Male Law Students and Police Trainees in Queensland, Australia: A Research Note," *Journal of Criminal Justice*, vol. 11, 1983, pp. 57-66, Ruth C. Engs and Kerry E. Mulqueeny found that law students used coffee significantly more than police academy students. Caffeine really does decrease boredom and relaxation, increase memory (at least for a while), improve mood, and increase attentiveness and the feeling of being vigorous, efficient, and full of ideas. (Wing Hong Loke, "Effects of Caffeine on Mood and Memory," *Physiology and Behavior*, vol. 44, 1988, pg. 371; H.R. Lieberman et al., "The Effects of Low Doses of Caffeine on Human Performance and Mood," *Psychopharmacology*, vol. 92, July 1987, pp. 311-12.) People have attributed their fame to caffeine. (See, e.g., Gary Larson, quoted in "The Far Side's Back!!" *Denver Post*, pg. F-1, col. 4, Dec. 30, 1989: "I don't know where my ideas come from. I will admit, however, that one key ingredient is caffeine. I get a couple cups of coffee into me and weird things just start to happen.") Some studies have even suggested that mind-over-matter powers are linked to the drug. ("Mind Over Matter," *Mysteries of the Unknown* (New York: Time-Life Books, 1988), pg. 61.) But beware the "Frodo's Ring" effect. In tests involving long word lists, subjects who have taken caffeine have shown inferior performance in the middles and ends of the lists. (William S. Terry and Barbara Phifer, "Caffeine and Memory Performance on the AVLT," *Journal of Clinical Psychology*, vol. 42, Nov. 1986, pp. 860-863.) High caffeine use seems to bring about a state in which, upon getting another "fix" of caffeine, the user experiences a significant *reduction* in the flow of blood to the frontal lobe of the brain. (Roy J. Mathew and William H. Wilson, "Caffeine Consumption, Withdrawal and Cerebral Blood Flow," *Headache*, vol. 25, Sept. 1985, pg. 305.) Before studying with coffee, consider the risk that caffeine, alone or possibly with other drugs (e.g., nicotine, alcohol), induces a state to which you must return before your memory will function properly with respect to the things you learned while in that state. (Geoff Lowe, "State-Dependent Retrieval Effects with Social Drugs," *British Journal of Addiction*, vol. 83, Jan. 1988, pp. 99-103.) Students who consume significantly more coffee than other students also feel noticeably more time pressure and get significantly less sleep. (Robert A. Hicks *et al.*, "Type A-B Behavior and Caffeine Use in College Students," *Psychological Reports*, vol. 52, Feb. 1983, pg. 338.) Caffeine has been shown to increase hostility, tenseness, nervousness, irritability, and anxiety — I *assume* you're still listening to me. (David M. Veleber and Donald I. Templer, "Effects of Caffeine on Anxiety and Depression," *Journal of Abnormal Psychology*, vol. 93, Feb. 1984, pp. 120-22.) Regular caffeine use does *not* necessarily lead to tolerance for caffeine-stress interactions. (James D. Lane and Redford B. Williams, "Cardiovascular Effects of Caffeine and Stress in Regular Coffee Drinkers," *Psychophysiology*, vol. 24, Mar. 1987, pg. 162.) Heavy caffeine users, when compared against, on one hand, ordinary university students, and, on the other hand, psychiatric patients, perform more like — guess who? — on standard tests of psychological health. (Jack E. James and John Crosbie, "Somatic and Psychological Health Implications of Heavy Caffeine Use," *British Journal of Addiction*, vol. 82, May 1987, pg. 508.) Note the phenomenon of schizophrenic patients who actually *eat* coffee. (E.g., John I. Benson and Joseph J. David, "Coffee Eating in Chronic Schizophrenic Patients," *American Journal of Psychiatry*, vol. 143, July 1986, pp. 940-41.) And do you know what else? Finland led the world in per capita coffee consumption, as of 1986, at 1.28 ounces per person per day in 1980, but the most expensive was Jamaican Blue Mountain, which costs $35 an ounce in Teaneck, where I'm sure Lipton's is cheaper. (Stout Guinness, *Guinness Book of World Records* (Toronto: Bantam Books, 1986), pg. 397.) Coffee can be used as a stimulant in shock cases if the victim is conscious and bleeding internally, although I'm not sure how you'd be able to tell that they were bleeding in there. (*The New York Public Library Desk Reference* (New York: Webster's New World, 1989), pg. 615.)

double over with stomach pains. To get to sleep at night during those months, I developed the habit of taking two sleeping pills every 10 minutes until I conked out. Sometimes it went on for hours. It was essential, though, because no matter what time I fell asleep, yesterday's caffeine would always hit me like a shock, first thing in the morning. Sometimes I'd find myself standing in the middle of the bedroom floor before I even realized that the alarm had gone off. I'm not kidding.

It's easy for me to say, now, that the coffee was not necessary. Then again, I don't have to sit still anymore, for weeks on end, and study that boring stuff. At the time, I was prepared to do whatever it took to keep myself in line. With the coffee, I felt grim. I kept my nose to the grindstone.

I do not think I will amaze you if I say that the coffee, and the pressure of studying, combined to make things a little, shall we say, *difficult* between my wife and me. This was a second big side effect of studying so hard for the exam. We had been married for six months by now, and it's definitely safe to say that, once the exam was over, so was the honeymoon.

I usually refused to talk to her when I was studying. When she disturbed me, I would snap at her, and as the weeks wore on, I sometimes found myself screaming at her. A quiet, frightened tone crept into her voice, and we found a distance between us that did not easily go away.

Problems with relationships during law school and the bar exam are hardly news.[239] Even those rah-rah Fordham law professors who say law school can be warm and caring have to admit that

> *The law school experience is awfully tough on relationships .... [M]ajor decisions concerning a relationship should not be made while in law school and certainly not prior to receipt of grades at the end of the first year.*[240]

The full effects upon our relationship did not come out

---

239. Clark & Rieker, fn. 95, pg. 32.
240. Calamari & Perillo, fn. 106, pg. 10.

until later. But the nightmares were there now. I dreamt that my wife wanted away from me, but that the law forbade a living wife to leave her husband — so she cut her own head off to escape. I dreamt that someone was moaning, and then realized that I was the moaner, and that I had gone insane. I found myself in a factory in which people were putting themselves into machines that transformed their bodies into piles of chipped flesh, laughing at me as they did it.

I did pass the bar the second time around. And that put me within reach of the goal: to become an attorney.

C. The Other Requirements for Admission

In New York and most other states, the bar exam is not the only requirement you must fulfill in order to be admitted to practice. Many states also require you to pass the Multistate Professional Responsibility Examination (the MPRE or the Ethics Exam for short). Compared to the Multistate, the Ethics Exam doesn't take so long to grade, it's much easier to pass, and all of the jurisdictions that require it will let you transfer your scores from another jurisdiction.

You may also have to obtain other elements of legal education before you're permitted to practice.[241] When I applied for admission to the bar in New Jersey, they gave me a bunch of booklets and required me to prepare some basic forms and papers, using the examples in the books as guides.

In addition to the academic requirements for admission to the bar, you have to pay a fee.[242] You may also have other minor paperwork requirements. But these pale against the amount of time and effort you must devote to that most obvious of all documents, the "Application for Admission to the Bar." With all of its attachments, my application for admission in New York consisted of 18 legal-sized pages.

The application is pretty bad in some states. Armed with

---

241. Beware the risk that these will make it tougher for you to begin in one state and move to another as bar examiners impose more state-specific requirements. See Roy T. Stuckey, "Preparing Lawyers for Law Practice: New Roles for the NCBE and the ABA," *Bar Examiner*, vol. 59, no. 2, May 1990, pp. 14, 44-45. (Note: NCBE is short for "National Conference of Bar Examiners.")

242. Except in the Virgin Islands. The fee ranges from $50 (LA, ND, and PR) to $600 (AK). (*Comprehensive Guide to Bar Admission Requirements 1989* (Chicago: ABA Section on Legal Education & the NCBE, 1989), pp. 36-38.)

the information you provide, the examiners may contact every high school and college you attended and every employer you've ever had (including the part-time and casual ones), as well as seeking three references for every place you've lived. They may ask about parking fines, child support obligations, bankruptcy, divorce, debts past due, bounced checks, your health, and even a "poor attitude."[243] The ABA actually encourages them to bother asking such broad questions as whether you have *ever* made "false statements, including omissions," been guilty of "misconduct in employment," or engaged in any "acts involving dishonesty."[244] Heaven forbid that you should have gone to see a campus shrink during your worst days in law school, because they'll want to know about it before they admit you to practice law, and they'll take that little visit seriously. They may want to know about buying sprees, reckless driving, foolish business investments, and "sexual behavior unusual for the individual,"[245] which may include not only homosexuality but ordinary heterosexual cohabitation or "living in sin" — and those sins can keep you from practicing law.[246]

I wasn't warned about any of this before I committed myself to a law career. Far from it. The official statements I heard were bland ones like this:

> *The usual requirements for admission [to the practice of law] are possession of good moral character and fitness, i.e., law abiding and free from drug or alcohol dependency ....*[247]

It would be one thing if everyone had to be a saint. But they do a miserable job of reviewing these applications. It's pretty much hit or miss. Only two out of every *thousand*

---

243. R.J. Gerber, "Moral Character: Inquiries Without Character," *Bar Examiner*, May 1988, pp. 16-17.

244. "Code of Recommended Standards for Bar Examiners," sec. III.13, *Review of Legal Education*, fn. 204, pg. 73.

245. Thomas A. Pobjecky, "Everything You Wanted to Know About Bar Admissions and Psychiatric Problems But Were Too Paranoid to Ask," *Bar Examiner*, Feb. 1989, pp. 18, 20.

246. Rhode, fn. 163, pg. 539; Gerber, fn. 243, pg. 18.

247. "Law As a Career," fn. 36, pg. 11.

applicants is denied admission at this stage.[248] The thing is, you don't want to be one of those two losers.

If you catch their attention, they'll be much harder on you than they are on practicing lawyers, even when the practitioner poses a much greater danger to the client than does the new admittee.[249] Thus, you can be kept from practicing law for hypersensitivity, rigidity, unwarranted suspicion, excessive self-importance, a tendency to blame others, or intemperate language.[250] But you don't want to go too far the other way, either. You can get into trouble for excessive immaturity, a lackadaisical attitude, or conveying the feeling that you lack interest in correcting yourself.[251]

As with the bar exam pass rates, there's no consensus among the states on this. For example, while an actual mental illness may not be enough to keep you out of practice in Nevada, mere "religious fanaticism" might X you in Arizona, Illinois, and Wyoming.[252] In one case, a conscientious objector was excluded because he could not swear to uphold the state constitution's requirement that he serve in the state militia in time of war.[253]

You'll find inconsistency even within states. Maryland denied admission to an applicant who had stolen sleeping pills and left the scene of an accident, but admitted a person who had been convicted as the driver of a getaway car in a bank robbery. Michigan once refused to admit a person who had violated a fishing license statute 10 years earlier, but admitted someone who had been convicted of child molesting and someone else who had spent several years in a maximum

---

248. Rhode, fn. 163, pg. 516. But after all this trouble for new applicants, they totally ignore what practicing lawyers do. "Clients' needs simply are no longer localized. Lawyers routinely jet across state boundaries to participate in transactions without the slightest concern for admission restrictions." (Lawrence A. Salibra II, "Counsel Seek Changes in Admissions System," *National Law Journal*, vol. 13, May 20, 1991, pg. S17, col. 1.)

249. Rhode, fn. 163, pp. 546ff.

250. Pobjecky, fn. 245, pg. 15. To take one case, that's true even if your past "irresponsible public accusations" are based on "an honest although *probably* misguided opinion of who was responsible for harassment [that you may have] endured while a law student." (Application of Ronwin, *Pacific Reporter 2nd*, vol. 555, July 6, 1976, pg. 317 (my emphasis). Reprinted at 113 Ariz. 357.)

251. Rhode, fn. 163, pg. 543.

252. Rhode, fn. 163, pg. 540.

253. Gerber, fn. 243, pg. 18.

security prison for conspiring to bomb a public building.[254]

The pretense of making sure that you are morally fit for the practice of law has aided in discrimination against women, minorities, and those who support unpopular causes.[255] Nevada asks you if you're a Communist. Tennessee requires you to list *all* organizations to which you belong, despite the fact that it's illegal for them to do so.[256]

Fortunately, I had no such problems. After filing the application, I waited a month or two, and then it was my turn to show up at the courthouse and have a little chat with someone about my application. He didn't seem to have read it. And I knew to expect that, because that was how it had been for my friends who had already been admitted. At worst, they had been asked to clarify one or two superficial points.

Then we got sworn in, me and the other people who had come to the courthouse that day for our little chats. I couldn't help recalling Arlo Guthrie and "Alice's Restaurant." But, finally, I was in. I was an attorney admitted to practice in the State of New York.

---

254. Gerber, fn. 243, pg. 19. Consider: "In Michigan, it is apparently illegal for an attorney not admitted in the state to give advice on the law of another state — including one in which he or she is admitted — while [the attorney is located] in Michigan, or to give advice on Michigan law while in any other state [apparently even if the attorney is admitted in Michigan]." (Salibra, fn. 248, pg. S20, col. 2.) Or how about this one: To buy a gun in Michigan, you have to take a test — and the answers are printed on back. ("True or False: This Is a Test?" *Time*, June 24, 1991, pg. 25.) To my friends at the U of M, I say: Good luck, and remember — many of your state's finest lawyers (perhaps including some on the bar admissions committee) got their legal training when the fine for possession of marijuana in Ann Arbor was five bucks.
255. Rhode, fn. 163, pg. 493.
256. Gerber, fn. 243, pg. 19.

§ 6. Getting Into a Firm

Any clown can get a job as a lawyer. The goal is to get a *good* job. It's a complicated process, and it starts early.

For me, it began at the end of my first summer. That's when it became important to land a spot with a good firm for the second summer, still nine months away. That next summer's job provides two things: (1) the name of a real, live law firm on your résumé, and (2) with any luck at all, an offer of permanent employment from that firm, to commence after taking the bar exam. Even if you didn't take that offer, having it would reduce your anxieties and increase your options.

A. Interviewing

The games begin in August and September. The first year of law school is over, and so is the crazy pressure. You know you can make it now. Armed with that confidence, you begin the second year knowing that you must get the job first and worry about the schoolwork later. The law school's "job fair" will attract hundreds of law firms, and you'll respond by donning your suit and peddling the flesh daily.

Law professors hate that. They complain about how "intrusive" the interviewing process is, with its absenteeism and distractions.[257] And, officially, the ABA backs them up. Strictly speaking, students who do not attend classes on a

---

257. Ely, fn. 111, pg. 659.

"regular and punctual" basis are in violation of ABA rules, and theoretically cannot receive credit toward graduation.[258]

But that's all ignored. You go for broke, because after a certain time, the opportunities fade away.[259] The best law firms like to fill next summer's openings by mid-autumn.

I saw this, and I responded by interviewing a lot and polishing my act. I learned to dress right, to talk more slowly, and to make my résumé look good. I discovered that interviewing was like taking an exam. You had to be sure to touch upon all the points that the professor wanted to see. Even if you didn't know what you were talking about, merely mentioning the right topics showed that you had your head on straight.

Most interviews consisted of a pretty tedious exchange of pleasantries, followed by an even more banal review of what you had done with your life, what you thought of law school, what your plans were, etc. Then it was your turn, and you got to ask the same old questions, one interview after another, about the firm's policy on something or other, the numbers of attorneys working in each of the firm's divisions, and the most interesting projects now underway in the firm.

In many cases, you could find this information just by looking at a handy book full of data that the law school distributed to each student. I hated asking my boring questions and hearing their dull answers, and I hated, even more, the thought that the answers were in the book and that both the interviewer and I knew it. When I'd ask something *really* obvious, I was sure that the interviewer considered me too lazy or stupid to open the book and find the answer for myself.

The fact was, I simply didn't know what else to say. When I started this job search, I had never even been inside a law firm like the ones I was trying to persuade to hire me now. I wouldn't have felt stiffer if the Wicked Witch of the West had transformed me into the Tin Man.

Once or twice, I tried a more direct approach, where I

---

258. *ABA Law School Rules*, fn. 117, rule 305(c).
259. "Initially, contact as many firms as possible. You can always decline an interview and it is better to have more than enough firms to see than to lose out by banking on just a few. Try to avoid interviews during school-year vacations and immediately before or after the holidays." (That is, interview during classes.) (William B. Stukas and Don H. Sherwood, *Career Placement After Law School Graduation* (Chicago: ABA Law Student Division, 1986), pg. 13.)

basically said something like, "Look, I don't have any idea what's important at this point. I just want to work in law for the summer, see if I can stand it, and then step back and do some serious thinking when the summer's over. I'm a smart fella, and I'll work as hard as the next guy, so why don't we go get a beer and just blow off the rest of the afternoon?"

Actually, if I'd had the nerve to blurt that out with some degree of confidence, it might have worked. The way I said it, though, it sounded pathetic. You can't ask interviewers for charity. It offends their sense of duty to their firm, and anyway they probably don't believe in it.

It was war in these interviews sometimes. One stuffy old guy informed me that the interview was at an end, after I implied that a few of my hardest-working classmates (like he'd probably been during law school) were also flaming jerks. In another, I'd been warned that the interviewer liked to make fun of people, so I let him get as far as chuckling at my résumé before I said to him, "Sir, your reputation precedes you. There's somewhere else I'd rather be," plucked my résumé from his hands, and walked out.

The follow-up interviews at the firms were sometimes even stranger. Half the time, I didn't know what the hell to do with myself. I'm quite a bit taller than a lot of the attorneys who interviewed me, and I felt kinda gawky when I tried to follow them around the firm at their slow pace rather than my customary gallop. Similarly, if I was too considerate and pleasant, I was afraid they'd think I was a bootlicker, but if I was too lively and aggressive, I risked being seen as a loose cannon. I couldn't bring up any subjects that interested me, because everything that interested me had nothing to do with what interested them. It was all just the damnedest thing.

Some follow-up visits had me going out to lunch with the whole gang and having a great time, while in other lunches I sat across the table from some stuffed shirt who was practicing to be God. Some firms put me in a pressure situation in which three partners would be grilling me at once, whereas other firms would let me cool my heels in the lobby for half an hour at a time while they forgot I was there. Ultimately, the ones that forgot who I was seemed to be the most willing to give me job offers, as though they had confused my résumé with that of another person whom they couldn't remember either.

After enough of this, I got pretty smooth at it, and landed some opportunities. But I had no depth, no way of deciding what to do. Never having worked in a law firm before, I did not know what was important to my future.

Except for the poverty-law softhearts, my classmates all seemed to want to go to the big, famous firms. Their logic was clear. Most people do not stay at their first law jobs for their entire careers. By starting at the best-known firms, they would have an excellent credential with which they could land top-flight positions in their next jobs.

I saw drawbacks in the big firms, however. They tend to have bad partnership odds.[260] Despite the claims of excellent training, I suspected that, the smaller the firm, right down to solo practice, the more you're on the line and the more quickly you learn.[261] I felt that big firms could push you into a degree of hasty, narrow specialization that smaller firms could never manage,[262] and that they could afford to let you become miserable,[263] whereas a smaller firm would have more of a need for you to turn out OK. Big-firm life seemed lonely, and big-firm lawyers seemed short on firm loyalty.[264]

I guess I also had the I-don't-believe-in-divorce attitude. I wanted to choose well and stay at my first job a long time. Thus, I wanted it to be friendlier than the big firms had seemed to me. Also, I hoped to have a life outside the job, which meant that I wanted to avoid the extreme working hours you find at many big firms.

So I decided to take my summer job at a small firm on Wall Street. It paid nearly as much as the biggest firms, and it seemed to offer the things I wanted. I accepted their offer in the autumn of my second year of law school, and turned back to my studies for the balance of the year.

---

260. D. Weston Darby, "Are You Keeping Up Financially?" *ABA Journal*, vol. 71, Dec. 1985, pg. 68.

261. See Jay G. Foonberg, *How to Start and Build a Law Practice* (Chicago: ABA Law Student Division, Section of Economics of Law Practice, Standing Committee on Professional Utilization and Career Development, 1984), pp. 6-7.

262. See P.J. Mode in "Associate Leveraging is Doomed," *American Lawyer*, Nov. 1985, pg. 10; "Business and the Law: $80,000 to Start Has Drawback," *New York Times*, Mar. 23, 1987, pg. D-2.

263. See James Rowan et al., "Shifting the Focus of Associate Training," *American Lawyer Career Guide*, fall 1989, pg. 47.

264. See Cohen, fn. 25, pg. 26; Rehnquist, fn. 154, pg. 44.

B. The Summer Experience

All my calculations about small firms versus big firms went out the window when I showed up at the firm to begin work in May. On my first day on the job, I was greeted with the words, "Congratulations! The Wall Street firm of Beekman & Bogue has just merged with the big Boston firm of Gaston Snow, and you, sir, are the very first new employee of the new megafirm Gaston Snow, Beekman & Bogue!"

That merger would eventually matter to me. During my first week on the job that summer, however, nothing could have been less important. I was far too concerned with sheer survival to worry about a gang of attorneys up in Beantown.

At the start, I was my own worst enemy. I was so psyched out that I could barely function. Here I was, making more money in a day than I had ever made in a week before. This was the first job I'd ever had where they made me wear a suit. There were all these lawyers and secretaries who seemed to expect me to know what I was doing. I was on Wall Street, and I was scared out of my gourd.

I started work on a Monday. The day before, a friend had said, "Aw, don't worry. They're going to show you your office, give you some pencils and paper, and take you out to a big lunch. You'll probably leave by 4 p.m."

She was wrong. At 9 a.m., they gave me a little brief to rewrite. A few people paused in my doorway during the morning, introduced themselves, and then moved on. Nobody stopped by at lunch, so I worked straight on through. Almost nobody stopped by in the afternoon, either.

I hadn't seen too many briefs before, and none in real life. I wasn't really sure how a brief of this type was supposed to look, but I was so eager to make a good impression that I didn't even consider admitting my ignorance and seeking advice. Instead, I kept going to the library and getting books that looked like they might be helpful, and then going to the lunchroom for more coffee. By 9 p.m., I was a basket case. Eventually, the partner who had given me the assignment came in, looked at what I had done, explained what he had wanted, took my version with him, and left. I was free to go home.

On the second day, a partner stopped by my office and invited me to lunch. "Finally," I thought. When firms had taken me out to nice lunches during the interviewing process, it had helped me feel more at home. I needed that kind of reassurance now. I looked forward to a good meal and a pleasant chat about myself and the firm.

As we walked out the door, I wondered where he would take me for lunch. They were laughing at me in Hell when he stopped at a Sabrett's hot dog pushcart down Wall Street, across from the Jesus Corner, where the preachers stood and lectured the brokers and bankers as they passed by. He ordered one, to go, with mustard and sauerkraut. Stunned, I did the same.

We brown-bagged it in Battery Park. It was a lovely day.

I'm no snob. I eat Sabrett's all the time. My ego just needed a bit of attention. And this partner was about to see that I got it. As we sat on the park bench, he started talking about how, most years, he was a member of the firm's hiring committee. "I wasn't on it this year, though," he said, staring directly into my eyes. "If I had been, some things would have been different."

Then we started to talk about me. He seemed amazed that I was from Columbia. "Did you really have the kind of LSAT score it takes to get in there?" he asked, with great doubt in his voice. He, himself, had gone to NYU.

By the time Wednesday arrived, I had begun to lose it. I was sure I belonged someplace else. Fortunately, during the previous summer, I had been taking classes in the business school, and had met a fellow who later walked out of a great investment banking job on his third day, complaining that nobody would talk to him. He was a really decent guy, and I now understood how he must have felt. But I remembered how everyone else had considered him a nut for that, and I was determined not to repeat his mistake.

It did get better. Friday came, and then the weekend. On Monday, the other "summer associate," as they called us, showed up. Her name was Ruth. We would be sharing an office for the summer. I teased her about being a princess, but I was glad she was there. She told me to shed my brand-new Yves St. Laurent polyester-blend suits, fresh from Barney's, in favor of seersuckers, khakis, and wool. We talked about law school and the people in this firm. I grew to like her a lot.

Which was too bad, because she grew to hate me. Oh, we

got along famously, right up through the end of the summer. But then they gave me a job offer and rejected her. She had left some work undone, and maybe had spent too much time on the phone with her friends. Probably just as important, I had arrived in our office first, and therefore had chosen the desk that was harder to see from the hallway. This meant that she was on permanent display for anyone passing by, whereas it was much harder to tell when I was goofing off.

Each big law firm works hard to persuade summer associates that life at the firm is quite pleasant. They take them out to four-star restaurants, to the ballet and the theater, and to Mets and Yankees games.[265] Some even go so far as to rent motel rooms off in the countryside somewhere and take everyone away for a weekend, as in, "Oh, Yum, I get to spend a whole weekend of my summer vacation with these people from the office." Instead of that, my firm was kind enough to fly Ruth and me to Boston for the megafirm's annual picnic.

The picnic was fun. They had a foot race, in which I ran, along with hot dogs and burgers and beer. Ruth and I had agreed to fly back to New York that evening, declining the firm's offer to arrange overnight lodging in Boston for us. So I found her, late in the afternoon, and asked when she thought we should head for the airport.

She was standing next to an associate from the Boston office. He looked pretty nerdy to me, but she seemed quite interested in him. She and I spoke for a couple minutes, and then she said, "You know, I think I'm going to stay in Boston tonight after all."

I assure you I'm no Gomer Pyle. But I looked at her, and then at him, and back at her, and my mouth dropped wide open. Fishing off the company pier? Dipping one's pen in the company inkwell? Surely Ruth did not intend to become a topic of gossip throughout the firm for the sake of a fling with this ... this *drip*. She took one look at me and said, in a tone of disgust, "Oh, hell, I guess I should go back to New York tonight." Later, she pulled me aside and said, "Hey — what

---

265. Compare the hiring tactics of Chinatown gangs: "The gang members drive up in fancy cars and scout out the boys who have potential .... They take him out for expensive dinners." (Donatella Lorch, "'Hong Kong Boy': A College Student, and a Ghost Shadow," *New York Times*, Jan. 6, 1991, pg. 13, col. 4.)

did you think I was going to do? Are you crazy?"[266]

To make things as pleasant as possible, the firm made sure that we didn't experience the boredom and pressure that afflict real-life attorneys. And they steered us away from the true bastards in the office, so that those people wouldn't color our impressions of the firm. In one lawyer's words,

> *A summer clerk would do well to ask himself why that senior partner ... says hello to him but not to the full-time associates. Does the partner remember the associates' names? ... [A]s a summer clerk you will rarely if ever be told of your shortcomings. Unless you screw up something serious — such as misspelling a partner's name in a memorandum — you will be told only that you did a fine job, made a lot of friends, and everyone is eager to have you back.*[267]

The law firms want to persuade young new attorneys to join the firm, and they succeed. After law students complete their summer clerkships, they typically affirm, overwhelmingly, that "The work that I received was interesting and challenging" and that "The work assignments I undertook and the results of my work product were adequately discussed with me."[268]

C. Clinching It

Autumn eventually rolled around, and then it was my turn to decide whether I'd had a decent summer experience.

I mean, I had. There was no question about it. I had made money, learned a lot, and liked the people with whom I had worked. I felt particularly close to one associate who had agonized over finding a hair style that would look "corporate" in the office by day but "punk" at CBGB's by night. She was

---

266. Perhaps I needn't have worried about her. A friend later told me that, during *his* firm's summer picnic, he'd gone off into the bushes with one of the female paralegals. Maybe this is part of the new associate's training. Maybe it would have helped me.

267. D. Robert White, *The Official Lawyer's Handbook* (New York: Simon & Schuster, 1983), pp. 59-60.

268. See, e.g., National Association for Law Placement (NALP), "Law Students' Opinion Survey, 1982," pg. 14, in which the affirmative answers accounted for 70-80% of all answers.

able to pick me out among the thousands of people at the New York City Halloween parade that year, despite the fact that I'd dyed my hair and painted my face. She was friendly, smart, and sensitive, and had been a real comrade-in-arms.

Others at the firm had been more restrained, but almost all had seemed genuinely decent. By contrast, I saw that some of my friends back at law school doubted that they would even be able to stand working with the attorneys they had met at their summer jobs.

So now that the annual autumn interviewing rites had begun once again at Columbia Law School, I really didn't see the point of trying to find another law job to replace the one I'd already been offered. Rather, what I needed to decide was whether I wanted to practice law at all.

If my classmates had raised that question, it would have implied that they were ready to scrap their careers. But with my half-completed MBA, I had the option of skipping the bar exam and spending the next summer, instead, in an MBA-style internship in the business world.

I suppose the outcome was never really in doubt. MBA employers wouldn't be interviewing my graduating class for another six months or more, and anyway, the economy was in a recession.

Just as important, I had spent several years, now, thinking of myself as a lawyer. Most of my friends were lawyers, and at that time most of my classes were in the law school. Losing the bird in the hand seemed foolish. Besides, I had acquired some expensive tastes and had learned to look down my nose at the less academically challenging, lower-paying (in most cases, anyway) jobs that my MBA friends were taking.

In the end, I caved in rather quietly. I called up the law firm and told one of the attorneys on the hiring committee that I was going to take their offer. "Oh, great!" he said. "We were really high on you." I hesitated when he said that, because the notion of these guys getting high on anything was pretty hard to take. Then I remembered that he had been in law school when his contemporaries were smoking hash and protesting the Vietnam war, and I realized that he had to be totally unaware of how funny his phrasing might sound. "Uh, good, er, great — well, then I'll be starting in January," I stuttered, "a little more than a year from now ..."

§ 7. Upward Mobility

You may recall that I criticized the practice of law because, among other things, it did not live up to its promise of giving me lots of money and excitement. But in my first months as a practicing attorney, after wrapping up law school and the bar exam, it looked for a while as though I would have all those things and more. These were the halcyon days of my legal career, and I now offer them a bit of praise.

When I started law school, people were talking about making $30,000 a year.[269] At graduation, three years later, it was $40,000. When I actually started work, it had risen even more. The "going rate" for new attorneys at the best firms seems to have stopped climbing, for the moment, but only after having reached the neighborhood of $90,000.

The money that you get from practicing law can propel you from the poverty you experienced during school into a new life aimed toward long-term financial stability. My wife and I quickly acquired a taste for trips to Europe, jewelry, furniture, a computer, a new car, nice restaurants, and better clothes. We appreciated the freedom to spend $50 to $75 on dinner without really thinking much about it.

On the relative extremes, at least, money buys happiness. In one survey, family financial decision-makers who were

---

269. See, e.g., Cohen, fn. 25, pg. 44: "The average salary for lawyers in this country is over $30,000 per year. Starting salaries in large law firms in New York City are now well over $20,000 per year."

asked, "Overall, how happy are you?" were 50 percent more likely to call themselves "happy" if their household incomes exceeded $50,000 than if they were below $15,000.[270] Certainly I was aware, along about this time, that, in a New York City winter storm, I'd rather be wearing my Brooks Brothers tweed overcoat than sleeping, homeless, on a piece of cardboard over a sidewalk grate.

Money makes time. With money, you can — indeed, with our work hours, you sometimes had to — hire a maid. You can pay laundry services and restaurants to handle chores on which you'd otherwise have to spend your own time.

Money makes confidence. You can go out drinking and be obnoxious, secure in the thought that you are the cream of the crop and that the only people who have what it takes to appreciate you are those fortunate few who can operate at your high level of intelligence and energy. When you and your drinking buddies slow down at the end of the evening, you can talk seriously about buying a piece of real estate or about how you might "get something going on the side" by way of a small business of your own.

As the *artiste* says, money makes taste. You can buy excellent wines and sit in the first row on Broadway. When you fool with expensive things for long enough, you eventually realize why they're expensive. They really are better than the cheap versions.

After a while, money makes necessities. You can't put up, anymore, with sending your kids to a public school, driving a cheap little car, wearing a watch or suits that are less impressive than those worn by your peers at the firm, and living in a neighborhood that makes your upper-class acquaintances cringe when they come to visit. If you get to this stage of refinement, you realize that you must do better.

Which is just what you do. Maybe you switch out of law into finance, and if things go well for you, you make dollars by the bushel. Or you might try to get into management. At the extreme, Steven J. Ross, head of Time-Warner, will wind up, by the year 2001, with as much as $1.1 *billion* in compen-

---

270. Mark Goodman, "Americans and Their Money: 1986," *Money*, vol. 15, Nov. 1986, pg. 162.

sation for his trouble.[271]

Even if you stay in law, you can do extremely well in the right firm or specialty. Many partners make over a million every year.[272] Other lawyers volunteer, or are forced, to accept payment from start-up clients in the form of stock, and are quite pleased to watch as some of that stock skyrockets.

At a good firm, even a new associate's perks can be nice. You may get a bonus for signing up, a year-end bonus, and a mid-year profitability bonus, plus an incentive bonus if you bring in a client. They might pay for parking, personal phone calls and photocopying, moving expenses, your bar review course, and your state bar application fee. Your secretary may type, copy, and send your outgoing personal and professional mail for you, as well as handle your American Express bill and other incoming personal mail if you'd rather not have it sent to your home. You can get lots of free lunches. Their retirement plan can add thousands to your net worth. They may buy you a computer, a speakerphone, a dictating machine, and other electronic toys. They may pay for your maternity or paternity leave. You'll have excellent medical, dental, life, and malpractice coverage. Over a period of years, all of these benefits can be worth many thousands of dollars to you.

There are other dollars that don't go into your pocket, but nevertheless improve your life and inflate your ego. Within two years after law school, classmates had already flown to Tokyo, Hong Kong, the Mideast, Paris, and London; some were long-term assignments. The clients paid for the flights, of course, and sometimes saved money by putting my classmates on the high-speed Concorde instead of having to pay their hourly rate for regular flights. Whether you're in the U.S. or abroad, the client pays for your meals while you're working, as well as for your limo ride home when you work late on his/her case, regardless of what it costs to get you to your residence way out in the suburbs. If you have to work overnight and have the nerve and the need to get out of the office for a couple of hours, you can bill the client for a hotel room nearby instead of making that expensive commute, and

---

271. Graef S. Crystal, "At the Top: An Explosion of Pay Packages," *New York Times Magazine*, Dec. 3, 1989, pg. 25.
272. See "What Lawyers Earn," *National Law Journal*, Oct. 1989, pg. 35.

can add breakfast and a fresh new shirt to the tab.

It can go overboard. I've known attorneys who've billed the client for flights to vacation spots or to their daughters' graduations. I've been at "working lunches" with a half-dozen other attorneys for which the client was billed more than $1,500 even though nothing of substance was accomplished. It says something about you when the client is willing to pay up to $7 per minute for your time, if you can spare it.

My classmates and I did not seriously doubt that we were smarter than almost anyone else anywhere. Sure, some of the people in graduate schools may have been brilliant in their subject areas, but it seemed to us that they couldn't see beyond their tiny little area of interest to realize how much they were missing for lack of money.

If you had any doubts about your importance, you'd lose them quickly after looking at what the firm does to make you as productive as possible. Paralegals, mailroom people, and a host of others wait at your beck and call. You can make a secretary spend 45 minutes trying to get a limo for you. You can keep a messenger waiting for an hour while you put together a document that needs to be rushed to another office.

Once you understand how important you are — and I don't necessarily mean to sound sarcastic, because some of the things you work on make a difference of millions of dollars, and can matter to hundreds, if not thousands, of people — you develop the habit of spending money whenever it seems necessary to make things happen. You order photocopies of everything for everyone, because it's faster and safer than trying to guess which copies will actually be read by whom. You don't hesitate to use Federal Express, at 10 or 20 bucks a pop, rather than ordinary mail, because you want to be sure it gets there — and *immediately.*[273]

Your sense of self-importance carries over into other activities. The law firm demands top-flight performance of you. So when you get involved in your local town's politics, for example, you're appalled at the sloppy thought and

---

273. In one disorganized firm, some lawyers even used Federal Express to move memos from one floor to another, rather than rely on the firm's internal messengers. At night, the documents would fly from New York all the way to the Federal Express center in Memphis, and in the morning they'd be delivered back in New York to a different floor in the same building.

low-quality work you find in the people who run the place. It's not hard to point out specific ways in which you could do a better job, and that helps you get elected or chosen for a position of power, if you want.

If you happen to test the waters in the job market, you'll be gratified to see how many people are interested in you.[274] Normally, they can't match the salary you'd get at your top-notch firm, especially if you're looking at opportunities outside of law and finance. But that only adds to the smug feeling of being in such high demand.

There's more to the good side of law than money. Law also tends to give its practitioners an unmatchable social ego boost. Suddenly, a place like New York City is your oyster.

When my wife and I split up, it was child's play to find women who would go out with me. Male or female, your Wall Street job proves that you're smart, motivated, and sensible. You're likely to be able to handle the duties and financial needs of a comfortable life and a family. As an added plus, working with words makes you witty, so that, all other things being equal, you'll be better rainy-day company than if you were a troll.

Beyond the money you make and the ego boosts, law can be exciting, even if the excitement is only temporary. There is, for example, a ritual known as "going to the printer."

It works like this. There are very tight rules on what the lawyers must put into certain kinds of documents, such as the papers that are required before a company can sell stock. These documents get prepared at specialized printing companies that charge huge amounts of money and produce work of extremely high quality.

To prepare the necessary documents, you wait until the stock market closes on the appointed day. At that point, you have the day's closing price for the stock. You then meet in a conference room at the printing company with a dozen other

---

274. "The business of major corporate law firms and, hence, their demand for associates, appears to be growing so fast that the traditional source of new associates — elite national law schools — no longer provide an adequate supply." (Gilson & Mnookin, fn. 161, pg. 589.) The drying-up of the big-money corporate takeovers of the 1980s has hurt some of the big firms (Ellen J. Pollock, "Slowdown Hits Legal Profession After 80's Boom," *Wall Street Journal*, Nov. 1, 1990, pg. B-1, col. 3), but I doubt that the underlying structure of the profession, and especially the demand for the "best" graduates, has changed significantly.

attorneys, accountants, and investment bankers, and you stay there, all night if necessary, until you've all agreed on every last detail in those documents and have reviewed a few samples of the final print. The printing people must get their educations at the feet of the saints, because you can sit there and be an absolute pig and insist that they bring you a filet mignon, an obscure kind of bottled water, an indelible green pen — anything you want — and they'll do it, even if it's 3 a.m. and they're dog tired.

Now, nobody else at the printer's thinks this is exciting. And neither will you, after the first time. But on that first evening, you feel that you're at the very heart of the world's highest finance, and everything about it is *so* impressive. At dawn, you fly to Washington, D.C., where you file copies of the printed documents with the SEC as soon as they open their doors. Once those papers are filed, it's legal to sell the stock that those documents describe. You get to a phone and call New York to tell them it's done, and you know that, moments later, $100 million worth of securities will cascade onto the selling floors of Wall Street.

I found my job exciting in other ways. I'd work on things one day and see them in the newspaper the next. The *Wall Street Journal*, far from describing distant transactions that meant nothing to me, was something that I read every day to see what was going on in my neighborhood. There were big deals afoot, and I was a part of some of them.

It was exciting just to be there: to work across the street from the New York Stock Exchange; to be at the office at 2 a.m. and know that, nearby, gold traders were doing war with midday competitors in Hong Kong; to watch the tickertape parades from high above Broadway at Trinity Church, where the confetti rains down by the ton when they celebrate a major national event; to walk out and stare at Federal Hall, where George Washington was sworn in as the first President; to stroll into the grand lobbies of Morgan and the other major banks; and simply to stand still and feel the financial power of the entire world throbbing through the pavement.

I think you get the picture. If you've got enough patience and money for law school, and your goal is to live a life that has as many different kinds of experiences as possible, you should try to include this one.

§ 8. Climbing

As I settled into the role of attorney, I found myself briefly lacking tangible goals. I'd gotten so used to having exams, interviews, and all those other school-related immediate pressures on me that it required some readjustment to deal with a lifestyle in which nothing more was expected of me than that I function as a lawyer and do my job well.

That was, however, a temporary phase. As it dawned on me that eight years could pass fairly quickly in this law firm environment, I became much more interested in a goal that had previously seemed distant, namely, partnership.

After you've worked in a law firm for a while, the possibility of partnership grows on you. It has its benefits, like making you a boss, giving you more money, allowing you to assign boring tasks to your associates, and notifying all the world that you've made it to the top.

So, within a year or two of being at the firm, you'll arrive at a certain level of consciousness. You'll know who's "in" and who's "out" in the eyes of the partners, and you will know much more about how to behave if you, too, would like to be a partner one day. There are a few things, in particular, that will make a big difference for you.

A. Be Perfect

If you want to "make partner," the first thing you must do is to be perfect. But it's not as easy as it sounds. In a law firm, being perfect does not mean being perfect.

As you probably realize, perfect people have perfect lives, which means you don't find them suffering as junior associates in Wall Street law firms. They're off smoking dope in Tibet, maybe, or floating on a cloud in heaven.

That leaves the rest of us screwups to handle the law in places like New York. It's a dirty job, but someone's got to do it. To make it all a bit more tolerable, we try to refrain from truly huge failures. We still make them sometimes, but they're frowned upon.

We have a funny way of discouraging errors, though. It probably wouldn't take too much brilliance to discover that people who work in a cooperative team effort tend to help one another avoid mistakes, while those who go it alone have no one to keep an eye on them and help them when they need it.

Some societies and some organizations seem to have recognized this. It continues to elude the legal community, however. Instead, on Wall Street, we reward the person who does the best job of *pretending* that s/he does not commit mistakes, and we punish those stubborn individuals who insist on admitting their shortcomings and who sometimes seek assistance when, in their best judgment, they'll need it to produce quality results.

As your guinea pig, I, for example, once made the terrible mistake of taking a half-finished document to a partner, showing him what I had accomplished so far, and asking him if I was on the right track. It was the silliest thing I could have done. Somehow, despite my words, he treated it as finished work. He criticized it harshly, and then took the project away from me and assigned it to someone whom he considered more capable of handling it properly.

Naturally, after a few of those experiences, I learned the time-honored, safe, and utterly inefficient approach of agonizing over projects for hours on end, taking my questions to relatively ignorant junior attorneys rather than to partners, and handing in my work only when I was as certain as I could be that it was perfect.[275]

Maybe I learned too much in business school. But I don't believe in human perfection. I believe in screwups: in learning from, anticipating, and managing them. That is, I believe that you get a more reliable mechanism when, instead of expecting people to do everything right, you give them feedback and set up intelligent systems that keep them from going too far astray.

But that's not how it's done in a Wall Street law firm. There, your rebuke comes only once a year, in your year-end annual review. It's as though the partners hated being punished by Santa Claus, in the dog days of each childhood December, for having been bad boys, and can now, finally, get even with the world by dumping upon their junior associates just when the Christmas spirit has reached its peak.[276]

As a young attorney, you can take steps to avoid screwups. For example, when you find yourself in a new situation, you can try to make yourself look good, and then get out at all costs, before anyone can hold you responsible for anything. You can also learn that worrying always helps, because it makes you think of solutions before trouble strikes, when you still have time for that kind of thinking.

Finally, it pays to understand that the partners in your firm will remember your mistakes much more than they'll appreciate your hard work. The wisest course is to assume that they're looking for an excuse by which they can simplemindedly view you as either a "winner" or a "loser." If that assumption proves to have been paranoid (see below), at least you'll have been prepared for the worst.

B. Be the Right Kind of Crazy

The dean of admissions at Columbia once told me that it might be nice to be well-balanced, except that being balanced seemed to make people mediocre. I don't know whether all deans of admissions would agree, but, if so, that would explain

---

275. See Rowan et al., fn. 263, pg. 48.

276. I still don't understand why they formally appraise your performance only once a year, but that's the way it is, and an awful lot of the associates in those firms are unhappy with that. See Ronald L. Hirsch, "Are You on Target?" *Barrister*, vol. 12, winter 1985, pg. 19.

some of what I saw during my years of practicing law.[277]

There's such a thing as being crazy like a fox. Consider, if you will, these guidelines for attorneys who wish to be successful negotiators:

> *Use two negotiators who play different roles [i.e., good cop, bad cop]. Be tough — especially against a patsy. Appear irrational when it seems helpful. Raise some of your demands as the negotiations progress. Claim that you do not have authority to compromise. After agreement has been reached, have your client reject it and raise his demands.*[278]

And there's also such a thing as a sensible level of paranoia. After all those years in law school, you begin to realize how much legal risk there is in the world.[279]

Besides paranoia, you can get a lot of mileage from aggression. According to the common advice given to attorneys, "If the facts are against you, argue the law. If the law is against you, argue the facts. If the facts and the law are against you, pound on the table and yell like hell." With enough energy and nerve, even a losing position can win.

I took these lessons to heart and applied them in everyday life. For instance, in the grocery store parking lot, some anonymous person once swung his/her car door against mine and put a little dent in it. I was already in the habit of carrying a small tape recorder in my pocket to record random thoughts, and after this experience, I made sure to record the license plate numbers of the cars I was parked next to before I went into the store. I was disappointed that no one else dented my car, but, as a second-best, I once arrived late for a flight, when they were already moving the jet away from the loading area, and was pleased to be able to shove the recorder

---

277. I studied on hallowed ground, for these purposes: Columbia now occupies the site of the old Bloomingdale insane asylum. ("The Moral Treatment," *Columbia: The Magazine of Columbia University*, vol. 16, spring 1991, pg. 43.)

278. Alvin B. Rubin, "A Causerie on Lawyers' Ethics in Negotiation," *Louisiana Law Review*, vol. 35, pg. 581, citing M. Meltsner & P. Schrag, *Public Interest Advocacy; Materials for Clinical Legal Education*, 1974, pg. 232 (my emphasis).

279. I always thought it would be interesting to study the question of whether attorneys are less likely to let the neighbors' kids play on their own children's backyard swingsets or to do other things that involve a risk of being sued.

into the faces of the airline people working at that gate, demand their names and statements of why the flight was leaving early, and stand there, yelling and threatening, until at last they informed me that the plane was coming back and I would be permitted to board after all.[280]

I learned to demand more and more from paralegals, secretaries, and word processing people, and to make it clear that they'd be held accountable if they weren't available when I needed them. I tried to be decent about it, but the work had to get done, and friendship came after performance on this job.

Not all attorneys considered it particularly important to be decent. In the worst cases, lawyers had, as one partner put it, a "screw the secretaries" attitude. One associate took it to the extreme, smiling as he told me that he had fired more than 30 secretaries in the past few years. And I can't tell you how many times I've seen secretaries crying.

Perhaps the classic example of human kindness in the practice of law was the partner who dismissed the employees of a newly bankrupt company (for which he was now responsible, as its attorney in bankruptcy) simply by telling them to get the hell out. An hour later, he had so forgotten about them and their lives that he could turn to me and say, "Hey, it's kinda fun here, running the ol' bucket shop."

According to the National Association of Disgruntled Attorneys (NADA),[281] associates are not exempt from similarly harsh treatment. When my classmates and I were interviewing during law school, we often compared notes on whether a particular firm had lots of "screamers," which was our term for partners who frequently yelled at their associates. The general attitude, even among non-screamers, is clearly that you are a hired hand, not a colleague, and that if a bit of abuse gets you down, your best bet is to find another job.

In case you were wondering, you don't take off these attitudes like a jacket when you find yourself outside the office. It is extremely difficult to keep your professional way of

---

280. "O! this woodcock, what an ass it is." William Shakespeare, *The Taming of the Shrew*, i.4.160.
281. I made it up. There should be such an organization, though.

thinking from dominating your entire life.[282] Many lawyers certainly have nobody but lawyers for friends. Too many of us found ourselves conducting cross-examinations in the kitchen at home, because we couldn't understand our own spouses and children until they learned to express themselves like lawyers (or until they walked out the door).

Sometimes, the rage of attorneys in top firms is more comical than threatening. I've seen partners yell so hard that they spit on themselves. When a typewriter ceased to function for one attorney, he responded by throwing it against the wall, pounding on it with his fists, and stomping on it until he had broken it to bits. I worked for a partner who hired some kind of Buddhist therapist, painted his office walls raspberry red, and began playing handball in there, in a desperate effort to relax. At least it was good exercise — after all, a waist is a terrible thing to mind.

At some point, though, you stop being crazy like a fox and start being simply crazy. When attorneys destroy typewriters or play handball on their raspberry-red walls, you know that they are either very senior, so that they don't have to answer to anyone, or very far gone, so that everyone's afraid to ask, or both. In fact, there is evidence that "a significant number of bar applicants and attorneys are afflicted with psychiatric problems."[283]

Along these lines, a couple of lawyers in my firm had speech problems. One of them had a hard time expressing himself, and sometimes even stuttered. The other one's problem was that he could not stop talking. As you might have guessed, they wound up working together in the litigation department. The one would talk for 20 minutes, and then pause for feedback; at that point, the other one would stammer and mumble, trying to think of what to say.

The garrulous one sometimes left three or four consecutive messages on my answering machine at home, because he couldn't deal with the machine's 60-second deadline before it would cut him off. In my first few months at the firm, before

282. Jerold Auerbach, *Unequal Justice: Lawyers and Social Change in Modern America*, pp. 62-67, reprinted in Hazard and Rhode, *The Legal Profession: Responsibility and Regulation* (Mineola, NY: Foundation Press, 1985), pg. 150.
283. Pobjecky, fn. 245, pg. 14, citing a 1979 survey by the National Institute of Mental Health and case law.

my workload got too heavy, he twice cornered me in my office at 6 p.m., blocked me from leaving, and started three-hour monologues about cases in which I had no interest — until, well past the point of caring anymore what he thought, I grabbed my coat and bolted for the exit.

The second time I ran like that, he went with me, right on out to the elevator, talking all the way. When it arrived, he actually climbed in with me, without his coat. Incredulous, I looked at him, my heart sinking, and asked, "You're going down?" "Oh, uh, no," he said, and then stepped out and just held the elevator door and continued to talk while the buzzer went off. I think the doorman, hearing the buzzer and the voices, must have feared some kind of emergency, because eventually another alarm sounded. At that point, my friend finally let the door go and I watched, in relief, as it closed.

I admit that Wall Street attorneys work under enormous pressures. But army generals, for instance, operate with the ultimate pressures on the battlefield, and yet, for the most part, our storybooks don't make them out to be lunatics. I don't know. Maybe it's that generals are dealing in life and death, hearts and minds, while many lawyers just pursue money, and maybe we all tend to take on the best and worst characteristics of the gods we worship.

The bottom line is that, if you wanted to make it to partnership, you had to absorb the proper amount of paranoia and intensity, but you couldn't let it carry you over the edge unless you were so darned good at your work that no one cared.

C. Get Positioned

I don't mean to stress the obvious, but in your climb up the ladder of success, you'll find it essential to position yourself politically. If you're a real turkey, you need a place to hide; otherwise, you should link up with a powerful partner who'll display your good points for all to see.

As a favorite of a leading partner, you'll get more interesting tasks, since this partner is probably important precisely because s/he brings in a variety of clients. It doesn't always work, but, all other things being equal, it's a better risk than working with some partner whose jobs are consistent, predictable, and absolutely guaranteed to make you snore.

Also, by working for the powerful partner, you gain an excuse to look down your nose at people who try to dragoon you into horrible labors. Law firms are full of junior partners and senior associates who have nothing better to do than slither into your office and demand your help on thankless tasks simply to avoid boredom or to remind you who's boss.

Political positioning includes a variety of other topics. Senior associates, for example, are so paranoid about the risk of doing something wrong, and thereby spoiling their chances for partnership, that they turn into androids for the year or two before the partnership decision is made. See no evil, hear no evil, speak no evil.

In some cases, the sense of position and rank can go too far. For example, I started work at the firm in January, rather than in the customary August or September. When a new associate joined the firm the next autumn, his eyes lit up when he heard that I had started late. "Oh," he asked, "you mean I'm only eight months behind you?"

I bow and defer to the many good books on the subject of proper political manipulation of the office environment.[284] Here, I mean only to say that you cannot ignore these things if you want to continue on your rise toward success.

D. Bill a Lot of Hours

If you're perfect, crazy, and positioned, probably the most important other thing to think about is the sheer quantity of work you do. Your firm charges an hourly billing rate for your time, and it's a lot more than they're paying you per hour, which means that they make money off you.

The first thing to know is that the firm can't charge the client if it can't prove you did the work. That proof requires written records. Thus, they tell you that, as they know, there will be times when your brain turns to mush and you waste many hours needlessly. Despite your shame for being so stupid, they say, you must resist your conscience and avoid the

---

284. Starting with Niccolò Machiavelli: "Princes ... have found more faith and more usefulness in those men, whom at the beginning ... they regarded with suspicion, than in those they at first confided in." (*The Prince*, written in 1513 (New York: Modern Library, 1940, 1950), pg. 79.)

temptation to charge the client for fewer hours. "We're only human," the firm suddenly admits, "and if we hadn't made these mistakes, someone else would have. It was all part of trying to do the job, and we charge for that."

In most cases, the firm assumes that you will do a lot of high-quality work each hour, so the real concern is with how many hours you work. Or, more accurately, not how many hours you work, but how many hours you *bill* to the client.

As this concern grows on you, you may change your accounting techniques. At first, for example, you might have kept track of each hour as you went along, charging the client only for those moments in which you felt productive. Once you become more sophisticated, however, you may simply sit back at the end of the day and subtract those few large chunks of goof-off time that you clearly remember taking. Memory being what it is, this change in technique can easily add an hour or more of billable time to each work day.

Naturally, you work at home or on the train as well as in the office, and you can bill for that. You can bill for putting your feet up and thinking about the client's situation. You can even bill for worrying about the client's problem while you're taking a shower, as long as it's high-quality worrying.

Creative billing is an art. You may have heard about the attorney who dies and goes to heaven. At the Pearly Gates, he tells St. Peter that he's only 38 years old, and that he's much too young to die. St. Peter pulls out some documents and says, "That can't be right. Judging from the number of hours you've billed your clients, you must be at least 75!"

Unbeknownst to many, though, there's nothing unrealistic about an attorney being at the office for, say, 10 hours, and yet billing for 15. It probably won't happen every day, but it can happen, for several different reasons. First, consider this advice from the *ABA Journal*:

> *[Let's say that] Client A calls and asks for information that requires one hour of research time. Therefore, Client A is billed for one hour .... The next day, Client B calls and needs the same information .... Client B should be billed for the same amount as Client A. There is value in the information [itself, not merely in the work that was needed to produce it] ....*

Also, a client should be billed at least the minimum (smallest increment) amount of time for short phone calls. This will take into account the "interruption" time of any other matter being worked on.[285]

At one firm where I worked, the policy was to bill in quarter-hour increments. I thus had the experience of seeing some attorneys charge the client a quarter-hour of time for the two-minute exercise of calling the client's office, being told that the client was not in his/her office, and asking the client's secretary to have the client return the call.

There's also "double billing." This happens, for instance, when your client requires you to fly someplace. Since you didn't prefer to be on that flight, you bill the client for it, even though you may not be working during the flight. But if you do decide to work — preferably for someone else, so that you don't have to deal with nasty questions when the client reviews the bill — well, then, you can bill the other client too. Presto! A four-hour flight produces seven or eight hours of billings. It's even better if you're working around the clock and flying to the West Coast, so that your 24-hour day produces, at the very least, 27 hours of billings.[286]

After you're done with billing your *hours* creatively, the firm may add its own touch to the *dollars*. If the client is ecstatic about what the firm has accomplished, the billing partner may take advantage of the client's apparent eagerness to pay by applying "premium billing." In one form, this consists of simply doubling the attorneys' ordinary hourly billing rates. (Since I didn't work in litigation, I don't get to tell you how happy the firm can be with contingency billing, in which they charge a flat 33 percent or 40 percent or more of the "take."[287])

But, as an associate, you don't worry much about the dollars. You just keep putting in the hours. Associates at most major firms are now expected to bill between 2,000 and

---

285. Robert L. Israeloff, "Look at the Time!" *ABA Journal*, vol. 75, Dec. 1989, pg. 88.
286. See, e.g., Goldberg, fn. 34, pg. 60.
287. Especially in those cases where the firm does very little work and arranges a very large settlement.

2,500 hours per year.[288] That's not usually put into writing, and it's possible to get away with less for a while. But neither is it the ceiling. I've known attorneys who have billed well more than 3,000 hours in a single year, and, according to legend, the garrulous one (see above) topped 3,500.

If you assume four weeks of vacation per year, and divide 2,000 hours by 48 weeks, you get an average of about 42 billable hours per week. If it's 2,500 hours, then the figure rises to 52 hours. That's eight to 10 hours a day, five days a week. It doesn't sound too hard.

You have to adjust that figure, however, to account for the spells of reduced work that happen during economic slowdowns and during the summer vacation months. Despite the lack of work on those days, you still have to be in the office, even if you're just sitting around reading law books. When the busy days return, you'll have to bill quite a bit more than eight or 10 hours a day if you're going to catch up with the target of 2,000 to 2,500 hours for the year.

Then, too, some hours won't be billable. It depends on the work at hand and your work habits, but by the time you include breaks (which you must have to avoid going batty) and important nonbillable tasks (e.g., meetings to discuss firm policies, or interviewing potential new attorneys), you may well average several nonbillable hours each day.

And no matter how many hours you're billing, some of them can't come between 9 a.m. and 5 p.m. You have emergency projects, last-minute demands by unreasonable attorneys and clients, trips to the printer, and all sorts of other required nighttime and weekend activities. It's not unusual to see associates work all day, work all night, and then work all the next day; a few even manage to go on for yet another night. When the work comes in, you have to do it.

Personally, I could usually work until somewhere between 2 a.m. and 5 a.m., but then I had to get a couple of hours of sleep or else I just couldn't function the next day. Unlike some firms, mine didn't have cots and showers for this purpose. There was a little storage room with a black vinyl couch in it, but it had no ventilation, and anyway it was full of

---

288. Goldberg, fn. 34, pg. 60.

wobbly stacks of empty cardboard boxes that kept falling on me while I slept. A couple of partners had couches, which I'd be tempted to call loveseats if it weren't for their locations, but they were too small to sleep on. So I would just stretch out, in my suit, on the floor of my office, with my Brooks Brothers coat as a blanket in the winter. One night, however, a security guard walked in with a flashlight and stepped on me in the dark. After that, I took to sleeping underneath a table.

Sometimes, especially after those all-nighters, I'd get partway through the day, and then have a desperate need to take a nap. I consoled myself with the thought that studies show people are more effective after that kind of midday break.[289] But I obviously couldn't sleep in my office, because (a) my office-mate would stare at me, and (b) people would come trooping in and think that I was goofing off, unless I closed the door, in which case they'd first knock, and then come trooping in and think that I was goofing off. So, instead, I'd sneak into that storage room with the sofa, climb onto it, load those blasted loose boxes onto my legs, and take a short snooze. I don't think anyone really knew where I was at those times, but I didn't feel I had any choice when the alternative was to spend the afternoon nodding off at my desk.

Not everyone is happy with the pressures on young attorneys to bill so many hours. Chief Justice William H. Rehnquist, for example, has complained:

> *Does such an associate have time to be anything but an associate lawyer in that large firm? ... It seems to me that a law firm that requires an associate to bill in excess of 2,000 hours per year ... is substantially more concerned with profit maximization than were firms when I practiced.*[290]

But others — including, most importantly, partners in law firms — aren't so sympathetic:

---

289. "Researchers say that the brain does fall into a lull in the afternoon, indicating an evolutionary predisposition toward napping ...." Natalie Angier, "Cheating on Sleep: Modern Life Turns America Into the Land of the Drowsy," *New York Times*, May 15, 1990, pg. B-8, col. 6.
290. Rehnquist, fn. 154, pp. 45-46 (his emphasis).

That's what we hear from students — that life for a young lawyer in a large firm is very stressful. I'm not sure that's accurate. I think a young lawyer has to be prepared to put in time. That's how young lawyers become good lawyers.[291]

In some jobs, young people say, "TGIF," or "Thank God It's Friday." In law, young attorneys say, "So Happy It's Thursday." That's because, when Thursday ends, there are only three more days left in the work week.

To summarize: Being perfect, crazy, positioned, and hard-working can go a long way toward advancing your career in your law firm. If you've got those things in place, all you've really got to worry about is doing your job. And that is a world unto itself.

---

291. Chicago lawyer Sanford Stein, as quoted in "Quotes," *ABA Journal*, vol. 73, Mar. 1987, pg. 31.

§ 9. Coping

I've been describing the big picture that might face you as a young attorney. But when you're quite finished with laying out your master plan from the lofty heights, you'll find everyone else impatiently waiting for you to climb down into the trenches and start struggling like the common, dogface attorney you are. That means that you have to do the work and deal with the people. This enterprise may lack grandness, but it's your job.

A. The Work: Pushing Paper

In this country, you have all kinds of attorneys and law-related tasks. And an awful lot of those tasks are basically paper-pushing.

If you haven't worked with lawyers, it can be difficult to understand how they can spend so much time playing around with paperwork. Our country's attorneys collectively spend well over *a billion* hours a year on this stuff.[292] You have to figure that it must be pretty complicated.

And it is. I found it frustrating to spend so much time on things that seemed so minor. And yet, when I looked at a specific task, I often wanted to spend even longer on it than

---

292. Working 2000 hours a year, a half-million attorneys would produce this figure. We may even be approaching two billion hours in the coming decade.

was customary, to be sure of getting it exactly right.[293]

Once, for example, I had to go to the offices of a company — let's call it NewCo — and undertake a "due diligence" inquiry. In a due diligence inquiry, you look through their books and papers and satisfy yourself that, according to their records, the things they're saying to you and your client about themselves are true.

At NewCo's offices, I looked at books that contained the certificate of incorporation, which showed that NewCo had originally been created as a Delaware corporation under another name. (Let's say their previous name was OldCo.) You'd want to double-check this by speaking with the appropriate governmental office in Delaware, but in the meantime, it was a good start to see this certificate in their books.

After that, the corporate books got more complicated, as I got into NewCo's by-laws and corporate resolutions.[294] I guess I didn't really understand what I was supposed to do. Or maybe I understood it too well.

As far as I could tell, my job was to look through all those resolutions, which filled seven or eight looseleaf binders, and make sure that NewCo's directors and officers had the legal authority to enter into this deal with my client.

For example, let's suppose that Joe Blow, John Doe, and Jill Snow signed a NewCo resolution on April 1, 1991, in which they claimed to be directors and agreed that NewCo should issue new shares of stock. And let's suppose that the people who bought that stock eventually voted, as shareholders, to permit NewCo to enter into this deal with my client.

Sounds OK, right? But what if Joe & John & Jill had not been properly voted into office as NewCo directors before April 1, 1991? In that case, they would not have had the power to issue that additional stock, which could mean those shareholders wouldn't be legitimate, and maybe their vote wouldn't count, and maybe it would be illegal for NewCo to

---

293. I wasn't alone in that. Consider the amazing number of hours that nine people at Cravath once devoted to a 20-page memo. ("A 312-Hour Memo," *Legal Reformer*, vol. 10, July-Sept. 1990, pg. 28.)

294. "Corporate resolutions" are formal, signed statements by the incorporator, the board of directors, or the shareholders. Resolutions may do harmless things, like stating that annual meetings will be held in February. But they can do more significant things, like giving the company's officers the power to sell a major portion of the company's business.

be entering into this deal with my client. These are things my client would want to know as soon as possible.

There were many other things like that to look for. It took me a long time to look through all those corporate books and consider all the various angles. I spent three days at it. I knew that other attorneys would finish a project like this in one day. They'd come in, open the corporate books, wave a magic wand over them, close them, and leave. But I sat there and agonized over every little thing, and the NewCo secretaries and managers snickered a bit louder every time I'd walk in or out. I felt like a dunce. Yet when I'd go back to my firm and ask people what I was doing wrong, they didn't seem to have any helpful suggestions.

Fortunately, I redeemed myself. I discovered that there was no document in the books authorizing NewCo to adopt the name "NewCo" instead of its previous name of "OldCo." As far as I could tell, the dotted line on my client's contract would have to be signed, not by NewCo, but by OldCo.

This shook them up, because they'd been doing business as NewCo for years. The Big Boys got really upset, and the secretarial smirks vanished. A sheepish clerk eventually walked back to my work area and handed me a corporate resolution that said what I wanted to see.

I mean, if you're changing your company's name from, say, "U.S. Steel" to "USX," you don't want to hire 1,000 sign painters, print a million brochures, spend a fortune on an ad campaign for the "new" USX, and then discover that the legal name "USX" is owned by a little guy who's been running a button-making company by that name, over in Dover, since 1939. While the signpainters' ladders are going up and the advertising agencies are buying full-page ads in the *Wall Street Journal*, the big-time attorneys are going to be on their knees in that little guy's living room, begging him to please sell them that corporate name.[295]

Anyway, that's one example of how you can spend an awful lot of time digging through mountains of paper. It never ceased to amaze me, how work expands to fool the time

---

295. This is only an example. USX and U.S. Steel were not involved in the deal I was working on.

allotted.

This three-day due diligence project was pretty minor compared to some of the paper-shuffling projects I found myself in. I began to develop a specialty in setting up stockbroker companies to buy and sell stock on the various exchanges. It involved researching and preparing hundreds of pages of forms with each exchange, each state's government, and the SEC.

I complained about the complexity of this work. I looked at it sometimes and said to myself, "For this I spent all those years in law school?" And I'd go home and stare at the copies of Dostoyevsky, Pynchon, and Camus on my shelves, and realize that I wasn't doing a lot with my education.

At the same time, though, I was becoming somewhat skilled in dealing with all those bureaucrats. If you'll pardon the German, my niche was becoming mein itch, in the sense that I liked the feeling of being a specialist in this broker-dealer stuff. Even though it may not have been enough to keep me from craving a siesta in midafternoon, at least it was a specialty, and I drew some pleasure from many months of just plugging along, doing my job, and drawing my paycheck.

B. The People

For me, the people with whom I worked were the most important and interesting aspect of practicing law. As I settled into the grind, I grew to believe that I would be stuck forever in the structure of the law firm, dealing with a few very distinct groups of players.

1. Clients

I had a variety of clients. But, as a rule, these were not the kinds of people you'd see coming in the door at the local Denny's restaurant for Sunday brunch. The clients we worked for were hard-nosed people who knew exactly what they wanted from us. I didn't get to experience much of the pleasure of serving, as a general practitioner might, in the role of watchdog for my client's welfare. Once our specific job was done, the client was gone.

So I worked for a tyrannical Napoleon, a little guy who was as mean as they come; for a Harvard Business School graduate who always apologized for bothering me when he'd call me at work or at home, any time of day or night, a half-dozen times a day, "just to check up on how things were coming along"; and for any number of others who, although less nasty or weird, were nevertheless all business when they dealt with me. At the rates my firm charged, I guess it was only to be expected.

I learned one thing very quickly: I was there to serve the client. This meant working all weekend, if that's what it took. I'd arrange to have documents delivered to clients at their homes, and to be in the office on Sundays and holidays — along with secretaries, word processing people, and messengers — to modify my copies of the documents as soon as the clients had had a chance to look at them and phone in their comments. If the client didn't call, and decided instead to spend the day drinking margaritas, that was my problem.

It may sound odd of me to say that, despite all this, the clients really weren't so important in my work. It's true, though. They'd come in or call every now and then, and I'd answer their questions. At some times, they absolutely dominated my schedule. But on average, the people in the office were the more important actors in my day-to-day job. It's different for partners, who must deal directly with their clients, but I was just a lowly junior associate.

2. Fellow Attorneys

The longer I hung around the law firm, the more I saw differences in the styles and abilities of the partners for whom I worked. Some could make the client relax, confident that everything was under control. Others specialized in providing quick and dirty service for the client who wanted the most bang for the buck. And still others, going in the opposite direction, were unsurpassed at providing utter thoroughness, for those clients who were facing the ultimate dangers and wanted no stone left unturned.

As I saw these things, and tried to apply what I was seeing to my own work, I felt that I really did want to become good at practicing law. It did not help, though, to realize that none of these attorneys provided a meaningful role model for me. Some were too arrogant or mean. Others made no sense. The closest I ever came was with a partner named Ed, who seemed to have become an authority in his specialty without either sacrificing the personal qualities that made him well-liked or ignoring his family's needs. But he kept me at a distance, so that no mentor-protégé relationship could develop.

If I had a hard time finding a role model among the partners, it was even worse with the senior associates.[296] One of them finally pushed me too far. It would be appropriate, I think, to refer to him here as "Bub." He had spent five or six years at the Boston office of my firm before transferring to New York. And now he needed to establish himself by making clear that I was his lowly assistant.

Bub had made a grand entry into the New York office by announcing, to the annoyance of nearly everyone, that he was absolutely certain he had passed the New York bar exam. We were all praying for him to fail. He didn't. But there were other opportunities to derail his choo-choo, and I, for one, took advantage of a few of them.

One time, Bub started getting on my back about a 40-page partnership agreement he had ordered me to draft for him. I had been working my tail off for other lawyers whose work I considered more important, and I simply did not have enough hours in the day to do this thing too.

He increased the pressure. In desperation, I decided to try an experiment. I handed a set of instructions to a paralegal[297] named Kate. She had had no formal legal training, but I asked her to work up a rough draft of the agreement anyway. I gave her an old agreement to use as a guideline, and hoped for the best.

Within a day or so after I handed her the instructions on this partnership agreement, she gave me back a finished draft of the document. I didn't even look at it, except to make sure that the words "Partnership Agreement" appeared on the first page. Instead, I just said a prayer, gave it to Bub, and waited

---

296. Everything is relative, but for someone like me, who had been at a law firm less than two years, an associate was senior enough to give me orders if s/he had been practicing law for at least four or five years.

297. A "paralegal" is a person who's halfway between a lawyer and a secretary. A paralegal doesn't have a law degree, and may not know how to type, but frequently does have a college degree, and sometimes also has some additional training in law-related matters from a paralegal school. See fn. 301.

for his response.

It was not long in coming. But it was not what I had expected. I figured he'd probably get to the middle of the second page and start screaming at the mess I had perpetrated upon him. Instead, as it turned out, Kate's old editing experience had come through. She had done a reasonable job of it.

So now Bub said that he just wanted, in the spirit of fatherly advice, to show me a few ways in which he thought I could improve my drafting technique. I sat down in his office, and we began to work through the document together. I quickly saw that, despite her general success, Kate had made a couple of hilarious mistakes, and I started to snicker. He asked me what I was laughing at, and I confessed the whole thing.

And you know what? He didn't get angry. Instead, he said, with a straight face, "Ray, I knew as soon as I saw this document that it could not have been something you would produce. I just knew you were capable of better work than this."

Although Bub and I didn't always hit it off, he was one of "us," the associates, and we all socialized together at times. And this was important to me. I understood my fellow attorneys much better out in the bars and restaurants, totally sloshed, than I did when I asked myself, in the office, whether I wanted to be like them. Depending on who went along, our outings would range from having elegant cocktails at La Tour d'Or to rubbing elbows with the traders and screaming over the din at The Bull & Bear.

It was interesting to watch this stuff, and to feel more involved with the big corporate deals and the various kinds of attorneys. I liked a lot of the lawyers I worked with: the punk-rock wonder woman; Bill, the social greeting partner who had been "high" on me; and Len and Rob and my other friends there. I liked another partner, with whom I worked on a few deals, for being such a friendly guy, even if he did mess things up for me sometimes, and I liked him even more when I heard, much later, that he had gotten thrown out after they caught him on his desk with, I think, a secretary.[298]   I liked the supposedly gay attorney whom I saw with a lovely blond — woman — at the bar at P.J. Clarke's at 5 p.m. on a sunny summer afternoon, just in time for happy hour, when both of us were supposed to be back at the firm working hard. These people were pretty tough on me sometimes, but if I caught them in their weaker moments, I genuinely enjoyed them.

3. Paralegals

To help with my mountains of paperwork, I sometimes enlisted the assistance of two different paralegals, namely, Kate, the former editor, and Gary, who wanted to be a playwright. After you've met a few paralegals like these, you start to contemplate the brain-drain that goes into the paralegal world:

> *If you want an interesting experience, go talk to your paralegal coordinator and ask for the 10 best résumés he has on his desk right now. At least in our firm, those résumés are breathtaking. We are looking at economics majors who were junior Phi Beta Kappas; we are looking at physics majors with A averages, English majors, historians, people who have written graduate theses .... After a while, some people stay on and you build a management structure around them.*[299]

You like to think that, say, a brilliant young physics major with an A average isn't permanently seduced by the money, and that s/he eventually goes back to school and does something with that brilliance. I sure hope so. In my experience, paralegal work might be defined as "that which is too boring for an attorney to do."

Paralegals occupied a sort of middle world all their own. They didn't tend to stay with the same firm as long as secretaries, and anyway seemed more replaceable than the secretary

---

298. Please keep your hands off the secretary's reproducing equipment.
299. Mode, fn. 262, pg. 11.

who gets to know his/her[300] boss very well.[301] On the other hand, since paralegals lacked law degrees,[302] they didn't
fare well in prestige comparisons against attorneys either.

This ghostlike status was sometimes painfully obvious.
One day, for example, a new associate arrived at the firm.
Bill, the social greeting partner, was walking this associate
around, introducing him to everyone. When he got to my
office, Gary and I were talking. Bill said, "Excuse me. Ray,
have you met Lee?" I said, "Yeah. Hi, Lee," and waved.
Lee waved back. Bill turned to go. Lee was still standing
there, expecting to be introduced to Gary. Bill stopped, looked
back toward Gary, obviously failed to remember his name, and
said, "Oh, uh, Paralegal, meet New Associate. New Associate, Paralegal." Poor Gary.

A few paralegals did have a more permanent status. In
particular, we often referred to Brenda as "para-Mom" because
she was responsible and stable. She had been with the firm for
a long time and probably would be there for quite a while to
come. She was in charge of a bunch of "para-pups" — that is,
college students and other junior paralegals who seemed to
come and go with the wind.

Paralegals like Brenda can easily be more capable, in
particular situations, than the attorneys who originally trained
them. That's because the paralegals have more time to learn
how to do things properly, and they keep on doing them and
learning new angles. They get trained from the ground up in
the nuts and bolts, whereas associate attorneys cost too much
per hour to justify educating them on some practical matters.

---

300. The pretense at gender neutrality is silly here. I never met a male legal
secretary.

301. Paralegals and secretaries sometimes do similar things, but with a sharp
eye, you can usually tell them apart. For example, the secretaries often get desks
out along the corridor, while paralegals get desks in a "para-pen" or even in their
own offices; top paralegals might have secretaries, but top secretaries don't
usually have paralegals; paralegals often have college degrees and career hopes,
or at least pretensions, outside of the world of law and law firms, while
secretaries usually do not have college degrees, tend to be career employees, and
often stay with a firm longer than the lawyers for whom they work. There are
things that you probably wouldn't ask a paralegal to do, like ordering lunches for
the people meeting at a conference or handling some of your personal matters,
either because the paralegal would be offended at being expected to do such
"non-professional" things or because the paralegal wouldn't be very good at it.

302. Except for a former lawyer I met who decided he'd rather be a paralegal
so that he could arrange his schedule to let him pursue his new career in acting.
Every now and then, I'd say, "Hey — where's Frank?" and they'd tell me he was
doing a commercial somewhere.

Following that philosophy one step further, a recent development at law firms is the hiring of nonlegal professionals (NLPs). Unlike paralegals, NLPs may cost as much as an attorney per hour but, by their specialized training, may handle the work more efficiently. Consider these words from a big firm's managing partner:

> *[A] quarter to a third of what many of our associates do ... can be done by a talented economist or MBA. We have just hired our first person like that. She is an economist in the international trade field. ... We compensate her like a young associate and she's got an office with a window.*[303] *I wish we had 10 more like her.*[304]

Given the limits on lawyers' practical knowledge when they come out of law school — and for years thereafter — it's not surprising that law firms are showing a greater interest, not only in hiring more paralegals (whose numbers are expected to double in the next 10 years), but also in employing economists and lobbyists, among others, to increase the range of services they offer to clients.[305] So if you'd like to get on the law firm bandwagon without having to become an attorney first, this is an angle to look into.

4. Secretaries

When you graduate from law school, you're lucky if you know where the courthouse is. Your practice will be filled with forms and documents you've never seen before and don't have the vaguest idea how to prepare. For these purposes, among many others, a legal secretary can be worth his/her weight in gold. With their assistance, you can get the job done without calling endless numbers of bureaucrats and plowing through mountains of books for the answers you need.

That's what secretaries *do*. But how about who they *are*? Wall Street is close to Brooklyn, so my secretaries tended to

---

303. This shows that she's not just another paralegal. Welcome to what counts on the law firm prestige ladder.
304. Mode, fn. 262, pg. 11.
305. Gibbons, fn. 33, pp. 70, 72.

be from that borough,[306] where rents are cheaper and where a lot of them grew up. And since I've mentioned Brooklyn a couple of times, I think it's time to give Kings County its due, if you'll pardon a brief diversion.

In 1636, Dutch settlers arrived at this piece of Long Island across the East River from Manhattan. They named the place after Breuckelen, in the Netherlands. Brooklyn grew. It became, in 1898, one of the five boroughs of New York City. Brooklyn now contains 2.3 million people, giving it more people than the cities of San Francisco, Boston, Denver, and Seattle combined. In population, Brooklyn, by itself, would be the fourth largest city in America, behind the rest of New York City, Los Angeles, and Chicago.[307]

Brooklyn has the broad parkways and the Promenade. It's the home of "Prizzi's Honor" and the original Mafia; of the disco in John Travolta's "Saturday Night Fever"; and of Neil Simon's "Brighton Beach Memoirs." When some American diplomats in Vietnam once tried to fool Ho Chi Minh, he asked them, in street-smart English, "What are you guys trying to pull?" He'd been a cook in Brooklyn. Babe Ruth ended his career in Brooklyn, as coach of the Dodgers. I'm told that Barbra Streisand was in the same high school graduating class there as Neil Diamond, who sang "Brooklyn Roads" after he moved to California.

On Mother's Day, the whole world returns to Brooklyn. My secretaries Marie, Susan, and Nereida, and my good friends Rena and Linda and Jim, all came from Brooklyn. I've met good cowboys and I've met good farmers, but I don't think I've ever met people with more heart than my buddies from the Big B.

But you don't want to go there. If you do, you're apt to get killed. The place is full of loonies. I may be a romantic, but only when it's safe. My friends survived their childhoods in that place, and maybe it made them more determined to be

---

306. New York City consists of five "boroughs." Each borough is a town that expanded to fill the borders of the county that contained it. Thus, the boroughs are Manhattan (New York county), Brooklyn (Kings county), Queens (Queens county), the Bronx (Bronx county, so named because it used to be Jacob Bronck's), and Staten Island (Richmond county).

307. U.S. Department of Commerce, Bureau of the Census, *County and City Data Book 1988* (Washington: Government Printing Office, 1988), pp. 354, 769.

good than they might have been if they'd grown up in a more pleasant world. I just wish they'd get out of there now and go someplace decent.

And maybe that's what the Brooklyn secretaries in my office were trying to do. Save up the money, get married, and move to Queens, or maybe Jersey, where life is better. All I knew was, I loved their accents. If the word ends with an A, you add an R to it. On the other hand, if the word ends in an R, you ignore it. So instead of "my sister Brenda," you get "my sista Brender." If this means that you have to drop a whole syllable, so be it: A "chest of drawers" becomes a "chesta draws." That creates the problem that a "drawing" must be a "drawring," because to the Brooklyn ear, it doesn't sound any better to skip lightly over the "w" in the middle of that word than it does to ignore the "g" in Long Island, which, as everyone knows, must be pronounced "Lawn Guyland," or (for those of us who like to tease) as simply "the Guyland."

Despite the pressures and the occasional conflicts in the office, I had fun gossiping with the secretaries and paralegals, sometimes joining them instead of the attorneys for a drink after work, and commemorating the higher moments in their lives, such as when Daisy celebrated, would you believe, her *sixtieth* anniversary of working as a secretary at the firm. The secretaries, like Brooklyn, were a world unto themselves, and with my farmland-and-law-school cultural baggage, I was never really able to explore those worlds like I wish I could have.

5. Chinese Waiters

I end this review of personalities on a high note. There remains this one class of person who had an important impact on my legal practice on Wall Street.

You have to figure, if a guy orders Chinese food delivered to the same office twice a week for two years, and if he always orders the same thing, you'll get to know him, even if you're a cold-hearted Chinese waiter in the stone tombs of Wall Street. Right?

Wrong. Such was not my luck. I always phoned in an order for fried dumplings, hot & sour soup, and tea. The same guy — I called him Won Ton Lee — always took my order, and yet he did not have a clue who I was. He'd claim to have problems with my credit card number. He'd forget the frigging tea. He'd refuse to deliver to my office. I couldn't believe it. After a morning of stressful corporate negotiations, I'd look forward to a relaxing lunch; instead, I'd get Lee, haggling with me in broken English about the notion of delivering a meal to 14 Wall Street. I'd remind him that he had delivered the identical order to me two days earlier, and then he'd agree to do it, as though it were a special favor to me.

On my last day at the Wall Street firm, I ate a dozen fortune cookies that had accumulated around my desk, just for good luck. And then, sure enough, a few weeks after I left the firm, my friends there told me that two well-dressed representatives of the Hunan Cuisine restaurant had made a personal visit to the firm, to find out what had happened to Woocok, the guy who used to order fried dumplings and soup twice a week.[308]

---

308. And tea, dammit, don't forget the tea.

PART III

DISLIKING THE SIDE EFFECTS

There's one final phase in the process of becoming a lawyer. It's a spiritual phase, not easily tied to a specific event that you and your buddies experience at the same time, like law school. It's not a requirement that some bar examiner imposes on you. But it will happen to you nevertheless, and by the time it's over, you'll be a different person.

The fact is, there's a ghost in this machine. Some of the most important things in our lives are the ones we didn't plan for, and maybe didn't even realize were happening at the time. So although you might start out with a simple idea of how to become a lawyer and what your life as a lawyer might be like, it's wise to make sure that your attitudes and goals don't turn into gremlins, running amok through your world. In this final part of this book, I offer a few ways in which that concern might become real for you.

§ 10. Wondering What You Are

By the time I had spent eight or nine months working in my first law firm job, some of the novelty had worn off, and I had started to take my status for granted.

That seems amazing to me now. I suspect that I may have fallen, myself, into one of those Black Holes of Confident Ignorance.[309] The fact is, when you start asking what it means to be a lawyer, you hear some peculiar answers, and you might like to ponder them before charting your future.

A. Defining the Legal "Profession"

As they say, law and medicine are the classical, "learned" professions,[310] where "learned" is pronounced "learn-ed," the old-fashioned way. I was delighted to be a member of this honored fraternity. And I accepted this definition of myself, at least for a while:

> *The commonly agreed-upon ingredients of a profession are twofold: (1) Membership [requires special] educational and licensure .... (2) Professions have the power of self-regulation .... Thus, law, medicine, theology, and accounting ... are professions. But*

---

309. See pg. 115.
310. See, e.g., Richard L. Abel, "Between Market and State: The Legal Profession in Turmoil," *Modern Law Review*, vol. 52, May 1989, pg. 308.

business, journalism and food preparation are not.[311]

Maybe if I had left law school with a wealth of useful skills and knowledge, I would have been proud to believe that definition for the rest of my career. But it just didn't fit, and I became more aware of that as time went by.[312]

I mean, what's this about "licensure requirements"? Sure, lawyers have a license to practice law. But did they have to have licenses to be professionals? If so, how did the members of "the world's oldest profession" get theirs? Do pro baseball players need a bat license?

I know it's nice, if you're a lawyer, to think that the only "real" professions are law and medicine, but that you can be generous and let your accountant friends believe that they're professionals too. But the truth is, I've known actuaries and financial analysts, and sometimes their entrance exams are tougher than the bar exams, license or no license.

And then there's the whole second half of that attorney's definition, which requires "self-regulation." I understand *what* it means. It means that professionals themselves get to decide who's admitted into the profession. But *why* should that be part of the definition? Here's a clue:

> *[P]rofessions are set off from other occupations by the requirement that they be relatively independent of control by laymen who, by definition, do not have the requisite training and skills to judge the work of professionals.*[313]

Now, that's an interesting thought. If you're a professional, they seem to be saying, then you *have* to be self-regulated. Laymen won't know whether you're doing your job properly. Only professionals will be able to tell.

Take, for example, an auto mechanic. This guy spends his

---

311. Robert B. McKay, "The Future of Professional Independence for Lawyers," *The Lawyer's Professional Independence: Present Threats/Future Challenges* (Chicago: ABA Tort and Insurance Practice Section, 1984), pg. 40.

312. For a general trashing of the notion that there's an ancient tradition of special training, self-regulation, and dedication to public service in the professions, see Nancy J. Moore, "Professionalism Reconsidered," *American Bar Foundation Research Journal*, vol. 1987, fall 1987, pg. 782.

313. Eulau & Sprague, fn. 43, pg. 133.

days scrounging around in rust, dirt, and grease. We can tell that he's no professional because you, a lay person, are fully able to get into your car when he's done and take it for a test drive. If it goes, he did it right; if it doesn't, he screwed up. This would not be possible if auto mechanics were professionals because, as we now know, "laymen ... do not have the ... skills to judge" the work of professionals. So I guess we should be glad that auto mechanics are not professionals.

Right?

Well, then, consider the example of your attorney. You go with her into the courtroom. She says some things to the judge and the other attorney. They all talk back and forth. After a while, you space out, and you remain that way until your attorney nudges you and says, "Psst — let's go." You go out into the hallway and say to your attorney, "Please tell me what happened. I did catch the part about life imprisonment, but, you know, I'm only a layman, so by definition I lack the skills to judge your work."

Right?

I'm sorry, folks, but it makes me punchy to talk too long about this concept that a layman can't figure out what a professional is doing. I agree that when the professional goes into the details and starts talking about camshafts and compression — I mean, motions and appellate review — well, when s/he starts talking that way, you might lose track.

But in the end, any moron can take one look and yell, "Hey — this is not my car!"

What can I say? I have my doubts. God did not reach down and touch me with His finger when I entered Columbia Law School. I was still more or less me. What I learned about the practical side of law, for the most part, did not come from law school, but from experience.

Well, after this fiasco, you won't be surprised to hear that the ABA did not exactly agree with that other guy's "commonly agreed-upon ingredients of a profession." Instead, they came up with this beauty:

> *[A profession is an] occupation whose members have special privileges, such as exclusive licensing, that are justified by the following assumptions: ....*

3. That the client's trust presupposes that ... self-interest is overbalanced by <u>devotion</u> <u>to</u> <u>serving</u> <u>both</u> <u>the</u> <u>client's</u> <u>interest</u> <u>and</u> <u>the</u> <u>public</u> <u>good</u>, and

4. That the occupation is self-regulating — that is, organized in such a way as to assure the public and the courts that its members are competent, do not violate their client's trust and <u>transcend</u> <u>their</u> <u>own</u> <u>self-interest</u>.[314]

In response to *that* definition, one lawyer asked, "If we try to see ourselves as clients see us, we shall wonder how to react to this definition. Should one applaud, sneer, laugh, or weep?" That lawyer went on to admit, sweetly, that this quote expresses "worthy goals."[315] But I fancy that it didn't conceal his belief — and mine — that the most-needed definition is a definition of "reality," as in, "Please shut up and look at our lawyers *before* you try to define them."

The more you read in the legal literature, the more you hope they do something about this problem quickly, because until they do, you'll keep seeing statements like this:

Since different sets of values underlie restrictions on the practice of divorce mediation by nonlawyers and lawyers, divorce mediation is not the practice of law when performed by nonlawyers. But when performed by lawyers, it is the practice of law.[316]

I'm not knocking the commentator. He's probably right. It just seems pretty funny.

What's going on, at this point, is clear. Nobody knows what in hell the legal profession is, other than that it's the thing that people do after they pass the bar exam.

---

314. Report of the Commission on Professionalism of the ABA, "'In the Spirit of Public Service:' A Blueprint for the Rekindling of Lawyer Professionalism," *Federal Rules Decisions*, vol. 112, Aug. 1986, pp. 261-62, quoting with approval Prof. Eliot Friedson of New York University (my emphasis).

315. Edmund B. Spaeth, Jr., "To What Extent Can a Disciplinary Code Assure the Competence of Lawyers?" *Temple Law Review*, vol. 61, winter 1988, pp. 1213-14.

316. Andrew S. Morrison, "Is Divorce Mediation the Practice of Law? A Matter of Perspective," *California Law Review*, vol. 75, May 1987, pg. 1155 (paraphrased).

B. Having Defined It, We Consider Its Special Needs

Welcome to legal logic.

You might think that, if we're having this much trouble figuring out what lawyers are, it might make sense to step back and ask why we need a single, separate profession called "law" rather than, say, a handful of different subgroups of lawyers that do quite different kinds of things.

But nooo. Whatever lawyers may become after they've finished law school and the bar exam, they want the rest of us to think law is special, so that we'll continue to tolerate their monopoly on legal services.[317] But they don't want it to be *too* much of a monopoly, like the electric company, because then the government might start to regulate it.[318] So they try to believe that, somehow, it's somewhere in the middle:

> *[T]he practice of law always has been a subtle blend of a "calling" such as the ministry, where compensation is all but <u>disregarded</u>, and the selling of a product, where compensation is <u>all</u> <u>important</u>.[319]*

But the real world is shaking, this tightrope is swaying, and the lawyers are about to fall off. I offer a comparison: the Old World versus the New.

1. The Way It Was

I wasn't around in the old days, but they seem to have had different attitudes back then.   I thought you might enjoy reading a few quotes, reprinted with permission from the *ABA Journal* ("the Lawyer's Magazine, published by the American Bar Association"), and from a 1951 article by Judge Learned (that's right — you know how to pronounce his name) Hand:

> *FORMER SUPREME COURT JUSTICE LEWIS POWELL: I graduated from law school in 1932. I had a heck of a time getting a job during the Depression. I took a job for $50 a month. I walked to work.*

---

317. McKay, fn. 311, pg. 42.
318. Abel, fn. 310, pg. 285.
319. Rehnquist, fn. 154, pg. 49.

In 1941, we were concerned about the outbreak of war in Europe. We made a number of speeches urging young lawyers to enlist. Almost all of them did.

ATTORNEY SIMON RIFKIND: I applied to law school in 1922. My first application was to Harvard. The only question they asked was whether I had a bachelor's degree. For financial reasons, I returned to New York and applied to Columbia. The critical difference between then and now was the level of anxiety. In 1922, I felt none.[320]

JUDGE HAND: It is the daily, it is the small, it is the cumulative injuries of little people that we are here to protect. Did you ever think of the problem that faced a person who had no knowledge of law or anything about it, when he suddenly found himself charged with breaking the law? For him, the law is a perfect wilderness — even the language is unintelligible.[321]

The mellowness of older people in the law[322] has to fade, now that the profession is growing younger.[323]   And many lawyers, of whatever age, now have a different attitude.

2. The Way It Is

You do still hear warm sentiments about the law.   But legal experts now tend to talk somewhat differently.

To illustrate it, I offer two opposing essays from the *ABA*

---

320. Goldberg (boxes: "Lewis Powell Remembers" and "Simon Rifkind Remembers"), fn. 34, pp. 60-61 (paraphrased).

321. Judge Learned Hand, "Thou Shalt Not Ration Justice," *Legal Aid Brief Case*, vol. 9, Apr. 1951, pp. 3-4 (paraphrased).

322. According to a study of lawyers who were aged 27-83, elderly lawyers are more able to reduce work stress by controlling the quantity and focus of their work, so that they have high job satisfaction and low rates of retirement. (Michael W. Meltzer, "The Reduction of Occupational Stress Among Elderly Lawyers," *International Journal of Aging & Human Development*, vol. 13, 1981, pp. 209-219.) Note also recent findings that "[n]ew studies show ... a sharp rise in people's altruism at midlife ...." (Daniel Goleman, "In Midlife, Not Just Crisis But Care and Comfort, Too," *New York Times*, Feb. 6, 1990, pg. B-1.)

323. A growing majority of lawyers have been practicing law for relatively few years. Today's graduating classes of more than 36,000 law students are much larger than the classes of less than 15,000 (before 1969) that produced today's older lawyers. (*Review of Legal Education*, fn. 204, pg. 66.)

Journal on the question of whether huge law firms are bad news. One commentator, Peter Megargee Brown, titled his essay, "Yes: Greed Is the Bottom Line." Against him, two legal consultants named Jack Kaufman and Bradford W. Hildebrandt wrote an essay entitled, "No: Big Clients Need Big Firms." My cut-and-paste job, which uses at least some of the writers' words to express their essays' concepts in dialogue form, is as follows:

BROWN: The pursuit of money for money's sake must be eradicated before it destroys the profession and, in turn, our entire system of justice. Many of the greediest lawyers are found today practicing in the megafirms.

K & H: The question of whether the rise of megafirms has endangered professionalism is provocative, but it misses the point. The real question is, are clients well-served by the megafirm?

BROWN: Twelve years ago, more firms were managed by an old-timer lawyer, and "management" consisted of making certain that everyone had enough pencils and legal pads. Today, firms are run by professional manager-accountants — the new barbarians — who often have no real knowledge of the profession.

K & H: The practice of law has become far more complex and diverse. Size has allowed the big firms to specialize, resulting in better client service and high-quality training to younger lawyers, along with state-of-the-art technology. We have fond memories of Mom and Pop grocery stores, but we would not shop in one today. Does the profession have any choice but to deliver what the clients desire?

BROWN: With the grant of monopoly from having a license to practice law comes the responsibility to use it for the good of all. Are we creating a breed of lawyers with no sense of history and narrow educa-

tion, riveted to their own self-interest?

*K & H: Not at all. Some megafirms have developed
significant <u>pro</u> <u>bono</u> programs that benefit society. As
long as lawyers follow the code of ethics and concentrate on providing the best possible service, it does not
matter what size firm they practice in.*[324]

I'll pass over the contrasting views on megafirms. Instead,
I draw your attention to a difference of attitude.

Consider, if you will, this question: As an attorney, if you
obey the Code of Professional Responsibility, is that good
enough? Or do you owe someone — the client, society, your
family, or yourself — an additional moral, or "gentlemanly,"
duty beyond what's required by that ethical Code?

For Mr. Brown, the answer seems to be that, yes, you owe
an additional moral duty. But for Messrs. Kaufman and
Hildebrandt, we don't have the luxury of indulging that
additional moral whim. Our clients are demanding, and we've
got to give them what they want, right up to the very edge of
the law. Indeed, that's what the Code expects. From that
perspective, competition is not an afterthought, but is, rather,
the organizing principle of the law, and everything good that
you do, as a lawyer, comes from your determination to
compete thoroughly.

The profession is pretty much following that approach
now. For example, the Supreme Court has struck down the
use of noncompetitive "flat rate" fee schedules,[325] and has
upheld lawyers' right to compete in advertising.[326] Clients
are more cost-sensitive.[327] Firms are hiring more professionals in management, finance, and marketing[328] to replace the
old-fashioned partnership approach of democracy and consensus. The largest law firm estimates that it will eventually

324. "Professional Responsibility: Has the Rise of Megafirms Endangered
Professionalism?" *ABA Journal*, vol. 75, Dec. 1989, pp. 38-39 (paraphrased).
325. Goldfarb v. Virginia State Bar, *United States Reports*, vol. 421, decided
June 16, 1975, pp. 773ff. Reprinted at 95 S.Ct. 2004, 44 L.Ed.2d 572.
326. Bates v. State Bar of Arizona, *United States Reports*, vol. 433, decided
June 27, 1977, pp. 350ff. Reprinted at 97 S.Ct. 2691, 53 L.Ed.2d. 810.
327. See Ronald Rotunda, "Demise of Professionalism Has Been Greatly
Exaggerated," *Manhattan Lawyer*, Mar. 29-Apr. 4, 1988, pg. 12.
328. Duncan A. MacDonald, "Speculations by a Customer About the Future
of Large Law Firms," *Indiana Law Journal*, vol. 64, summer 1989, pg. 595.

employ more than 5,000 attorneys,[329] and the legal staffs at some corporations are bigger than entire law firms.[330]

If anything, the competition will intensify as the rules change. There is now a chance that huge companies like Sears will be allowed to open law offices, squeezing the profit margins of today's local firms. A lot of smaller firms are hurting anyway: They must buy expensive computers and make other investments to remain competitive, but can't generate as much income from those investments as the bigger firms.[331] Indeed, it's been said that you now need 200 lawyers to have a top-quality general practice firm.[332]

The good news is, this competition saves you money when you go to a lawyer. The bad news is, it saves your adversary money too.

Actually, there's more bad news. Remember People Express? For a while there, we had an orgy of airline competition. But then, son of a gun, everyone merged into everyone else, and now it's not so clear what all that competition has given us. Are you ready for the day when Hertz and Avis dominate the legal industry?[333]

Individual lawyers aren't so happy with the switch from the Old World to the New World. We're talking about an environment, nowadays, like this: Lawyers scream, engage in personal attacks, and even get into fistfights in the courtroom; a majority of them agree that civility has deteriorated; they routinely fail to return one another's phone calls; they make huge demands for papers to be used as evidence, with no intention of actually reviewing those papers; and they adopt, as a standard tactic, the stance of opposing whatever the other side does or asks for. One judge quit the bench after deciding that the courtroom had simply become too nasty. Her words? "Life is too short."[334] Consider:

---

329. Goldberg, fn. 34, pg. 59; Gibbons, fn. 33, pp. 71-72.

330. See, e.g., the listing of hundreds of attorneys employed by IBM in *Directory of Corporate Counsel* (Clifton, NJ: Prentice-Hall Law & Business, 1987), vol. I, pp. 787-98. See also AT&T, Mobil, etc.

331. Gibbons (box: "How Small Firms Will Fare"), fn. 33, pg. 73.

332. Tamar Lewin, "Smaller Firms Are Vanishing," *New York Times*, Mar. 9, 1987, pg. D-2, col. 1.

333. That's not so far-fetched. It's been projected that as few as 20 law firms will dominate the profession by the year 2000. (Gibbons, fn. 33, pg. 71.)

334. Examples in this paragraph come from Milo Geyelin, "Lawyers Object to Colleagues' Rudeness," *Wall Street Journal*, June 24, 1991, pg. B1, col. 3.

It's gotten to the point where lawyers will shut off their fax machines at 5 p.m. on Friday so that the other side won't send a notice at 11:30 p.m. about a Monday morning hearing.[335]

[W]hat used to be a gentleman's profession, relying upon a code of honor more stringent than the professional ethics, has degenerated into a hostile, backbiting environment ....[336]

Law is no longer about having a good time, serving people and doing interesting, important work. It's about making money.[337]

If you're not making at least $200,000 a year after 10 years of being a small practitioner, you're in the wrong business. Working as a small-firm lawyer is too hard if you're not making a lot of money at it.[338]

Don't get me wrong. We can complain, but nobody has any good ideas for how we might go back to the gentlemanly old practice of law. We're in the deep part of this competitive toilet bowl now, and the only way out is down the tubes. Hold your nose and hang on.

And really, it's not all bad. Personally, I've been a client, and it sounds much better to me to think that lawyers have to scramble for business, and have to please me and charge fair amounts, than to let them sit up on their haughty thrones and do with me what they wish. But being a lawyer in this competitive environment? That's a different matter.

---

335. Texas Supreme Court Justice Eugene Cook, as paraphrased in "Reining in Rambo," *ABA Journal,* vol. 75, Nov. 1989, pg. 43. See also e.g., Crouch, fn. 209, pg. 413.

336. Arron, fn. 44, pg. 46.

337. Alan Morrison, a public interest lawyer and director of Public Citizen Litigation Group in Washington, D.C., as quoted by Goldberg, fn. 34, pg. 59.

338. James A. Jennings, quoted by Gary A. Munneke and Frances Utley, "Is There Life after Your First Job?" *Barrister,* vol. 12, summer 1985, pg. 21.

§ 11. The Original Plan; the Revised Plan

As a lawyer, you may discover that the tough, competitive nature of your work can affect the very values and goals that took you into law school in the first place. Like one of those brilliant college term paper ideas that begins to look increasingly stupid as the clock approaches 3 a.m. on your deadline all-nighter, you may find that your life contains some noticeable contradictions as your legal career develops. I say this to you now because it's a risk you should be aware of from the outset, even though years may pass before it takes hold.

A. *The Plan?* On to a Professional Career! *The Reality?* They Drop Like Flies!

There are few good statistics on attrition — that is, on dropout rates — in the process of becoming a lawyer. And, of course, we can't know in advance what will happen to you. But we can estimate what goes on.

To begin with, how many people consider going to law school? We don't know. But we do know that the LSAS prints up about 700,000 copies of the LSAT application booklet each year.[339] Some copies probably go to ambitious college sophomores who just want to fondle them. Other copies collect dust on the shelves of deans' offices. Still, with 13

---

339. According to a spokesperson for the LSAS with whom I had a phone conversation on June 25, 1990.

million people going to college in the U.S. each year,[340] it seems safe to guess that at least 350,000 copies must get into the hands of people who are trying to decide, at that time, whether to take the test and go to law school.[341]

Next, to get a nice average, let's consider the people who actually did take the LSAT during the ten-year period between June 1976 and May 1986.[342] On average, about 112,000 exams were given during each of those years.[343] The LSAS says that about 20 percent of those exams were repeat tries,[344] which means that, on average, approximately 90,000 people took the exam each year.

So what has happened to those people? Let's consider a representative sample of one-ninetieth of that group, or 1,000 of the people who took the exam sometime during that ten-year period.

First off, on average, a year after taking the exam, 575 of those 1,000 people had applied to ABA-approved law schools,[345] but only 460 had actually gotten in.[346] Of the remaining 540 out of our original 1,000, some gambled on non-ABA-approved schools;[347] some may have decided to get an honest job after graduation; and some probably went to med school. One little wrinkle: Note that the 460 who I say had "gotten in" to ABA schools had actually gotten in and had also survived the hair first month of law school. I can guarantee, from watching my own classmates, that others do drop out

---

340. *Statistical Abstract*, fn. 205, pg. 131, table 211.

341. LSAS won't say how many people get copies, and probably doesn't even know for sure itself how many non-duplicated names are on its mailing list.

342. More recent statistics are available, and they look even tougher than the story I'm about to tell. More than 135,000 people took the LSAT in each of the two years from June 1988 through May 1990. I used the 1976-86 period because we know more about what happened to those people, as you will see.

343. *Review of Legal Education*, fn. 204, pg. 66.

344. From the same phone conversation as in fn. 339.

345. The text at fn. 2 suggests that, for every eight people who get into ABA-approved law schools, two more try, but fail, to do so.

346. For the 10-year period from June 1977 through May 1987, the average first-year enrollment at ABA-approved law schools was about 41,000, which is about 46% of the 90,000 LSAT-takers.

347. Non-ABA schools are not necessarily bad. The ABA's reasons for denying approval may not reflect on the schools' overall quality. Some non-ABA schools exist within larger colleges or universities. Some can be affordable. Those of us who have had the experience of studying under famous professors might envy those whose low-prestige professors actually speak plain English. And some state bar admissions rules are quite open to graduates of non-ABA schools. For instance, in 1990, 40% of the people who took the California bar exam were from non-ABA schools, as were about 20% of those who took the Georgia exam. ("1990 Statistics," *Bar Examiner*, May 1990, pg. 17.)

during that month, and therefore do not show up in the ABA's data, which is not compiled until Oct. 1 of each year.[348]

The next step was to make it through law school. Combining both full- and part-time groups,[349] the first-year survival rate at ABA-approved schools was about 91.5 percent. So for every 460 people who were enrolled on Oct. 1 of their first year, only 421 were still there a year later. And then, in turn, for every 421 second-year students, another 15 (3.5 percent) dropped out during their second years, and another five (about 1 percent) in the third year,[350] leaving 401 ABA-approved law school graduates out of the original 1,000 applicants in this typical group.

At this point, our ABA-approved law school graduates were rejoined by their peers who had gone to non-ABA schools. It is difficult to say exactly how many people have graduated from non-ABA schools.[351] Using 1990 data, however, we might estimate that, for every 10 people graduating from an ABA school, one person graduates from a non-ABA school.[352] On this basis, our beginning group of 1,000 typical law school applicants would turn into a group of 441 law school graduates (with 401 from ABA schools and 40 from non-ABA schools).

The next step for these people was to take the bar exam. Not all of them did. I've known JD/MBAs and others who've decided, after graduating, that they would rather do something else. I have no idea how many people decide not to take the bar exam, but let's just suppose it's a nationwide average of 3 percent of law school graduates, which means that 428 of our

---

348. See first footnote to chart, *Review of Legal Education*, fn. 204, pg. 66. This leads to a simple request: If you've just started law school and are planning to drop out, please wait until October, so that you can become a law school statistic. I appreciate it.

349. Full-time students outnumbered part-timers, nationally, about five to one throughout this period.

350. Calculated by comparing the number of people enrolled in the first year of law school during the 10-year period of 1977-86, against the number of degrees awarded to those people when they graduated during the 10-year period of 1980-89. The numbers of part-timers (who began earlier or left later) even out.

351. The ABA appears to have had some difficulty gathering this data from the non-approved schools (see footnote to chart, *Review of Legal Education, Fall 1983*, similar to 1990 issue (fn. 204), pg. 69). In 1984, they gave up trying.

352. The *Bar Examiner* (May 1991, pg. 17) shows 52,416 bar exam administrations taken by ABA-school graduates in 1990. It also shows 5,047 non-ABA grads taking the exam, with five states failing to provide non-ABA data.

original 1,000 did take the exam.[353]

The next big question, then, is this: How many pass the bar exam? The statistics at this point are really screwed up, but it is possible to estimate that 77 percent of the people who took the bar exam for their first time passed it.[354] That means 330 of our group passed on their initial attempt.[355]

How about the 23 percent (98 people) whose first stab at the exam missed? Despite the lack of useful data, one can estimate that another 41 out of our original 1,000 LSAT-takers returned to the land of the living by passing the bar exam after taking it multiple times.[356] Thus, a total of 371 were ready, at some point, to go on to the next step, of gaining admission to the practice of law in one or more jurisdictions.

Despite the lack of accurate and complete statistics directly from the bar examiners, two fairly recent studies support the general picture I have painted. I will refer to those studies as the "Georgetown study"[357] and "NALP Survey."[358] Both are skewed in favor of people who liked, or excelled at, law school and/or the bar exam.[359] Even so, they suggest that as

---

353. Note that they may take it in more than one jurisdiction, or may take it more than once. There are no statistics on how many such duplicative exams are given, according to a spokesperson at the NALP with whom I discussed the matter by phone on June 13, 1991.

354. Based on *Bar Examiner* data for the three exam years from June 1987 through May 1990. (See fn. 225.) On a nationwide total basis, as *The Bar Examiner* reports, bar exam pass rates were very stable during the 1980s.

355. Again, this is an average. It could be much lower or higher for any particular state. To dispel one myth, California does not have the lowest pass rate. In 1990, for example, seven other jurisdictions had lower pass rates than California's. California's rate may also be affected by the surprising variety of non-ABA law schools available there.

356. Arbitrary working assumptions: (a) The pass rate for repeaters remains constant over multiple tries at the recent national average of 42%; (b) the percentages of people who attempt the exam on each of the second, third, and fourth tries are, respectively, 75%, 50%, and 25% of those who failed the previous try; (c) a statistically insignificant number of people try more than four times; and (d) 13.3% of bar exam takers never pass. (See fn. 360.) Results: The numbers per 1,000 of those who take and pass the exam for the second, third, and fourth times are, respectively, 74 take/31 pass, 22/9, and 3/1. Note: If 77% pass the first time, and only about 87% ever pass, then, of those who ever pass, eight out of nine do so on the first try.

357. Marilyn Tucker et al., "Whatever Happened to the Class of 1983?" *Georgetown Law Journal*, vol. 78, Oct. 1989, pg. 153.

358. Gail G. Peshel, *National Association for Law Placement Class of 1988 Employment Report and Salary Survey* (Washington: NALP, 1990).

359. The Georgetown study's survey went to 535 graduates, of whom 207 responded. (Pg. 156.) Despite a recent nationwide first-time pass rate of 77%, fully 96% of these passed the first time; a third of them had been on Law Review; with high accuracy, only 14% had been in the bottom quarter of their graduating classes; and (compare fn. 360) none of them were unemployed. (Pg. 176.) The NALP Survey questionnaire went to all 35,701 people who graduated in 1988, but

many as 15 percent of law school graduates never pass.[360]

There are no statistics on how many people are admitted to practice. As with the bar exam, the state bar admissions committees tell only how many admissions there were, and that double-counts the many attorneys who obtain admission to two or more jurisdictions. But using the estimate that only 0.2 percent fail to become admitted to the bar after passing the exam,[361] I would suggest that, of our original sample of 1,000 applicants to law school, we are now dealing with a round pool of about 370 survivors (i.e., 84 percent of the 441 graduating from law school) who were admitted to the practice of law.[362]

So what happened next? Using the class of 1988 as a representative group, the NALP Survey found that 2.3 percent (9) of our survivors peeled off into part-time legal work,[363] leaving 361 full-time lawyers. Of these, 7 percent (25) went to the legal staffs of corporations. About 3 percent (11) went into public interest law, never to be seen again; 12 percent (43) went into government, never to be paid again; and 1 percent (4) went into law teaching, never to be understood again.[364]

---

was answered by only 72% (25,714) of them, and has been criticized for underrepresenting the less successful graduates, as I learned in my phone call to NALP. (See fn. 353.)

360. Only 84.7% of those who answered the NALP Survey questionnaire were working in legal (or possibly paralegal) positions, and 7% were unemployed. (Pg. 1.) The Georgetown study's statement that only 4% of its relatively more successful respondents had not passed the bar on the first try meshes with its finding that only 6% had taken nonlegal jobs after graduation. (Fn. 357.) One scholar has observed that as many as one out of seven never pass the bar exam. (Stuart Duhl, ed., *The Bar Examiner's Handbook*, 2d ed. (Chicago: NCBE, 1980), pg. 18.) More dramatically, of those who first took the California bar exam in July 1985, the percentage of those who had given up or had still not passed after as many as five more tries were: 14% (non-minorities), 24% (Asians), 33% (Hispanics), and 45% (blacks). (Ramsey, fn. 120, pg. 23.)

361. See text at fn. 248.

362. I do not know what rates applied in the past. But using rates from the 1980s, we have 370 survivors, out of 460 first-year students at ABA schools and an assumed 46 others at non-ABA schools, for a survival rate of 73% from first-year enrollment through bar admission. Given 755,694 people who had actually made it through the process and had become attorneys by 1990 (see fn. 205), this suggests that about a million people now living may have spent at least some time in law school — that is, that there are more than a quarter-million law school dropouts in the U.S., before subtracting those who went back a second time.

363. Pg. 1. They may have returned to full-time legal work later, but probably were at least matched by others who left full-time work.

364. Note that no category is identified for a full 37% of the ones who responded to the questionnaire. I, and everyone else, assumes that they come proportionately from the groups that are represented in the data. At present, 70% of all practicing lawyers end up in private practice, 8% in government, 3% in judicial positions, and 13% in other salaried jobs. (See *Statistical Abstract*, fn. 205, pg. 182, chart 309.) (See text at fn. 379 regarding the remainder.)

Not quite 13 percent (46) went into judicial clerkships. But that lasts for only a year, and then they're out and looking for a job again. And most ex-clerks want to work on the cutting edge of the law, which almost guarantees that they'll be going into private practice, along with more than 64 percent (232) who did that directly out of law school.[365]

Anyway, on with the story. Allowing for a couple of the judicial clerks to do other things, I'd say we're looking at a group of about 270 young lawyers who more or less start their permanent careers in private practice.

But what does that mean? It means, based on the NALP Survey,[366] that a half-dozen of our survivors started their own practice; groups of about 12 to 14 percent (33 to 39 each) went into the several different NALP categories of firms in the range of 11 to 100 lawyers; and the remainder, consisting of two large groups of identical size (77 lawyers each, or about 29 percent of the survivors), went in totally opposite directions. One group went to firms of 10 or fewer lawyers (which I'll call "very small"), and the other to firms of more than 100 ("very large").

Not that those two groups are identical in all ways. According to the Georgetown study, people in the top half of the class supply about three-fourths of all graduates who go to very large firms, while those in the bottom half provide about two-thirds of all lawyers who begin their careers in very small firms. And new lawyers of ages 25 to 29 constitute three-fourths of those who go to very large firms, while new lawyers aged 34 and over supply only 2 percent.[367]

I thought you might appreciate a closer look at what happened to those survivors who went on to the big law firms. To that end, I have studied the data for Debevoise & Plimpton, one of America's premier law firms.[368]

---

365. These jobs were not all offered at the same time. More than 3/4 of those in the top quarters of their classes had their job offers by the end of the autumn of their third years, whereas 87% of those in the bottom quarters had to wait until after graduation for their offers. (Georgetown study, fn. 357, pg. 181.)

366. Based on intelligible responses, that is, which involves assuming a proportionate distribution of those who indicated "firm size unknown" and "branch office." I am not helped by the fact that the NALP's own percentages under "private practice" don't quite add up.

367. See Georgetown study, fn. 357, pp. 177-78.

368. See, e.g., James B. Stewart, *The Partners: Inside America's Most Powerful Law Firms* (New York: Simon & Schuster, 1983). I picked Debevoise

For simplicity, let's divide the group of very large firms into two groups ("very large" and "truly huge"), with half (39) of our 77 survivors going into truly huge firms. Debevoise, with its 300 lawyers, would probably fall into the truly huge category. And let there be no doubt about which survivors get into that kind of firm: We're talking, now, about the Harvard-Yale-Columbia[369] crowd for sure.

So what happened to the 39 people, out of every 1,000 LSAT-takers, who wound up at truly huge firms like Debevoise sometime during the past decade?

Briefly, I find[370] that Debevoise made four to seven new partners each year during that 10-year period. That contrasts against 28 to 65 new associates hired each year; not surprisingly, more than 200 associates left during the decade.

If you'd like to track a specific example, consider the fates of the 60 associates who started at Debevoise in the two years of 1981 and 1982.[371] Nine of them (15 percent) made partner.[372] Three others took on some other status (e.g., "senior attorney"), and seven others were still there as associates after eight or more years, for a total of 19 (32 percent) who, in some sense, had survived that long.[373]

Thus, 41 out of those 60 (i.e., two-thirds) did *not* stay at Debevoise for eight years (by their choosing and/or by the

---

merely because it was one of the few big-name firms that provided full lists of names in *Martindale* (fn. 18) for every year through the 1980s.

369. Funny how easily that phrase comes to my lips. I do mean, of course, to include the other top-name schools here too.

370. By analyzing the lists of names provided in the *Martindale* (fn. 18) for the New York office (including people from other offices who are listed there) for each year from 1981 through 1990. See also the questionnaire that Debevoise prepares every year, available from the NALP. Note that the firm's responses to that questionnaire may exclude laterals and other offices and may include those of e.g., the class of 1981 who did not arrive at Debevoise until e.g., 1985.

371. As indicated by the *Martindale* (fn. 18) entries published in 1982-83. Three others arrived during those years, but made partner within a couple of years after arriving, suggesting that they had already survived for a number of years at other firms, and that they had been hired with more of an eye toward eventual partnership than would be the case with fresh law school graduates.

372. Five made partner after six years, two after seven, and two after eight. Of course, times change. Debevoise is bringing in far more associates than it used to, even though it isn't making a lot more partners. If our 39 heroes were to arrive at Debevoise at the end of the 1990s, recent trends suggest that they might constitute only 1/5 of the 200 new associates arriving each year, and could therefore expect to split 1/5 of the 11 partnership slots that, based on trends during the 1980s, might then be opening up each year.

373. Using the 1990 *Martindale* (fn. 18). I assume a few of these might have been told to stick around in hopes of being considered for partnership again the next year, and that others were in the process of finding new jobs.

firm's). The average stay, for those who left, was 3.1 years. Almost 40 percent of the departers left after only one or two years, and another one-third left after three years.[374] Only one-sixth of the departers stayed more than four years.[375]

If you'll recall, I was tracing what happened to 1,000 typical LSAT-takers. I got as far as saying that 39 of them ultimately went to work at truly huge firms. So now, using the Debevoise example, you might speculate like this: In the 1980s, 10 of the 39 left their truly huge firms within their first two years there, another nine left in their third year, and eight more left in the next several years after that.[376] The 12 who stayed for eight years or more divided fairly evenly, with half becoming partners and the other half hanging around — for a while, anyway — as associates or as "senior attorneys."

It's important to point out that life does not end for those who do not make partner at truly huge firms. Debevoise is an excellent name to have on your résumé, even if you stay for only a year or two. And I doubt Debevoise is much different from any of the other top-name firms: The odds are tough, but the credential looks good.

The real point is this: If you're even vaguely thinking about partnership in a big-name firm, you might want to look at my rough estimate — that only five or 10 out of every 1,000 LSAT-takers will actually make it to partnership in that kind of firm — and decide to develop a backup plan. The legal profession operates by a tough logic nowadays, and a lot of grand career plans do change along the way.

B. *The Plan?* Security, for Those Who Make It. *The Reality?* Nausea, When They Make It & Hate It.

Most lawyers do not go to the huge firms. It makes sense, then, to back up and look at a different kind of attrition. What

---

374. These data probably understate attrition. I assume the firm would not make a record, in *Martindale* (fn. 18), of those associates who might arrive in January, for instance, after the *Martindale* report for the new year has been filed, and who might then leave late that same year, before the next *Martindale* report.

375. These rates vary from firm to firm. They also vary in the same firm from one year to the next. Of those who arrived at Debevoise in 1985, for instance, 2/3 had already left by 1989.

376. I'll leave it to you to decide what the turnover does to morale and close friendships among associates, long-term planning by the partnership, and efficiency for the client.

happens to the 361 people, out of every 1,000 LSAT-takers, who become full-time lawyers of any type?

There are two ways to answer that question. One is to give you some more statistics, which I'll do first, and the other is then to tell you some stories. In talking about the statistics, remember this: I do not have 361 actual names, but these statistics are built on real lives, and for that reason I will talk about them in actual terms — that is, not about what *might* happen to such people, but about what actually *is* happening.

1. The Numbers Tell the Story

I'm not here just to hand out bad news. Please remember, as I fork over the negative statistics, that there are a large number of people to whom the dark side does not apply.

Having said that, about one-third of our 361 lawyers (32 percent, or 116) would think twice before deciding to become lawyers, if they had it to do over again, and another 5 percent (18) absolutely would not choose law again.[377] A full 42 percent (152) have seriously considered leaving law.[378]

It is less certain how many actually do leave the law, or when they do so. On the question of "when," the studies all show young lawyers to be the least happy, so I assume that most of those who quit do so sooner rather than later. And on the question of "how many," estimates (excluding those who've died) range from 6 percent[379] to 15 percent[380] and up.[381] For that matter, it is difficult even to know what is

---

377. Georgetown study, fn. 357, pg. 187. Note that while 34-38% of those in the bottom 3/4 of the class would think twice, only 17% of those in the top quarter of the class would. Recall, again, that this study under-represents people in the bottom quarter of the class, so that perhaps the text here should show worse percentages than those that I have copied from the Georgetown study. It may also be appropriate to consider the difficulty that respondents might have in admitting that they have made a career mistake.

378. Georgetown study, fn. 357, pg. 185. The most doubtful groups: 47% of women, of lawyers aged 25-29, and of those who work in law firms; and 57% of those who were in the bottom quarters of their classes.

379. *Statistical Abstract*, fn. 205, pg. 182, table 309, shows 6% of all lawyers as "inactive or retired." As I learned in a phone conversation with an ABF spokesperson on July 15, 1991, that percentage is based on the number of attorneys who file statements of inactivity or retirement with state bar associations. As such, it almost certainly understates the number. Not all attorneys bother (or even wish) to file such statements, which may require you to do absolutely no legal work.

380. Arron, fn. 44, pg. 46, citing a long-term Harvard Law study.

381. Consider the suggestion that as many people leave the law out of dissatisfaction (i.e., in addition to mortality numbers) as arrive each year. (Arron,

meant by "leaving the law." Do lawyers continue to count as lawyers, for these purposes, if they become paralegals? How about if they do part-time legal work while supporting themselves in some other way?

I have not found good statistics on this. If you'll pardon me for taking the middle ground, though, I will proceed on the assumption that, by this point, of the 361 people who became attorneys, 10 percent (36) have turned to something other than the full-time practice of law, leaving us with 325 full-timers.

Of those 325, 25 percent (81) plan to change jobs in the next two years;[382] 41 percent (133) have changed jobs within two years of graduation; and 51 percent (166) answer "undecided" or "no" when asked whether they plan to stay in their current jobs for long.[383]

About 26 percent (85) of our 325 lawyers have tried cocaine. Five percent (16) are problem drinkers who also suffer from "statistically significant elevated levels of depression," a combination that is "highly predictive of suicide attempts and relapses," and another 27 percent (88) are divided, nearly evenly, into either problem drinking or depression, but not both. Under the applicable definition, most of the "depressed" ones are having suicidal thoughts. There is no data on attorney suicides, but experts have observed that attorneys' typical isolation could be expected to encourage them to act on those ideas. I remind you, these are people who started law school with approximately the same level of depression as the average American.[384]

If our 325 lawyers stay in the law for full 25-year careers, about 24 of them will be disbarred or suspended or will resign from the bar.[385] About 96 malpractice suits will be brought

---

fn. 44, pg. 46.) See also fn. 205.
   382. Hirsch, fn. 276, pg. 18.
   383. Georgetown study, fn. 357, pp. 178, 183.
   384. The information in this paragraph comes from Benjamin *et al.*, fn. 113, pp. 240-42 (including their fn. 31). All of these percentages are two to four times higher than the percentages that apply to the population as a whole.
   385. Using 1984-88 annual average of 1,907 disbarments, suspensions, and resignations from the bar (i.e., not just from a job) as compared to total lawyers in 1985. (See fn. 205.) (Standing Committee on Professional Discipline and Center for Professional Responsibility, *Statistical Report: Sanctions Imposed in Public Discipline of Lawyers 1984-1988* (Chicago: ABA, 1989), pp. 25-26.) Not all states were similar here (e.g., California, with 22% of all disbarments and 18% of all suspensions). Assumes no multiple sanctions of any one attorney, i.e., that it is difficult to simultaneously quit and get suspended and disbarred.

against them.[386]   Some of those troubles will result from substance abuse: At least 27 percent — maybe far more — of all cases of attorney discipline[387] involve alcohol abuse, and perhaps 60 percent (36) of lawyers who suffer from substance abuse will be sued for malpractice.[388]   In one survey of managing partners at Denver law firms, the large majority said that they had worked with at least one partner whose personal problems (especially involving alcohol and marriage) had impaired his/her performance, and that, in more than a third of those cases, the lawyer eventually left the firm.[389]

Figure it out, folks. A good percentage of the people who become lawyers find that it eats them up inside. If you're not sure you'll still be standing when this party ends, you'd be smart to consider a low-commitment preliminary visit as a secretary, maybe, or a paralegal at a law firm.

2. Being There

In the end, no matter where you go, there you are — and you're still a lawyer. The law is not something you step in on the sidewalk and then scrape off your shoe. As you'll see, the law sort of sticks to you, like chewing gum on your bus seat.

I have experience on this point. The first job I took after leaving the practice of law was a position with a major New York legal headhunting — i.e., executive recruiting — firm.

As a headhunter, I found myself trying to fill some interesting positions. For one of them, I got on the phone with

---

386. Using the annual average of 5,817 suits in 1981-85 (ABA Standing Committee on Lawyers' Professional Liability, *Characteristics of Legal Malpractice: Report of the National Legal Malpractice Data Center* (Chicago: ABA, 1989), pg. vii), increased by 33% to account for missing data (e.g., greater number of suits now than then; partial or complete failure of several large insurers to report; lack of data on uninsured suits and on those for which no claim was filed).

387. Attorney discipline includes disbarment, suspension, public reprimand, resignation or probation from the bar, fines and other monetary penalties, and an order to take and pass an ethics exam, among other things. See Ann Hagedorn, "Lawyers Have High Rate of Mental-Health Woes," *Wall Street Journal*, Nov. 30, 1990, pg. B-1, col. 2 for a report that, in New York, more than half of all disciplinary cases involve alcohol or drugs.

388. Benjamin *et al.*, fn. 113, pp. 243-44.

389. Stephanie B. Goldberg, "Lawyer Impairment," *ABA Journal*, Feb. 1990, pg. 32. Note the study of 12 alcoholic lawyers in a New York inpatient alcohol treatment service: As compared to 350 non-lawyer alcoholics, the lawyers tended to have *many* other psychiatric problems, to be highly resistant to treatment initially, and to evoke negative feelings in the staff people. (Richard Frances *et al.*, "Lawyers' Alcoholism," *Advances in Alcohol and Substance Abuse*, vol. 4, winter 1984, pg. 59.)

important partners from major law firms. At first, they'd treat me like dirt. I'd tell them that, actually, I was looking to fill a spot for an investment banking firm. They'd warm up a bit. Then I'd mention the huge salary and bonus, and, what do you know, they'd suddenly be a lot more eager to meet me. Next thing, they'd be sitting across the table, and I'd be asking them all kinds of questions that I had been just dying to ask when I was a lowly associate.

For the most part, headhunting was a sad business. Every day, I'd talk, in person and on the phone, with literally dozens of attorneys at all stages of their careers. Some were young people who'd been in the law for only a year or two. Some were senior associates who were pretty obviously not going to be made partners at their firms and who were facing the fright of the "up-or-out" tradition. And some had gotten off the ordinary law firm career track from junior to senior associate to partner, and wanted to get back on.

I guess it was like seeing a movie of your own screwups played and replayed before your eyes, 20 or 30 times a day. It made me want to be God in this job, or at least to have magical powers. For the younger attorneys, I wanted to be able to hand out a gift of time, to take them back to the start of their legal careers and let them re-think their decisions. And for the older ones, I wanted to be able to concoct an attorney's Garden of Eden, a place into which they would walk, with résumés in hand, and be greeted with warm shouts of welcome as they were led to people who desperately needed the hard years of experience that they had accumulated.

I don't want to make my role at this job seem sweeter than it was. Along with their tough situations, some of these people were nasty. You may have felt sorry for them, but that's the last thing they wanted from you. If anything, your sympathy only made clear that you were not buying their cool, relaxed stories about how they had decided to try something new in their lives — as though it were a mere coincidence that they were coming to you only now, just as their classmates were being made partner or their firm was falling apart.

In a few cases, I thought I might be able to find something for them. But in the vast majority of cases, I couldn't. They didn't have the background that it took to land the top-flight jobs that we handled. Like all headhunters, we dealt with experienced people only, so I had nothing to offer the many who wanted to switch to a nonlegal job, or even to a different specialty within the law. As poignantly phrased by Terry Louise Fisher, the co-creator of the TV show "L.A. Law,"

> *We get stacks of letters from attorneys who want to work on the show — as writers, "consultants," as gofers on the set — anything. I guess there are a lot of lawyers out there who really don't like to practice law. All the time I did "Cagney and Lacey," I didn't get those letters from cops.*[390]

And yet, despite the complaints that you hear from these attorneys, nothing happens. They may be diligent in every other way, but somehow they cannot bring themselves to tackle their own career problems. Instead, they get comfortable, settle down with their salaries, and stay in law after all. They slowly stop griping and, eventually, may even be the *least* tolerant of other attorneys' gripes.

There are good reasons why many dissatisfied attorneys don't actually leave the law. Most don't have MBA degrees to fall back on, for example, and I'll bet that most don't pursue many different kinds of nonlegal jobs. Also, of those who do, few will accept big cuts in prestige and salary.[391]

As an attorney, you're used to being coddled. You come out of the simplistic world of school and go straight into a job that pays a lot and gives you a level of prestige that other people get only after years of work. It can be perplexing to see how complicated the nonlegal job market is, and to discover, for perhaps the first time in your life, that potential employers are fully able to think that you are not so amazing.

Young attorneys indulge in lots of pipe dreams to avoid this ugly reality. Besides imagining that they could get a job on a corporation's legal staff and then switch easily over into management, they like to think that clients will try to entice them away with attractive offers of employment as business partners. In the real world, though, if your clients want to

---

390. Anthony Monahan, "Who Puts the Law into 'L.A. Law'?" *Barrister*, vol. 15, spring 1988, pg. 8 (his emphasis).
391. Arron, fn. 44, pg. 47.

hire you at all, they'll want you as a lawyer, not as a partner. The clients who really *could* offer you an attractive nonlegal job won't be in the habit of thinking, "Gee, s/he looks frustrated. Maybe I should give him/her a new career." If they see your dissatisfaction, they'll probably avoid you, lest you let your unhappiness foul up their legal work.

I mean, it's not as though successful businesspeople have a hard time finding people who'd like to be their partners. They've got friends, friends' kids, their own kids ... the list goes on. Lawyers do get offers to go into business, but the offers are rarely attractive. When it comes to the task of finding jobs after law, for those who wind up going in that direction, I can say only that there are no handouts.

C. *The Plan?* Superior Training.
The Reality? Too Much Intensity.

As the joke goes, when you practice law, you have to deal with the dregs of society — and their clients. In that spirit, kindly consider this quote from an article in the *ABA Journal* about criminal law practice in Miami:

> *"A criminal lawyer's dream come true," says attorney Roy Black. "What interests the true professional are the most unusual and arcane cases, and that's what we have in Miami." Attorney José Quinon agrees. "Two years ago, I got a case where the guy intended to kill the president of Honduras. You don't see that kind of case anywhere else."*

> *What sets Miami apart is its abundance of extraordinary crime — a singular mixture of sensation and intrigue. Miami's underworld is so right and slimy it has become a cliche to call the place Casablanca. What a great place to be a lawyer.*

> *It's possible, in a climate like this, to lose track of just how rich a vein Miami's criminal defense bar is working. Quinon is co-counsel in the Lehder drug trial. The publicity is great — the witness list includes Walter Cronkite. So many lawyers offered their*

services to Lehder that prison authorities had to appoint a secretary for their precious prisoner.[392]

After you read that, you can understand why scientists have recently decided to use attorneys instead of monkeys for laboratory tests. It seems that attorneys have several advantages over monkeys for these purposes: There are more of them, they're more like human beings, and there are things that a self-respecting monkey just won't do.

What happens is this: Lawyers are trained according to the theory that more is better. More complexities, more intelligence, more hours of hard work, more caffeine. But when they come up against real-world problems, their intensity leads them to focus so much on the details that, unless there's a lot of spare time and a huge amount of coffee available, they may never be entirely ready to appraise the big picture.

I'll give you an example. After I left the practice of law, I scratched around in various jobs (including the headhunting spot) for more than a year. I finally succeeded, however, in landing a Lotus position, if you will, preparing Lotus 1-2-3 spreadsheets for a tax-oriented law firm.

My purpose in this job was to take the place of a guy named Johnson, who was going off to seek fame and fortune elsewhere. When Johnson explained my duties to me, he seemed arrogant. He said, "I do the spreadsheets in summary form, and I don't go into a lot of detail on the calculations, because the lawyers here don't understand what I'm doing, and if I try to explain it to them, they just get bogged down in it."

My approach, by contrast, was to provide everyone with full details on everything. It was up to them to decide whether to read it, but this way I was covered. Besides, I believed that everyone made mistakes, and that full disclosure of the background information made it easier for us all to find those mistakes before they did any damage.

Technically, I'm sure I was right. But practically, I was wrong, for two reasons peculiar to lawyers. First, the more information they get, the more they want. As long as Johnson

---

392. Dave Von Drehle, "Ohhhhh, Miami!" *ABA Journal*, vol. 74, Apr. 1988, pp. 62-66 (paraphrased).

had kept things vague, the lawyers had been too busy to go looking for trouble.   But once I implied that they should understand what I was doing, they got nervous and began to explore.   As a result, my projects grew from Johnson's one-page spreadsheets into these giant data verification nightmares, as the attorneys insisted on getting only the most exact inputs for every single calculation.

And second, my full-disclosure approach made me look bad.   You'd think I'd learn after a while.   You may recall my story about the partner who had seemed eager to treat my rough draft as though it were a final version, and to criticize what he considered a shoddy effort.   In the same way, when the attorneys in this firm began to see mistakes in my spread-sheets, they weren't ready for it.   Johnson's less detailed presentations had concealed the nitty-gritty calculations.

In short, the attorneys may well have had superior analytic abilities, but they went so far with them that the clients wound up paying a lot more than the projects deserved.   Maybe law school does give you superior training, but only for its own purposes.   While you're busy polishing some skills, others will get rusty.   You don't get something for nothing.

D. *The Plan?* Legal Self-Sufficiency.
The Reality? Hidden Costs.

Some people go to law school to learn how to handle their own legal affairs.   Maybe they're tired of getting yanked around in court.   Maybe they are thinking of starting their own businesses and want to nail down all angles.

These are not dumb motivations.   Law school might help with these things.   But there are some respectable costs and risks in self-representation for anything more significant than small-claims court.   If you become an entrepreneur who falls back on legal skills once in a while, you won't be nearly as experienced in the courtroom as a regularly practicing attorney. Even the best lawyers hire others to represent them sometimes.

After losing patience with my first divorce attorney, I took over the case and handled most aspects of my own contested divorce.   And as the philosopher said, "A divorce is essentially the absurd."[393] I spent two years at it, produced a paper file that weighs 60 pounds, and learned a lot about matrimonial practice. But how frequently do you hope to use that kind of knowledge for your own purposes? Once every couple of years, at best. All I knew was that, in retrospect, even though I had won some important points, I had basically lost two years' worth of free time for the sake of self-defense.

In the most pessimistic view, it worked out like this: I married a woman whom I wouldn't have married if I hadn't gone to law school; I did it mostly because she was a steady friend during some tough years when I needed that. Having married her, I drove a wedge into the relationship because of my commitment to pass the bar exam and succeed at the firm, no matter what it meant to her needs or wishes. As I furthered my legal training, I became increasingly tough on her. When we broke up, I did not shrink from a highly confrontational course. When she responded by hiring an equally confrontational attorney, I upped the stakes by pretending that I had nothing more important to do than to fight her. I won, but I also lost.

Nothing is free. Litigation has its price, and when you figure in all the hidden costs, it may not be cheaper for you to learn how to handle your own cases or to live your life as though you were free to sue whenever you'd like. Litigation really can lead you away from your primary goals. Law, like anything else, is much easier to practice on someone else.

---

393. Sumac Trebla, *Athip of Mythiputh*, pg. 93.

§ 12. Trying to Remember Human Attitudes

Some time has passed since my successes and failures in law school, in law firms, and in handling my own lawsuits. During that time, I have made some progress back up the road I came down, toward deciding whether I got sidetracked, in law school, from things that were once important and should be again.

I'm still working on that question, but I can offer a few comments that may elevate the discussion from the everyday stories I've been telling to the philosophical level you'll need to consider in making your career decisions. In posing these thoughts, I talk as an outsider, referring to attorneys as *them* rather than *us*. This seems appropriate, whether you're a future law student or a potential ex-practitioner.

A. Self-Evident Rights

My question for you is: Where is your energy best spent in resolving the law-related issues you face? Can you redress the injustices I'm about to describe by becoming a lawyer instead of something else? If I were ever on a radio talk show,[395] these are the points I'd press most vigorously:

---

395. Such as, the Will Toop Hour.

1. The Right to Screw Up

When you were young, you probably knew some kids who were always being made fun of. If you laughed at them long enough, they got mad and went off to tell the grownups on you.

In a way, nothing has changed. As it turns out, you should have been nicer to those little twerps, because they grew up and became attorneys, and now they're pissed. They're no more tolerant of your laughter today than they were 30 years earlier, when they were kids.[396]   In their daily business, they'll trample, without hesitation, on your world's happiness.   To them, blithe living is a Black Hole;[397] it's inscrutable, and therefore meaningless.

The practice of law, like leprosy, is totally serious. But the seriousness does not persuade me that either the plague or the profession represents the way things should be. Any kid out of law school can hope to impress people with the glint in the eyes and the set of the jaw. It takes a champ, I believe, to back up and say, "Hey, I'd prefer to laugh."

Lawyers will be quick to object that they are among the wittiest members of our society. And it's true, for some of them. But after a while, you start to get a feel for what attorneys think is funny.

For example, do you remember how, in the old films, James Bond's car had a rotating license plate with numbers from different countries? When someone would copy down his number, he'd just rotate to another one. Well, if lawyers had written that part, instead of seeing our hero in high-speed races across international frontiers to get away from the bad guys, we would have watched him rotate to the "Handicapped" plate while parking at a fire hydrant.

I don't think most lawyers like fun when it involves the risk of liability, as in high-speed races, or when it comes in the form of gaiety and silliness. They prefer word plays and at

---

396. "'What starts the process really,' Mr. Nixon once recalled, 'are laughs and slights and snubs when you are a kid. ... But if you are reasonably intelligent and if your anger is deep enough and strong enough, you learn that you can change those attitudes ....'" (Godfrey Hodgson, reviewing Tom Wicker's book *One of Us: Richard Nixon and the American Dream* in "Staying Power," *New York Times Book Review*, March 10, 1991, pg. 14, col. 1.)

397. See pg. 115.

least some of the other things that pass for wit. They like jokes in which someone gets shafted. And they especially like a story about a good screwup.

But I don't think it's fair for them to laugh at screwups. You may recall my complaint that, as a practicing attorney, I found myself working with people who had a strange need to pretend that errors did not happen. If screwups are bad, then it makes no more sense for these lawyers to laugh at them than for a nun to giggle at a penis joke.

The problem for humor — or, depending on how you look at it, for the law itself — is that the law can't take a joke. When you screw up, you may do something very funny, but it may also be grounds for a lawsuit. This is why lawyers don't like practical jokes. My temptation to put trick blackface soap in the toilets at the Wall Street firm was so farfetched, so likely to result in dismissal, that I never even tried.

What can I tell you? There's a place for errors in everyday life.[398] And not just the funny ones. Even the painful ones are essential to progress. People who look like they're mistaken have a nasty habit of turning out to be right sometimes. For example, I hear that the Japanese take the long view when they're entering an industry. That gives them enough spare time to allow for an occasional screwup. And this seems wise. You can't be trying to win every competition at every moment.

It's easy to say that we learn from our mistakes. But it's also easy to condemn someone for one foul-up. Lawyers, in particular, are paid to make everything out of one mistake and ignore the progress that the defendant has been making and the good that s/he has been doing otherwise.

The law in America, as it's now taught and practiced, acts as though we have an infinite amount of leeway to attack those who get out there and try to accomplish something. And that's wrong. We like screwups, and we need them.

We are very far from the day when you can go into court and say, "Yes, I tried something, it didn't work, I screwed up, I know what I did wrong, and I'm thinking about making a few

---

398. If we didn't believe that, we'd never put up with a situation in which even the best trial judges in the country are found to have been mistaken, upon appeal, in at least one out of every six cases. (Forer, fn. 58, pg. 151.)

changes and trying it again." That is unfortunate for the sake of progress in our society and for adopting the long-term perspective we'll need if we wish to remain competitive — and much more so if we wish to *enjoy* competing — in this world.

2. The Right to Live According to an Unwritten Code

The law insists that you "get it in writing." That's wise, of course, to prove that there was an agreement and to help you avoid misunderstandings. But let's not pretend that contracts make the world go 'round.

On the contrary, I can go through an entire week without signing anything. But I can't go through a day without 100 implicit understandings with people. For example, at the grocery store, I don't have to say a word, but everyone reasonably assumes that I haven't come to play floor hockey with the frozen fish or bring the checkout line to a halt by trying to pay with Swiss francs.

We observe those understandings without being forced to. Nobody's going to sue us for breaking them. They're just part of an unwritten code of civilized behavior that almost everyone follows, century after century.

Naturally, it's the court's job to write down the facts of a case. When you go into the law library, you see that they've produced an awful lot of books full of facts, and yet, somehow, there are always new cases that haven't occurred before. I guess we shouldn't be surprised if it'll take an infinite number of volumes of law to capture all possible human legal experiences.

When you go too far with the notion that what counts is the written law, then you allow your bad people to insist that, if it's not in the written law, they don't have to worry about it. You also have the unfortunate experience of seeing lawyers and written documents intrude in places where they're perhaps better left out.

Possibly the worst example of such intrusion is the antenuptial (pre-marriage) agreement, like that which my ex-wife and I had. It seems prudent to have such an agreement, because a lot of people who didn't think they would ever get divorced do wind up separating from one another. But it's still awfully uncomfortable. When you raise the idea of an antenuptial agreement with your future spouse, you (and s/he) can easily wonder, in the delicate days before marriage, if you've begun to have doubts about your future together.

And then the lawyers arrive, yours and his/hers, and suddenly everyone's attention is on everything that can go wrong. Admit it: When you compare what you're trying to accomplish in this marriage against what you're doing with these lawyers, it's as though you're running in two opposite directions simultaneously.

It's worse than that. As I discovered, some spouses eventually attempt to persuade the divorce judge that they were forced to sign the agreement, and an excellent way of defeating that claim will be to prove that the two of you negotiated hard — or, better yet, fought bitterly — over this agreement before you signed it, demonstrating that you knew exactly what you were doing.

One matrimonial lawyer may have been correct in saying that "[Clients] don't realize that prenuptial agreements don't kill romance. They just suspend it for a short time."[399] But even if he's right, the real question is whether the law knows exactly what it is doing when it encourages you to suspend your romance.

We've got another Black Hole here. We let lawyers rush in and talk about how their antenuptial agreements don't really disturb love. The implication, of course, is that lawyers understand which things do and don't disturb love.

But that's nonsense. Humans certainly don't understand love. We do some of the damnedest things to find it, and when we do have it, we do even sillier things to lose it. It may be that love is just a little blank spot in the law's understanding of reality. Or it may be, instead, that when you step into this Black Hole, you find that there are whole galaxies within the realm of love, enough to keep you busy exploring for the rest of your life. This is certainly how people talk when they're in love. Who are we to imagine that anyone, and especially lawyers, will ever understand it?

It's one thing for lawyers to set out rules that describe the

399. Albert N. Podell, as quoted in "Quotes," *ABA Journal*, vol. 73, Mar. 1987, pg. 31.

necessary limits of conduct for everyone, whether they're lovers or not. Thus, for example, it's reasonable to prohibit murder under almost any circumstances. But that's an easy example. The closer the lawyers come to disturbing things that they don't understand, the more dangerous it becomes to let them go on with their endless written rules and arrangements. They don't know what effect they'll have, and they lack the self-restraint to know when to stop.

We've got an ambitious legal system. It sticks its nose into everything.[400] But who says that's how it's got to be? It's not at all clear that its nosiness is really doing us a big favor. To use the present example, everyone recognizes that divorce is often more of an emotional problem than a legal problem.[401] Even the justice system treats divorce that way, putting it into a separate court of its own. So how about the thought that it really doesn't belong in the hands of judges and lawyers at all?[402]

Cooperation and mutual concern have always counted for more, in everyday contacts among human beings, than have written documents and lawyers, with their odor of confrontation. Sometimes, obviously, there's no special concern between people. But in a surprising number of the most important cases, there is. Your mom, for example, didn't sign up anywhere to raise you. Nobody beat the businesspeople of bygone America until they admitted, sobbing, that "the customer is always right." These people arrived at their wonderful attitudes voluntarily, out of a mix of common sense,

---

400. And it's quite conscious of doing so. (See, e.g., William L. Prosser, *Law of Torts*, 4th ed. (St. Paul: West Publishing Co., 1971), pg. 3, fn. 13, describing a case from England in the year 1703 as "a famous case, if only because of Chief Justice Holt's declaration that for every interference with a recognized legal right the law will provide a remedy." On the parallel development of the medical profession, see John Kaplan, *The Hardest Drug: Heroin and Public Policy* (University of Chicago Press, 1983), pg. 41.)

401. See, e.g., Stephen Cretney, "Family Courts: A Symposium: I. Inquisitorial or Adversarial?" *Adoption and Fostering*, vol. 10, 1986, pp. 32-34. I had to chuckle at one in which a spouse won visitation rights to see, not a child, but a cockatoo. ("Quotes," *ABA Journal*, vol. 76, Jan. 1990, pg. 32.)

402. There are alternatives. Suppose, for example, that it were up to you to choose your own church or synagogue, get married in it, and be bound by its rules of marriage and divorce. If you didn't like any particular religion, you could get married by the justice of the peace, and then perhaps today's divorce laws would apply to your case. You'd have the option of choosing from a variety of handlers, and over time some ministers (or psychologists, or social workers), and some views about marriage, would tend to develop a track record of success in keeping couples together and/or making their breakups more civilized.

duty, and care.

I'm not saying there's no place for written laws or agreements. There's plenty of need for them, without pretending that they can capture all of human experience.

Naturally, when you have a tool that explains a certain kind of reality, you can be tempted to apply it to everything. For example, physicists may be right in saying that the world consists of subatomic particles, just as lawyers say that everything is, or should be, governed by principles of law.

But I think physicists must have more common sense than lawyers. I don't see physicists pretending that they can just grab the principles that guide subatomic particles and use them to provide a meaningful guide to, for example, the workings of the human mind. Lawyers, by contrast, don't hesitate to apply their insights to *everything*, as though written laws and agreements do, or should, rule all human interactions. And with enough aggressive lawyers, we might indeed see that kind of nightmare world someday.

But that's not what we want. Now, and then, and forever, it will always be crazy to give, to the law, such unstoppable power to rule things it does not understand.

3. The Right to Receive Humane Legal Assistance

Lawsuits often deal with the most intense, sensitive matters of your life, and yet lawyers and law firms are as cold as ice and judges act like they don't care if you live or die. Your friendliness or good intentions won't necessarily warm up the situation, either.

As a client, I have been repeatedly appalled at how my lawyers have seemed so indifferent to the real details of my cases. For a while, I thought that was because I was such a novice and didn't know what was really important. I wanted to believe in my attorneys, and tried to avoid second-guessing them. Eventually, however, you learn that, sometimes, the attorney who seems so unconcerned about the things that seem most important in your case really *is* unconcerned, and that those really *are* the most important things in your case.[403]

It's always amusing to hear one attorney express surprise

---

403. See, e.g., Stein, fn. 60, pg. 264.

at the way another attorney acts in a *personal* lawsuit. I've heard such phrases as, "You're a lawyer, but you're acting just like a typical client." Or, as a couple of lawyers described it in the *ABA Journal,*

> *Sending out legal bills is a difficult process. Reviewing and paying them, I will certify to you, is significantly worse.*

> *An associate in our firm was sued for malpractice. He had a very different goal for the litigation than the firm did. The definition of "winning," for the firm, was finding the cheapest, quickest, easiest way out, while for the associate, it was vindication. He was warned not to volunteer information, but when he got into the courtroom, he made speeches. I was stunned to find that in a lawyer. He turned out not to be much different from any other bright, interested client.*

> *It is infinitely, infinitely more difficult to be a client than an attorney.* [404]

Unique among the industries in our market-oriented economy, the law acts as though the goal is to turn off, disappoint, and get rid of the customer. There are no guarantees or warranties. There's no "truth in justice" that requires your attorney or the court to give you full information on what is happening to you. [405]

And that's dumb. Treating consumers well is what makes our economy grow and leads to improvement of our products. What's good for America is good for business. Surely it makes no sense to let the legal system use sales tactics that would be considered tacky, if not downright illegal, in other industries. But what is it, if not a bait-and-switch, [406] when

---

404. Don J. DeBenedictis, quoting William C. McClearn (managing partner of the Denver firm Holland & Hunt) and James H. McConomy (a partner with Reed, Smith, Shaw & McClay in Pittsburgh), in "The Law-Firm Defendants," *ABA Journal,* vol. 76, Jan. 1990, pg. 35 (paraphrased).

405. Richard K. Burke, "Truth in Lawyering: An Essay on Lying and Deceit in the Practice of Law," *Arkansas Law Review,* vol. 38, 1984, pg. 23.

406. "Bait-and-switch" refers to the practice of offering a great bargain to get customers into your store, but then telling them, when they arrive, that you've run

attorneys promise, or let you believe, all kinds of good things about what you can get from your lawsuit, and then, after you've paid a lot of fees, gradually lead you to see how tough it'll be to really win anything. Not to mention the high-pressure sales tactics in which they tell you that the judge is unavailable and that you'll have to wait forever for a trial date; but then, the moment you cave in and decide to settle your case, the super-busy judge is miraculously available, and they get you to agree to everything as quickly as possible.[407]

When consumers lack confidence in the legal system, they'll tend not to use it if they don't have to. That means two things: Lawyers will not do as much business as they could, and consumers will not get from the legal system what they need.

4. The Right to Be Meek

Let's suppose that I belong to a certain passive religion. My religion believes that it's wrong to argue. Thus, people in my religion do not sue, and when we are sued, we automatically give up everything. Obviously, an adversary system of justice gives us no justice at all.

You don't need to go that far to understand what happens to the meek and the sweet people in this country. They lack the sheer blood lust that it takes to enjoy litigation and to continually come up with hostile, aggressive approaches to their problems. A hardened jerk will almost always get more from the legal system than would a meek person. Even in their own defense, the meek will avoid using the system, so that, rather than protecting the innocent, it becomes a useful weapon for the attacker, allowing him/her to pretend to be civilized.

It may be irritating to meet people who are this passive. You want them to wake up and become practical. But, ultimately, that's not for you or me to decide. People have a

---

out of that item but that you'll be glad to sell them something "similar" (on which you make a better profit).

407. Or, as it's put by Abraham S. Blumberg, "The Practice of Law as a Confidence Game," *Law and Society Review*, vol. 1, June 1967, pp. 19-20, in the criminal law context, "All court personnel, including the accused's own lawyer, tend to be coopted to become agent-mediators who help the accused redefine his situation and restructure his perceptions concomitant with a plea of guilty."

right to live the way they want. Before we give a jerk the power to invade a meek person's life, there ought to be a good reason for it.

And anyway, you can't force people to become tough and realistic if they aren't built for it. In "To Kill a Mockingbird," Atticus Finch ultimately agrees that the town weirdo, who turns out to be a good guy, is so shy that he must be shielded from the publicity he'd suffer if he were to be put on trial for killing the bad guy. Moral of the story: If you insist on making sweet people tough just so that they do a better job of protecting themselves in court, you wind up with the psychological equivalent of a Vietnam soldier's comment: "It became necessary to destroy the village in order to save it."

You can't really fault meek people for avoiding the legal system. It disrupts their peace and contentment for the flimsiest reasons, but restores their domestic bliss, if ever, only after a bitter struggle. Litigation, for these people, is not just a matter of paperwork. It exposes them to a whole world of meanness from which they've been marvelously free. Throwing them into this pit shouldn't be done lightly.

Lawyers and judges might not understand this point. Remember how I said that "thinking like a lawyer" involves accepting a set of attitudes that lay people won't understand? A couple of them come into play here, such as: If in doubt, you should request more information, not less, about a person's business affairs or private life; ordinary people are wrong in not being political, cynical, and paranoid; and it's wrong to avoid fighting in defense of your rights.

In the end, the legal system demands realism of everyone. To my mind, that reeks of political persecution of the meek. They've got a right, I say, to be spacy and sweet.[408] Those people create the domestic situations that enable the rest of us to go out there and work hard. The longer our system of law

---

408. Not to underestimate those who don't always play with a full deck. One scientist, whose ideas "have influenced a generation of the nation's top computer scientists" and "has made significant contributions in virtually every area of [IBM's] business" is so dizzy that "he sometimes leaves unlaundered shirts stuffed in his filing cabinet" and once tossed $4,000 worth of his stock certificates in the trash can. (John Markoff, "A Maverick Scientist Gets an I.B.M. Tribute," *New York Times*, June 26, 1990, pg. C-1, col. 4.) This is the kind of genius whom we need desperately, but who might screw up something as mundane as a lawsuit because he can't get the hang of filling out the forms. What's more important?

and legal education is permitted to go on making us mean, the fewer there will be who'll have the strength, or even remember how, to be trusting and relaxed toward others.

They say the price of liberty is eternal vigilance.[409] But eternal vigilance by *everyone* leaves no time for liberty. It is essential for our kind of society that a large number of us have the right to live innocently, and that we limit the freedom of lawyers to attack that innocence without first evaluating the merits and consequences of their attacks.

5. Other Rights

There's a right to know the law. Some people don't want to discover that they've been breaking the law without knowing it. Others don't want the police to have an excuse to harass them just because they're oddballs. Some simply don't want to try a business idea, or invest money, or take a risk, and then hear some judge tell them that, even though there was no law on the subject before, it's now officially declared to be an illegal activity.

There's a right, I think, to like my fellow man. I can't do that if I've got to view him as a potential adversary. On the contrary, competition somehow manages to bleed through from one area of life into another, and especially if I'm playing to win. I want to be able to assume that the other guy is thinking good things about me, if he's thinking of me at all. We show, over and over, in the foxholes and the bars, that that friendly attitude comes naturally — at least when our training in hyper-competition isn't befuddling us.

We have a right to some personal dignity. It's not fair that we should be less protected if, by failing to complain constantly, we make it possible for some future judge to look back and say, "Well, he wasn't griping then, so it must not have bothered him." Along those lines, there's a right to obtain a decent resolution of minor disputes without having to blow them up into federal cases before the courts will pay attention to them.

I'm sure there's a right to work hard and save money, without automatically becoming a target for everyone who

---

409. Thomas Jefferson or John P. Curran — see Bartlett's, fn. 56, pg. 397.

wants to take advantage of your desire to get back to work by yanking you around in the courts until you pay a nuisance fee to get rid of them. And there's got to be a right to run a business without being victimized by the courts.[410]

Finally, and most offensively to my legal friends, I suspect there's a right to be inarticulate. Sometimes you just don't know what to say. That happens when you're shocked. It also happens when you're dealing with the really important things, for which you sometimes can't find adequate words. There really are those times, you know, when a lack of words is the way to go, when explanations would take too long or just wouldn't capture the instant simplicity of the situation.

B. Conclusions

It is not difficult to wrap up the situation in the law as we now confront it, and to present to you an image of what you're doing, in the big picture, if you become a lawyer and do nothing to improve the legal system.

1. A Study in Anarchy

There's no sign that legal experts are keeping up with recent changes, such as the transformation of the legal profession into a business. Only the wildest optimist would see any reason to believe that, beyond keeping up with the changes, the experts are making sure that the legal system of the future will be *better* than the one we have now.

Our legal system takes great precautions to make sure that the truth comes out in trial, and then forces nearly everyone to avoid a trial by settling out of court. On the criminal side, it announces a goal, like reformation, and then fails, and then announces another goal, like deterrence, and fails at that, and then announces another goal ... You've got a system in which they encourage dishonesty because it will supposedly bring you

---

410. If you have a big company, you can afford to hire a lawyer full-time at $60,000 a year, or about $30 an hour, and you'll keep him/her busy. But if you have a smaller business, you won't have that much legal work, and will instead have to hire an independent lawyer or firm, at rates of $100+ an hour. Besides being a target for private citizens who are defended by lawyers willing to sue you on a contingency fee arrangement, you're also a target for bigger businesses that would like to make life hard for you.

the truth. You spend a tremendous amount to obtain justice in even the simplest cases.

Let's face it, folks. Many of us believe that "Power tends to corrupt and absolute power corrupts absolutely."[411] By being too nosy and ambitious, our legal system has greedily claimed more power than it can manage. Consider:

> **an·ar·chy** *1. Absence of any form of political author-ity. 2. Political disorder and confusion. 3. Absence of any cohering principle, as a common standard or purpose.*[412]

By that definition, we now have a situation of anarchy in our legal system. Sure, the courts struggle mightily over every last comma and citation in their grapplings with the law's specific rules. They reach highly precise conclusions and defend them with exhaustive logic. But when you ask bigger questions — what does it all mean? where is it going? — you discover that nobody has any answers. No one's in charge.

Many judges and lawyers like it this way. They even think they're defending our system of government. But I have my doubts. I'd say they're defending chaos. What they love about our legal system is so far removed from the sensible, fair government we were promised in our high school civics classes that I can only call them anarchists. It would be different if we had enough time and money to pursue all the issues that seem important to them. But that would take infinite supplies of those two unfortunately rare commodities.

Those who designed the legal system like the fact that, in the ways that matter to them, it is so orderly and logical. But their priorities are not ours. They may make it perfect accord-ing to *their* needs, but by going too far in the directions that matter to them, they don't go far enough in the directions that matter to the rest of us. All too frequently, they leave us worse off than we were to begin with.

For 200 years, our Declaration of Independence and our Constitution have been the envy of the world. Unfortunately,

---

411. Lord Acton, as quoted in Bartlett's, fn. 56, pg. 615.
412. *American Heritage Dictionary.*

the ways in which our legal system has developed the concepts contained in those documents have not always worked out in the direction of liberty and justice for all. When the Iron Curtain fell, Eastern Europeans sang the praises of those old documents, but, unlike their eagerness for Hollywood movies and American technology, the masses noticeably did *not* cry and scream until they were given, say, a Czechoslovak equivalent of the American jurisprudential bureaucracy.[413]

It is important that we straighten out these matters, even though it might be possible for the legal system to continue to muddle through by ignoring them. American business has power around the globe. American law firms are taking prominent positions in other countries. And American law schools are training record numbers of foreign students in American views of law.[414]

All over the world, people are looking to us for guidance in concepts of liberty and democracy. We should make sure we're proud of what we're handing out to them, so that we can live up to their hopes, as we did in the old days.

2. The Law for Me Now

I regret that space has not permitted a more detailed response to this objection: that I have found it very easy to criticize the process of legal education, but that I would find it much harder to outline, in detail, how I would change it. Still, some readers will agree that the process is so silly that any moron, including me, could improve it, and others may be content with the thought that, if you always had to know exactly how things would turn out before you ever instituted any changes in anything, an awful lot of improvements in this world would be postponed indefinitely.

Like other ex-lawyers, I have mixed feelings. Clearly, the experiences described in this book were largely available to me only as a lawyer. I learned, I had fun, I met interesting people, and I obtained training that does come in handy in

---

413. "Jureaucracy," to coin a word. See Thomas L. Friedman, "For the Nations of Eastern Europe, The U.S. Is More Symbol than Model," *New York Times*, June 30, 1991, sec. 4, pg. 1, col. 1.
414. Lisa Green Markoff, "Law Schools: A New Onslaught of Foreigners Enrolls for Advanced Degrees," *National Law Journal*, Dec. 18, 1989, pg. 4.

some places, even though I have had to unlearn a lot of it for other purposes. I don't mind the low-intensity regret that things might have been better for me if I'd made a different choice. The main thing was not to perpetuate a bad situation, once I perceived it to be such, by trying to hang on when it was time to go.

So I went — sort of. I still do some legal work, but this book probably tells you that my big ambition — one I ignored during all those years in law school and practice — is to do more good for the people who need or deserve it.

I didn't write this book to offer a general review of the legal system, nor to publish my memoirs. I have tried, rather, to give you a gut-level feeling for how it can all work out in practice. Your experience cannot help being very different from mine, if only because you'll now be much keener to avoid unnecessary mistakes. It really is possible to go wrong in this profession, and it's a huge waste that so many young attorneys actually do go wrong.

I hope this book forces you to understand the questions that have mattered to me, and to arrive at good reasons why you won't repeat my errors. If you come away from this thoughtfully, with either a decision not to go to law school or a strong determination to outdo me as you become a lawyer — to take the bar and beat me, as it were — then it will have accomplished its purpose.

Get the Latest Scoop

I've learned a lot of things about lawyers and legal education. Unfortunately, not all of those things could fit into this book. The footnotes contain as much as I could cram into them, but there's a lot more that I would have liked to tell you and couldn't.

In a gesture that may be good for both you and me, the publisher of this book has given me a couple of pages, here, on which I could offer to provide further information on topics of special interest to you. I have responded to that offer by dividing my additional information into about two dozen reports. Each report addresses a specific topic, or responds to a particular need, that some prelaw students have. They are:

Getting into Law School
  1. *Latest Information on Top Law School Admissions*
  2. *Reading List: Choosing a Law School, Getting In, and Surviving*
  3. *Critical Analysis of Your Favorite Law School (specify school)*
  4. *Financing a Legal Education: Cost-Benefit Projections*
  5. *A Four-Year Calendar: From Law School Application to the Job*
Getting through Law School
  6. *Thoughts on Joint Degree Programs, with a Focus on the JD/MBA*
  7. *The Past Year's Best Articles on Legal Education (bibliography)*
  8. *Law-Related Organizations and Periodicals to Know About*
  9. *Which Courses? Preparing for the Bar, the Job, and Everything Else*
Life after Law School
  10. *Admission to the Bar in Your State (specify state)*
  11. *Law Career Options in Your Target City or State (specify city)*
  12. *Salaries of Lawyers: A Comparison of Multiple Data Sources*
  13. *Trends in Big-Firm Partnership Opportunities*
  14. *Hours vs. Dollars: How Many Billable Hours Before You Croak?*
The Process: Complaints, Concerns, and Alternatives
  15. *The Paralegal Option, Short- and Long-Term*
  16. *Legal Education: The Way It Should Be*
  17. *Alternative Ways of Getting a Legal Education*
  18. *Reform: A Guide to Sources for Changing the Legal System*
Psychological Aspects
  19. *The Healer: Career Thoughts for Those Who Want to Counsel*
  20. *Developments in the Study of the Psychology of the Lawyer*

If you liked this book, you'll definitely like these reports. You can get them for $2.50 each plus 75¢ per report for postage and handling. (Colorado residents: Add 7% sales tax.) If you order four or more, I will give you, at no extra charge, two issues of a semiannual newsletter, published in autumn and spring. This newsletter contains whatever information I consider appropriate on topics that are important at those times of the year, such as developments in the LSAT, applications, law school, the legal economy, etc.

I reserve the right, of course, to discontinue any or all reports, and to end the special offer for the newsletter, at any time according to my own best judgment. If that happens, you'll get your check back. On the other hand, as seems more likely, I will add new reports if readers' questions and comments seem to warrant it.

I'll send the latest list of reports whenever I fill an order. The list is also available if you'll send me a stamped, self-addressed envelope. Make checks payable to Raymond L. Woodcock and send all orders and inquiries to me at:

P.O. Box 1421
Denver, CO 80201

Please allow 3-4 weeks for delivery.

No matter whether you order reports or not, don't hesitate to write. Your comments and questions will influence the content of newsletters, reports, and future revisions of this book. And if you have nice things to say, you'll make me feel good. What's more, if you're famous and important and buy lots of reports, I'll beg the publisher to print your remarks in block letters on the front cover of the next revision.

And having said that, I think it's time for me to take the bar and beat it.

INDEX